Combining social history with literary criticism, James Krippner-Martínez shows how a historiographically sensitive rereading of contemporaneous documents concerning the sixteenth-century Spanish conquest and evangelization of Michoacán, and of later writings using them, can challenge traditional celebratory interpretations of missionary activity in early colonial Mexico.

The book offers a fresh look at religion, politics, and the writing of history by employing a poststructuralist method that engages the exclusions as well as the content of the historical record. The moments of doubt, contradiction, and ambiguity thereby uncovered lead to deconstructing a coherent conquest narrative that continues to resonate in our present age.

Part I, "The Politics of Conquest," deals with primary sources compiled from 1521 to 1565. Krippner-Martínez here examines the execution of the Cazonci, the indigenous ruler of Michoacán, as recounted in the trial record produced by his executioners; explores the missionary-Indian encounter as revealed in

continued on back flap

REREADING THE CONQUEST

REREADING THE CONQUEST

Power, Politics, and the History of Early Colonial Michoacán, Mexico, 1521–1565

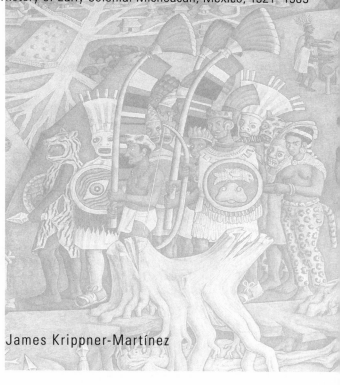

James Krippner-Martínez

The Pennsylvania State University Press
University Park, Pennsylvania

Library of Congress Cataloging-in-Publication Data

Krippner-Martínez, James, 1962–
    Rereading the conquest: power, politics, and the history of early colonial
    Michoacán, Mexico, 1521–1565 / James Krippner-Martinez
      p.   cm.
    Includes bibliographical references and index.
    ISBN 0–271–02129–2 (cloth : alk. paper)
    1. Indians of Mexico—Mexico—Michoacán de Ocampo—Missions. 2. Indians
    of Mexico—Mexico—Michoacán de Ocampo—History. 3. Michoacán
    de Ocampo (Mexico)—History—16th century. 4. Michoacán de Ocampo
    (Mexico)—Historiography. 5. Tarasco Indians—Missions. 6. Tarasco
    Indians—History. I. Title.
F1219.1M55 K75 2001
972'.3702—dc21

                                                            2001021477

It is the policy of The Pennsylvania State University Press to use acid-free paper for
the first printing of all clothbound books. Publications on uncoated stock satisfy the
minimum requirements of American National Standard for Information Sciences—
Permanence of Paper for Printed Library Materials, ANSI Z39.48–1992.

CONTENTS

PREFACE

On October 26–27, 1990, my long-standing interest in religion and politics became focused on the history and historiography of the sixteenth-century missionary evangelization of Michoacán. On these dates I attended an extended series of lectures, speeches, a play, and public ceremonies in Morelia and Pátzcuaro that commemorated several decisive moments in Michoacán's early colonial history. All of these activities in some way referred to Vasco de Quiroga, who served as the region's first bishop from 1538 until his death in 1565. They included the 450th anniversary of the Imagen de Nuestra Señora de la Salud, the Virgin cherished as the patron of Don Vasco's village-hospitals; the anniversary of his decision to make the village of Pátzcuaro the center of his ecclesiastical administration; the 425th anniversary of his death; and the 450th anniversary of the founding of the Colegio de San Nicolás, the first seminary/college on the American continent and precursor to the contemporary Universidad Michoacana de San Nicolás de Hidalgo.[1]

These events culminated in the transfer of Vasco de Quiroga's mortal remains from a safe in the baptistry of the Basilica de Pátzcuaro to a new, more prominent mausoleum in the same location.[2] Prior to October 26 and 27, 1990, I had embarked on the first stages of research for what was intended to be a dissertation on Catholicism and regional political culture in the late colonial era. At the time, graduate training in social history and an interest in liberation theology shaped my perception of the Mexican colonial past.

1. Francisco Miranda, *Don Vasco de Quiroga y su Colegio de San Nicolas* (Morelia, Mexico, 1972), 39–40.

2. *La Voz de Michoacán* (Morelia, México), October 26, 1990, 9-A, 1-B, 9-B; *La Jornada* (Mexico City), October 28, 1990, 14; Francisco Martín Hernández, *Don Vasco de Quiroga (Protector de los indios)* (Salamanca, 1993), 261; Manuel Toussaint, *Pátzcuaro* (Mexico City, 1942), 126.

I considered Vasco de Quiroga and the other missionary "defenders of the Indians" to be precursors of the martyred Latin American Church of the 1970s and 1980s, in a manner that now seems excessively linear though not entirely incorrect.[3] As I rode the bus from Mexico City to Morelia, and then from Morelia to Pátzcuaro, I became increasingly curious about the various ways that Don Vasco was remembered more than four centuries after his death.

In Pátzcuaro, I found the cultural politics demonstrated by the joint participation of the Catholic Church and representatives from the traditionally anticlerical Mexican State to be the most remarkable aspect of the entire experience. This indicated that the public distance between these institutions— notable since the liberal reforms of the nineteenth century, and deepened after the Mexican Revolution (1910–17)—had been substantially reduced, the result of a rapprochement engineered by the Vatican and the Salinas administration.[4] As anyone who struggled to find a hotel room and avoid overpriced souvenirs during those days in Pátzcuaro can testify, this particular construction of memory in reference to the sign "Vasco de Quiroga" also revealed something about the promotion of tourism and the commodification of the past in late-twentieth-century Mexico.[5]

In the pages that follow we will see how political and economic considerations have influenced the production of a specific historical narrative over more than four centuries—the story of the Castilian Catholic evange-

3. On the significance of the martyrs, see Jon Sobrino, "The Winds in Santo Domingo and the Evangelization of Culture," in *Santo Domingo and Beyond,* ed. Alfred T. Hennelly, S.J. (Maryknoll, N.Y., 1993), 165–235, esp. 178–80.

4. For an understanding of the circumstances that made this type of rapprochement possible, and for the complicated history of the Church/state relationship in Mexico, see Michael Tangeman, *Mexico at the Crossroads* (Maryknoll, N.Y., 1995), 67–87; George W. Grayson, *The Church in Contemporary México* (Washington, D.C., 1992), 65–90; and Peter Lester Reich, *Mexico's Hidden Revolution* (South Bend, Ind., 1995), esp. 105–12. A classic work demonstrating a pattern of cooperation between the elites of Mexico's postrevolutionary ruling party and the upper echelons of the Catholic church is Jean Meyer, *La cristiada* (Mexico City, 1973), vol. 2, *El conflicto entre la iglesia y el estado—1926–1929,* 303–80. For a recent, innovative interpretation, see Marjorie Becker, *Setting the Virgin on Fire* (Berkeley, Calif., 1995).

5. On commodification, tourism, and the "ethnographic voice," see Eric Van Young, "Conclusion: The State as Vampire—Hegemonic Projects, Public Ritual, and Popular Culture in Mexico, 1600–1990," in *Rituals of Rule, Rituals of Resistance,* ed. William H. Beezley, Cheryl English Martin, and William E. French (Wilmington, Del., 1994), esp. 344, 367–68; Nestor García Canclini, *Hybrid Cultures,* trans. Christopher L. Chiappari and Silvia L. López (Minneapolis, 1995), 145–83; and Robert V. Kemper, "Urbanización y desarrollo en la región tarasca a partir de 1940," in *Antropología social de la región purépecha,* comp. Guillermo de la Peña (Zamora, Mexico, 1987), 67–96.

lization of Michoacán, Mexico, from 1521 to 1565. Though decisive in terms of my own representation, these contextual influences do not exhaust the full symbolic meaning of this history, in the present or in the past. Nevertheless, when they are demonstrably present, intellectual honesty requires that they be recognized, rather than denied or ignored. Only then will we be able to confront the unresolved disputes of the past, develop new understandings in the present, and move toward a better future.

ACKNOWLEDGMENTS

The end of the process of writing a book is far easier to determine than its beginnings. As the author tests old assumptions and new ideas, various institutions, scholarly communities, and individuals are engaged. In the end, all of these influence the text that emerges in print. All are deserving of thanks, though realities of space mean that only a select few can be mentioned by name.

As a graduate student at the University of Wisconsin–Madison, I had the good fortune of studying with Thomas Skidmore, Francisco Scarano, Florencia Mallon, and Steve J. Stern. All of them helped me think through the issues addressed in this book, perhaps in ways they never realized. Steve J. Stern deserves the greatest thanks, for his firm insistence that I push myself to meet the highest standards (his), combined with his willingness to let me find my own way. Among the many friends and fellow students sharing graduate school, Sarah Chambers and Sinclair Thomson played especially important roles in the production of this book. Sarah encouraged me to present my work publicly at an early date, despite my reservations, and then provided the opportunity to do so. Sinclair read and commented on the entire manuscript, thus providing invaluable constructive criticism at a time when it was sorely needed. To both, the sincerest thanks!

In Mexico, Armando Escobar, Francisco Miranda, and Carlos Herrejón provided kind encouragement to a novice historian. One of my regrets is that our conversations were so limited by family and financial constraints. At Haverford College, my current home, I have enjoyed the friendship and support of a wonderful scholarly community. Over the years, Susan Stuard, Paul Smith, Lisa Graham, Bethel Saler, Rajeswari Mohan, Ulrich Schoenherr, Richard Freedman, Kim Benston, Laurie Hart, and Roberto Castillo-

Sandoval read and commented on various parts of the manuscript. In addition, Roberto Castillo-Sandoval was always available to help with difficult translations, and never complained about my habit of calling on the spur of the moment, regardless of the time. I do remain convinced that there is a material basis to cultural production. Without Haverford College's substantial financial assistance for this project, through faculty sabbatical, research, and travel grants, *Rereading the Conquest* could not have been completed. I will always be profoundly grateful for this institutional support.

Of course, teaching in a small college in a large metropolitan area leads one into dialogue with colleagues from other institutions. Over the years I have benefited from conversations with Madhavi Kale, Sharon Ullman, and Jane Caplan of Bryn Mawr College; Howard Spodek and Arthur Schmidt of Temple University; Richard Warren of Saint Joseph's University; Miguel Díaz Barriga and Aurora Camacho de Schmidt from Swarthmore College; Ann Farnsworth Alvear from the University of Pennsylvania, and Maghan Keita from Villanova University. Arthur Schmidt deserves special thanks for his thorough reading of the entire manuscript, twice. His comments resulted in a vastly improved final product. Aurora Camacho de Schmidt also helped with the manuscript while demonstrating that one can balance a flair for translation and a profound commitment to social justice. Finally, it has been my pleasure to share similar scholarly interests with Cynthia Stone of the College of the Holy Cross. Our knowledge of the *Relación de Michoacán* will be greatly enhanced by her forthcoming book. A study of Vasco de Quiroga by Fernando Gómez (University Press of America, 2001) appeared after this book had gone to press and thus could not be consulted.

Librarians and archivists are the unsung heroes of the research process, and I am indebted to several. These include the staffs of the libraries of the University of Wisconsin–Madison; the University of California–Davis; the University of California–Berkeley, and especially UC–Berkeley's Bancroft Library; and the University of Pennsylvania. Special thanks must go to the library staff of Haverford College, and especially Margaret Schaus, who always responded cheerfully when I began a conversation by stating "Margaret, I know I've seen this somewhere." The staff of the Archivo General de la Nación in Mexico City provided a congenial research environment and valuable assistance with the illustrations in this book, and the slides for the cover illustration were kindly provided by the Biblioteca Pública de Pátzcuaro. Of course, editors are to writing what librarians and archivists are to research.

I have enjoyed the good fortune of working with the editorial staff of Penn State University Press, especially Sandy Thatcher and Cherene Holland. The superb copyediting of Andrew Lewis resulted in a far more presentable text. In addition, a previous version of Chapter 1 has been published in the *Colonial Latin American Review,* as have versions of Chapter 2 and Chapter 5 in *The Americas.* I am indebted to the editorial staff and anonymous reviewers of these journals, whose comments helped clarify my thought.

One last set of influences remains to be acknowledged. My mother, Sheila Krippner, instilled a love of learning and a respect for intellectual work at an early age, and at crucial moments encouraged me to persevere in this task. My father, George Krippner, taught me not to fear the refinement of faith through reason. His insistence on the value of informed and nuanced argument, whether one is debating history or writing an appeal, has served me well over the years. My children, Diego and Fiona Martínez-Krippner, helped me rediscover the beauty of life while reminding me that many things are more important than books. Olivia Martínez-Krippner, my long-term friend, companion, and spouse, has lived with this project from the first rough ideas in graduate school through the publication of this book. She always believed the book would be published, even when the author had his doubts. Her presence can be noted in every line, and I will always be grateful for her love and support. All of these individuals, and many more, have contributed to the book. Of course, any errors that remain are my own.

Rereading the Conquest is dedicated to Olivia, Diego, and Fiona, with the hope that the joys of our shared past will be surpassed in an even better future.

INTRODUCTION

History is not a substitute for social praxis, but its fragile
witness and necessary critique.
—Michel de Certeau, *The Writing of History*

Rereading the Conquest is a regionally focused study of religion,
politics, and the writing of history. In it I evaluate the selective
recording in historical documents, and inevitably partial reconstruction by historians, of crucial moments in a specific historical
narrative: the story of the Castilian Catholic evangelization of
Michoacán, Mexico, from 1521 to 1565.[1] I hope thereby to con-
tribute to recent scholarship questioning celebratory accounts of
sixteenth-century missionary activity, while also engaging long-
standing and recently revived debates about history and the historical imagination.[2]

1. It was in 1521 that the Spaniards first contacted the indigenous peoples of
Michoacán, and in 1565 that Vasco de Quiroga died. The following works detail
this history: Bernardino Verastíque, *Michoacán and Eden* (Austin, Tex., 2000);
José Aparecido Gomes Moreira, *Conquista y conciencia cristiana* (Quito, 1990);
Enrique Florescano et al., *Historia general de Michoacán*, vol. 2, *La colonia*
(Morelia, Mexico, 1989); Delfina Esmeralda López Sarrelangue, *La nobleza indígena de Pátzcuaro en la época virreinal* (Mexico City, 1965); Helen Perlstein Pol-
lard, *Taríacuri's Legacy* (Norman, Okla., 1993); J. Benedict Warren, *The Conquest
of Michoacán* (Norman, Okla., 1985), and (Fintan B.) Warren, *Vasco de Quiroga
and His Pueblo-Hospitals of Santa Fe* (Washington, D.C., 1963); and Miranda,
Don Vasco de Quiroga. On sixteenth-century Castilian Catholicism, see Stafford
Poole, C.M., *Our Lady of Guadalupe* (Tucson, Ariz., 1995), 19.
2. On history and objectivity, see Michel de Certeau, "The Historiographical
Operation," in *The Writing of History*, trans. Tom Conley (1975; New York, 1988),

Rereading the Conquest consists of a series of autonomous essays arranged in chronological sequence. Each essay is an analysis of representations of important events and actors during the first generation of the "encounter" between the indigenous peoples of Michoacán and the initial wave of Spanish soldiers, settlers, and missionaries.[3] Collectively, they demonstrate how historical context and the subjective nature of writing influenced the documents containing traces of this history, as well as the interpretations of historians put forth over time.[4] The result is a succession of tentative understandings and truth claims based on the character of specific written records, rather than a spurious claim to have mastered the past.

The conquest of Michoacán began almost immediately after the fall of Tenochtitlán in 1521. The region's location directly west of Mexico's central valley had long influenced its history. Indeed, the long and successful Purhépecha/Tarascan struggle to maintain autonomy from the bordering Mexíca/Aztec empire prefigured initial indigenous responses to the Spanish

56–113; Michel-Rolph Trouillot, *Silencing the Past* (Boston, 1995), esp. 1–30; Gesa Mackenthun, *Metaphors of Dispossession* (Norman, Okla., 1997), 3–140; Walter Mignolo, *The Darker Side of the Renaissance* (Ann Arbor, Mich., 1995), esp. vii–25; Mario J. Valdés and Linda Hutcheon, *Rethinking Literary History—Comparatively,* American Council of Learned Societies (ACLS) Occasional Paper No. 27 (New York, 1994); and Steve J. Stern, "Paradigms of Conquest: History, Historiography, and Politics," *Journal of Latin American Studies* 24 (1992): 1–34.

3. Unlike other Mexican regions, primary sources in the indigenous languages of Michoacán for this era have yet to be discovered, thus granting even more importance to the few Spanish sources that exist. Gruzinski, *Conquest of Mexico,* 75. Considerable debate exists over the proper designation for Michoacán's indigenous people during the colonial era. See Alfredo López Austin, *The Rabbit on the Face of the Moon,* trans. Bernard R. Ortiz de Montellano and Thelma Ortiz de Montellano (Salt Lake City, Utah, 1996), 91–98. A sense of the contours of the debate can be gained from Verastíque, *Michoacán and Eden,* 9–11; Cynthia Leigh Stone, "A Fragile Coalition: The 'Relación de Michoacán' and the Compiling of Indigenous Traditions in Sixteenth-Century Mexico" (Ph.D. diss., University of Michigan, 1992), 9, and "Rewriting Indigenous Traditions: The Burial Ceremony of the *Cazonci," Colonial Latin American Review* 3, nos. 1–2 (1994): 87–107; Pollard, *Taríacuri's Legacy,* 15–16; J. Benedict Warren, "Writing the Language of Michoacán: Sixteenth-Century Franciscan Linguistics," in *Franciscan Presence in the Americas,* ed. Francisco Morales, O.F.M. (Potomac, Md., 1983), 308; Francisco Miranda, "Estudio preliminar," in *La Relación de Michoacán,* ed. Francisco Miranda (Morelia, Mexico, 1980), xxxii–xxv, (unless otherwise indicated, all quotations from the *Relación* are from this edition); and Ma. del Refugio Cabrera V. and Benjamín Pérez González, *El estado p'urhepecha y sus fronteras en el siglo XVI* (Morelia, Mexico, 1991), 17–18. I am persuaded by Verastíque that the least problematic designation is Purhépecha-Chichimec for the entire indigenous population, and Purhépecha for the dominant group.

4. On the preservation of "traces" of the past in written documents, see Paul Ricouer, *Time and Narrative,* vol. 3, trans. Kathleen Blarney and David Pellauer (1985; Chicago, 1988), esp. 116–26.

presence.[5] The first contact between Spaniards and indigenes in Michoacán occurred as early as February 23, 1521 (this date is likely, but not confirmed). In 1522, Cuinierángari—known in Spanish documents as Don Pedro, and the adopted brother of the Cazonci, or indigenous ruler—traveled to Mexico City to meet with Cortés. In that same year, a military expedition led by Cristobal de Olid passed through the region. More detailed surveys of Michoacán were produced by Antonio de Caravajal between the years of 1521 and 1526, and these corresponded with and facilitated more sustained efforts at Spanish settlement. Franciscan missionaries, who dominated the regional Church during its first decade, left Mexico City for Michoacán in 1525.[6]

The role of the Catholic Church in the colonization of Michoacán has long been recognized as distinctive.[7] The consolidation of the institutional church, and the colonial order in general, received a decisive boost during the brutal campaign of the conquistador Nuño de Guzmán, which passed through Michoacán in 1529–30. This process was completed during the administration of Vasco de Quiroga—a member of the secular clergy (i.e., a priest who was not a member of a particular religious order, unlike the regular clergy) and Michoacán's first bishop. One result of this more sustained colonial presence was the writing of documents, and the beginning of the construction of a historical archive. It is here that our inquiry begins.

The book that follows is divided into two parts. The first part, "The Politics of Conquest," consists of three chapters. These chapters are based on primary sources produced during the era of conquest and early colonization, selected for their importance in subsequent historiography. Chapter 1, "The Vision of the Victors: History, Memory, and the *Proceso* [1530]," examines the execution of the Cazonci as recorded in the trial record produced by his executioners, namely settlers led by Nuño de Guzmán. Here I argue that the execution of the Cazonci demonstrated the consolidation of Spanish authority in Michoacán and describe the tense political dynamics of the initial occupation of Michoacán, including a significant amount of intra-Spanish rivalry as various factions sought to gain control of the region in the 1520s. I also

5. Pollard, *Taríacuri's Legacy*, 87–108; Alfredo López Austin, *Tarascos y Mexicas* (Mexico City, 1981).

6. The best summary of this history remains Warren, *Conquest of Michoacán*, esp. 24–101. See also Florescano, *Historia general de Michoacán*, 2:1–54, and López Sarrelangue, *La nobleza indígena de Pátzcuaro*, 21–80.

7. Robert Ricard, *The Spiritual Conquest of Mexico*, trans. Lesley Byrd Simpson (1933; Berkeley, Calif., 1966), 65–68.

show that Nuño de Guzmán did not act alone when he killed the Cazonci. Rather, he carried to completion a project initiated by settlers frustrated at various forms of indigenous resistance. Indeed, Nuño de Guzmán's actions were not aberrant, as later history portrayed them, but quite functional for the founding of the colonial order. This poses a deeper question: What does it mean to condemn, in isolation, the violence of an individual participating in the violent invasion and colonization of previously occupied lands? I conclude Chapter 1 by suggesting that the image of Nuño de Guzmán as deviant has served, in the sixteenth century and subsequent accounts, to cast the behavior of his opponents and the entire process of colonization in a more favorable light.

In Chapter 2, "Alterity, Alliance, and the *Relación de Michoacán* [1541]," I explore the "encounter" between missionaries and the indigenous peoples of Michoacán as reflected in the *Relación de Michoacán*. This text was compiled and edited by a Franciscan missionary between 1539 and 1541 at the request of Viceroy Antonio de Mendoza. It consists of testimonies of the indigenous male elite about the indigenous past, from the origins of the Purhépecha through the arrival of Spaniards and the execution of the Cazonci. Here I evaluate the *Relación de Michoacán* as an artifact of early colonial church/state and indigenous interactions. I contend that this document could be produced only as the result of a political alliance between missionaries and indigenes against other colonizing factions, one that cohered in the 1530s following the Cazonci's execution. Indigenous collaboration in its production presupposed an acceptance of Spanish rule. The version of the past it puts forth can be read as an attempt to enhance the status of the local male indigenous elite in the eyes of the colonial state. I show how the Franciscans and indigenes developed those shared interests and the temporary alliance that allowed the creation of this text and conclude by assessing the influence of this relationship on regional political culture during and after the colonial centuries.[8]

In Chapter 3, "The Writings of Vasco de Quiroga," I examine the writings of Vasco de Quiroga, Michoacán's first bishop, who served in that position from 1538 to 1565. Vasco de Quiroga intervened in sixteenth-century debates over Indian slavery and later became an important figure in Mexican

8. Susan Kellog, "Hegemony Out of Conquest: The First Two Centuries of Spanish Rule in Central Mexico," *Radical History Review* 53 (1992): 27–46, details this process in central Mexico.

Catholic, national, and international scholarship. Here I seek to explain Vasco de Quiroga in terms of his own sixteenth-century milieu, based on a close reading of his writings. I concede that for his time and this place, influenced as it was by the socioeconomic institution of the *encomienda* and the feudal ideology that created and sustained it, aspects of Vasco de Quiroga's intervention were humane. Nevertheless, substantial evidence drawn from these sources also reveals that profound ethnocentrism and an authoritarian paternalism permeated his thought. Since Vasco de Quiroga's writings provide the most tangible link to his actual practice currently available, they point toward a harsher reality than the heroic image revered today. I conclude Chapter 3 by noting that Vasco de Quiroga shared much with his fellow colonists, including those—such as Nuño de Guzmán—commonly portrayed as his opponents.

In the second part of this book, "Reflections," I investigate depictions of these events and figures created at the distance granted by the passage of time. Chapter 4, "Representing the 'Spiritual Conquest,'" is based on the *Crónica de Michoacán,* a massive late colonial work (ca. 1788) written by the Franciscan intellectual Pablo de Beaumont. Beaumont's *Crónica,* intended to instruct Franciscans about their own history, has been recognized widely as the single most important source detailing the sixteenth-century Franciscan evangelization of Michoacán. In Chapter 4 I show that Pablo Beaumont's *Crónica* is a late colonial, conservative creole representation of the Franciscan evangelization of Michoacán. It is a text riddled with irony, or at least fertile ground for ironic readings. Beaumont's celebration of the sixteenth-century "spiritual conquest" was composed within a context of late colonial decline. During the eighteenth century "Bourbon reconquest," Beaumont's Franciscan order lost privileges they had maintained in Michoacán during the two centuries since the initial evangelization efforts. Here I contend that Beaumont's attempt to demonstrate the continued necessity of Franciscan evangelization reveals an unintended subtext of indigenous rejection. His claim that the end of Christian conversion justified the means of armed conquest provides an example of a scholar appropriating the past to render massive violence acceptable—indeed, morally commendable—for his contemporaries.

In Chapter 5, "Remembering Tata Vasco," I historicize the emergence of Vasco de Quiroga as a legendary figure. Here I detail the multiple meanings that have been assigned to his legacy from the mid-eighteenth through the late-twentieth centuries, thus demonstrating how an image from the colonial period continued to resonate in various "historical presents." In the chapter I argue that the heroic image of Vasco de Quiroga circulating today is a product more of colonial discourse and creole nationalism than of the events of the sixteenth century. This is not to deny the significance of Vasco de Quiroga's sixteenth-century experience, only to call into question unsubstantiated assumptions about indigenous responses to Vasco de Quiroga's evangelical efforts during his lifetime. Taken together, Chapters 3 and 5 reinforce and provide additional support for those who have sought to qualify and even challenge the largely heroic narrative of the founder of the regional Church.[9] Collectively, all of these essays demonstrate the inevitable influence of power and politics on the history and historiography of early colonial Michoacán.

9. Most important among these cautionary works are Verastíque, *Michoacán and Eden;* Gomes Moreira, *Conquista y conciencia cristiana;* and Anthony Pagden, "The Humanism of Vasco de Quiroga's *Información en Derecho,*" in *The Uncertainties of Empire* (Aldershot, England, and Brookfield, Vt., 1994), 133–42.

Part One

THE POLITICS OF CONQUEST

1

THE VISION OF THE VICTORS

History, Memory, and the *Proceso contra Tzintzincha Tangaxoan* [1530]

> Every trial, each interrogatory yields its share of data, provided
> that one knows how to evaluate what the filter of writing, the
> aims of the investigator, the questioning of the judge, the in-
> tervention of the notary and the escribano or the chances of
> preservation have been able to add to (or subtract from) the
> original account.
>
> —Serge Gruzinski, *The Conquest of Mexico*

On February 14, 1530, along the Lerma river in west-central Mexico, a band of Spanish soldiers—accompanied by local settlers and
allied Indians and led by the conquistador Nuño de Guzmán—
executed the Cazonci, or ruler, of the indigenous peoples of Michoacán, Tzintzincha Tangaxoan. The execution of the Cazonci
has long been considered one of the most infamous events of the
Spanish Conquest of Mexico.[1] In this chapter I analyze the account of the Cazonci's trial, torture, and death in the *Proceso,* a
judicial record submitted to royal authorities by the men who

1. The event is well known and has been frequently mentioned in the literature.
For some recent examples, see Rodrigo Martínez, "Los inicios de la colonización,"
in Florescano, *Historia general de Michoacán,* 2:39–73, esp. 65–71; Warren, *Con-
quest of Michoacán,* 84, 223, also available in Spanish as *La conquista de Michoacán;*
Tzvetan Todorov, *The Conquest of America,* trans. Richard Howard (1982; New
York, 1984), 96–97; and López Sarrelangue, *La nobleza indígena de Pátzcuaro,* 51,
54–55. Older sources include Jose López-Portillo y Weber, *La conquista de la
Nueva Galicia* (Mexico City, 1935), 159–65, and J. H. Parry, *The Audiencia of New
Galicia in the Sixteenth Century* (1940; Cambridge, England, 1968), 21.

killed him.[2] This document contains statements from the conquistador Nuño de Guzmán, several other Spanish soldiers and settlers, and the accused and other elite male indigenes, as translated and transcribed by Spanish functionaries. It provides a fascinating lens into the initial years of the Spanish colonial presence in Michoacán.

The *Proceso* details a decisive moment in the conquest of Michoacán. As we shall see, it is a source marked by what it excludes, as well as by what it contains.[3] When this document is analyzed in a manner sensitive to each of these dimensions of representation, it becomes possible to challenge two widespread and misleading images of conquest that superficial readings of the *Proceso* have helped to perpetuate: the "passive Indian," acted upon but not capable of responding to the trauma of conquest, here symbolized by the Cazonci; and the brutal conquistador, whose actions are defined as aberrant and even pathological in a manner that obscures the utility of extreme violence for supposedly more humane forms of colonization, in this case Nuño de Guzmán. These images retain a vitality in the conquest historiography of Michoacán—especially in the case of the "passive Indian"—that has been thoroughly challenged in other Latin American regions by the now firmly established "new social history" of the last thirty years.[4] I hope to revise our understanding of the conquest of Michoacán, while introducing methodological questions of interest to social historians and literary critics alike.

Given its hurried and extremely summary quality, historians have debated the *Proceso*'s validity. The argument has centered on the question of whether it came into being after the fact, as a way of lending a veneer of legality to Nuño de Guzmán's act, or whether it does indeed record an actual trial that occurred prior to the Cazonci's death.[5] While I believe that the latter position is correct—and the debate not irrelevant—the significance of this dispute has

2. France V. Scholes and Eleanor Adams, eds., *Proceso contra Tzintzincha Tangaxoan el Caltzontzín, formado por Nuño de Guzmán año de 1530* (Mexico City, 1952).
3. Gayatri Chakravorty Spivak, *In Other Worlds* (New York, 1987), 118, 121–22, and *The Post-Colonial Critic* (New York, 1990), 43; Beatriz Pastor, "Silence and Writing: The History of the Conquest," in *1492–1992: Re/Discovering Colonial Writing*, ed. René Jara and Nicholas Spadaccini (Minneapolis, 1989), 121–63, esp. 121–24.
4. Florescano, *Memory, Myth and Time in Mexico*, 65–99; José Maria Rabasa, *Inventing America* (Norman, Okla., 1993), 3–22. I am grateful to Steve J. Stern for pointing out that the conquistador Francisco de Chaves played a role similar to that of Nuño de Guzmán during the conquest of Peru. For information on Chaves, see John Hemming, *The Conquest of the Incas* (London, 1970), 248–49, 262.
5. Warren, *Conquest of Michoacán*, 223; Scholes and Adams, *Proceso*, 11–68.

Figure 1   "Here it is shown that [...] the captains of the natives went out to en-
counter Cristóbal de Olid and his captains and [...] they went to give the news to the
King Caltzontzin [...] who was in a dance [...] and he received them gladly." In
Beaumont, *Crónica de Michoacán,* copy of 1792 (translated by the author). Archivo
General de la Nación.

been overstated. Regardless of its validity as a legal document, the *Proceso* is an
authentic source for the study of colonial ideology. As Tzvetan Todorov has
pointed out, "The important thing is that the text be 'receivable' by contemporaries, or that it is regarded as such by its producer. From this point of view,
the notion of 'false' is irrelevant here."[6] As we shall see, there are reasons for
criticizing aspects of Todorov's work. Nevertheless, his insight concerning
"truth" and "falsity" in terms of the reception of colonial texts—be they judicial records or chronicles—is useful, and certainly applicable in this instance.
Nuño de Guzmán, his allies, and many of their Spanish contemporaries certainly considered their version of the trial, torture, and execution of the
Cazonci to be "receivable," whatever else it may have been.

Inevitably, my investigation privileges the "vision of the victors," since it
relies so heavily on the account produced by Spanish soldiers and settlers.

6. Todorov, *Conquest of America,* 54.

Historians, especially those looking back over almost five centuries, tend to favor written sources of information. This has the effect of marginalizing those—for reasons of language, or social power, or both—whose entry into the historical record has occurred only in severely compromised ways, as the result of processes they may influence but do not control. However, in this instance the privileging of dominant visions exists only in the sense of taking this text as the entry point for analysis. Virtually all colonial texts, even those that on the surface appear to be the most "European," contain frequently neglected traces of the indigenous presence.[7] My analysis of the *Proceso* engages these traces, and in so doing unsettles interpretations that tend to reproduce the perceptions of the conquerors themselves.[8] Perhaps ironically, one result of my investigation will be a more nuanced understanding of the role of the conquistador Nuño de Guzmán in establishing the regional colonial order.

I do not intend to provide a complete reconstruction of the Cazonci's execution, and even less a comprehensive history of the early years of the Spanish and Indian "encounter" in Michoacán. Rather, I seek to generate a series of partial insights by examining the influence of unequal relationships of power on the construction of one document and to utilize these insights to revise existing interpretations of a specific conquest history. My approach has been influenced by the historically minded literary criticism of scholars such as Peter Hulme, who argues that "the venture, it should be said, is archaeological: no smooth history emerges, but rather a series of fragments which, read speculatively, hint at a story that can never be fully recovered."[9] In this chapter I do not provide a "smooth history," nor do I "fully recover" a story from the past. Instead, through the painstaking consideration of the evidence and exclusions contained in the judicial record of the Cazonci's trial, torture, and execution, I argue that this was a contested moment in an ongoing struggle to establish and maintain colonial power, one that did not end with the Cazonci's death. We can recognize the plausibility of this interpretation while also acknowledging that it has been built on a distant and distorted source, at least one step removed from the reality it claims to represent.

7. Rolena Adorno, "Discourses on Colonialism: Bernal Díaz, Las Casas, and the Twentieth-Century Reader," *MLN* 103, no. 2 (March 1988): 239–58; Inga Clendinnen, "Fierce and Unnatural Cruelty: Cortés and the Conquest of Mexico," *Representations* 33 (Winter 1991): 65–100.

8. Todorov, *Conquest of America;* Warren, *Conquest of Michoacán;* Hugh Thomas, *Conquest* (New York, 1993).

9. Peter Hulme, *Colonial Encounters* (London, 1986), 12.

The Conquerors' Text

On February 23, 1533, in Toledo, Spain, Sancho de Canego, acting in the name of Nuño de Guzmán and following repeated requests from royal authorities, produced a notarized version of the Cazonci's trial record.[10] This document actually contained three parts: a lawsuit prosecuted by Francisco de Villegas against the Cazonci between January 26 and January 28, 1530; an investigation by the Spanish settler Bernaldino de Albornoz against Don Pedro—the adopted brother of the Cazonci, as he was named in Spanish documents—and two Indian interpreters identified as Gonzalo Xuárez and Francisco, dating from June 25 through June 28, 1529; and a record of the trial and execution of the Cazonci, carried out by soldiers under the command of the conquistador Nuño de Guzmán, between February 5 and February 14, 1530.[11] Nuño de Guzmán, and his allies, undoubtedly compiled this entire document in the hope of proving that the Cazonci's execution met the requirements of Spanish law. They needed to do so because they were under attack from other colonial factions, and they must have known that the execution would be controversial.[12]

The trial record itself is extremely brief, consisting of only sixty-eight pages in modern typescript. This brevity—and the fragmentary, at times contradictory, quality of the materials contained within it—precludes the analysis of anything as unitary as a "Spanish colonial worldview." However, it is possible to note some changes in Spanish concerns and attitudes during the short time it took to compile this collection of statements. This is an overwhelmingly European source, despite its inclusion of some indigenous testimonies. The process of translation and transcription into a formal legal document seriously constrained the final accounts, especially the indigenous voices, presented in the text. This is not to argue that the source is without value, but rather to note that we must begin our examination with a frank recognition of its limitations.

For example, the document sent to royal authorities as the trial record of the Cazonci was not an original, but a copy of a copy, made almost two years after the execution.[13] Therefore, all of the Spanish testimonies contained in

10. Scholes and Adams, *Proceso*, 11.
11. Ibid., 11–36, 36–44, 44–68
12. Ibid., 6–9, 11.
13. Ibid., 11, 68.

this source passed through at least two "filters"—the original composition of a written judicial record, and any alterations or omissions introduced in the copying process after the fact—while, as we shall see, indigenous testimonies passed through at least four, and possibly five. Since we lack the original, we cannot determine the extent of the editorial influence of these Spanish notaries. We can, however, state with confidence that—at the very least—this process of transcription into a formal legal document gave the final version presented to royal authorities a certain distance from the event.

In addition, none of the Indian witnesses spoke or wrote Spanish. This means that their accounts had to be processed by a translator, at a time when Spaniards had been familiar with Tarascan (Purhépecha) for only—at the very most—a little over eight years. The *encomendero* Francisco de Villegas, one of the first Spaniards to settle in the region, claimed that he had possessed Indians there for only "five or six years, a bit more or less."[14] Thus one can legitimately question the accuracy, and certainly the subtlety, of the translations provided. The text identifies Juan Pascual—whom at one point in the text Nuño de Guzmán indicates is a native—as an "interpreter of the Tarascan language," and the man responsible for translating indigenous testimonies. Martín Gómez is listed as the translator for the Cazonci's final sentencing.[15] At no point in the text does Juan Pascual sign the text, and his inability to write is frequently mentioned.[16] Thus, at a minimum, all of the indigenous testimonies translated into Spanish by the illiterate Juan Pascual were transcribed by someone else, most probably the notary Hernando Sarmiento, before being copied and sent to the Crown.[17]

The trial record of the Cazonci lends itself to one last point regarding the complexities of translation. In the investigation by Bernaldino de Albornoz, care is taken to identify the Indians Gonzalo Xuárez and Francisco as "naguatlatos," that is, speakers of Nahuatl, the dominant indigenous language in the central valley of Mexico and the one most familiar to Spanish conquistadores. In the section of the document produced by Nuño de

14. Ibid., 12, 36, 45, 48, 50, 58.
15. Ibid., 12, 23, 45, 47 (identified as Indian), 55, 61, 64, 65, 66 (Martín Gomez).
16. Ibid., 61. See also 47, 58.
17. The sections of the document attributed to Francisco de Villegas and Nuño de Guzmán name Hernando Sarmiento as the public notary present during the composition of the trial record. The investigation by Bernaldino de Albornoz, submitted as evidence for the Villegas lawsuit, lacks a notary's signature, although it contains a passage referring to "I, the said notary . . . ," most probably Sarmiento. Ibid., 11, 68, 37.

Guzmán, an Indian named Guanax is referred to as a "naguatlato chichi-meca," that is, a Nahuatl-speaking member of the seminomadic peoples who populated the northern frontier of the Aztec and Tarascan kingdoms, but also as a "naguatlato tarasco," or Nahuatl-speaking Tarascan.[18] Clearly, he spoke Nahuatl, although the Spaniards may have been confused about his political affiliation. Thus it is likely that a third language was in play for at least some of the indigenous accounts recorded in this document. One can even plausibly envision an additional layer of translation—from Purhépecha or Tarascan into Nahuatl, or vice-versa, then into Spanish—for at least parts of the indigenous testimonies, prior to transcription by a literate Spaniard. For example, the trial record at one point notes that Juan Pascual interpreted the following complaint from the Cazonci: "He said that he was accustomed to be lord of this [province], but that now he is like a *macegual*."[19] The translator, or transcriber, here inserted the Nahuatl term *macegual*—which refers to the laboring or commoner strata of the population—instead of the term *purhépecha*, which Spanish colonial dictionaries claim at that time had an equivalent meaning in the Cazonci's native, and most probably only, lan-guage.[20] All of these factors related to translation, and the influence of tran-scription into a formal legal document, undermine strictly literal readings of this source.

This is not to say that the testimonies contained in this document are fraudulent or valueless. However, the information provided must be viewed as partial, incomplete, and selective—or better yet, selected. After all, the Spanish colonials decided which questions were asked of all the informants, thus decisively controlling the information obtained. Essentially, this docu-ment consists of Spanish charges against the Cazonci and other Indian elites and information elicited to support these claims. The entire process of its composition—from the selection of witnesses, to the presentation of ques-tions, through translation and transcription into a formal legal document—influenced the content of the final representation. Recognizing this reality is the starting point for our investigation.

18. Ibid., 39, 47.

19. Ibid., 20.

20. This substitution of *macegual* for *purhépecha* can also be noted in Maturino Gilberti's *Arte de la lengua de Michoacán*, ed. J. Benedict Warren (1558; Morelia, Mexico, 1987), 115. See also his *Diccionario de la lengua tarasca*, introduced by José Corona Núñez (1574; Morelia, Mexico, 1983).

Illusions of Conquest

By his own admission, Nuño de Guzmán killed the Cazonci, known to the Spanish as Don Francisco.[21] This was despite the fact that, at least initially, he had peacefully greeted Spanish colonial forces.[22] The reality of Nuño de Guzmán's harsh treatment of him, combined with the Cazonci's relatively benevolent posture, has led many to consider the latter a hapless victim, overwhelmed by forces he could barely comprehend.[23] This notion of an immediate and complete victory is based on a superficial reading of the conquerors' perceptions, and it has reinforced a bias that is deeply imbedded in the historical record. For example, the great nineteenth-century historian William H. Prescott cited Cortés in his attempt to explain why the Cazonci initially received Spaniards peacefully.[24] According to Prescott, when the Cazonci arrived in Mexico City, formerly Tenochtitlán, after Cortés's military triumph, "the Indian Monarch gazed with silent awe on the scene of desolation, and eagerly craved the protection of the invincible beings who had caused it."[25] Virtually all historians today would find it ridiculous to cite Cortés to discover the Cazonci's thoughts. Nevertheless, far fewer would challenge Prescott's underlying themes of Spanish invincibility, or the portrayal of Indian capitulation as immediate, total, and complete.

This deeply rooted, yet deeply false image of Indian passivity during the initial colonial encounter in Michoacán also surfaces in J. Benedict Warren, who claimed that "the colonial sources that are now available give some evidence that the native king did not honestly fulfill the obligations he had assumed by the acceptance of Spanish sovereignty and the Christian faith."[26] He based this conclusion entirely on his reading of the trial record of the Cazonci, the existence of which had been mentioned in various colonial sources, but never confirmed—or used as the basis for historical investigation—until its discovery and subsequent publication in 1952.[27] However,

21. Scholes and Adams, *Proceso*, 67.
22. López Sarrelangue, *La nobleza indígena de Pátzcuaro*, 21–46; Warren, *Conquest of Michoacán*, 24–72; Hernán Cortés, *Letters from Mexico*, ed. and trans. A. R. Pagden (New York, 1971), 266.
23. Todorov, *Conquest of America*, 96, 97.
24. On Prescott, see Thomas, *Conquest*, xiv–xvi.
25. William H. Prescott, *History of the Conquest of Mexico* (1843; Philadelphia, 1860), 236.
26. Warren, *Conquest of Michoacán*, xii; see also 239–41.
27. Scholes and Adams, *Proceso*, 7–9.

there is absolutely no evidence in the trial record, or any other colonial sources, that the "native king" defined his obligations to Spanish colonialism according to the norms of the colonizers. The evidence that we have demonstrates that some type of relationship between the Cazonci and representatives of the colonial state existed, but provides no basis for unraveling the meaning which the Cazonci assigned to this affiliation. Thus there is no way to assess the sincerity of the Cazonci's attempts to fulfill what the conquerors believed to be his obligations. If we attempt to do so, we only accept the Spanish definition of this relationship, a hazardous stance—to say the least—since colonial situations are so notoriously fraught with misunderstanding.[28]

While we lack direct evidence revealing the Cazonci's perceptions of the initial colonial encounter, there is much to suggest that he viewed his early alliance with the Spaniards—specifically with Hernán Cortés and his allies—as a limited partnership among equals, defined according to his own needs and obligations. The Cazonci established a close relationship with Hernán Cortés soon after the successful Spanish military occupation of Tenochtitlán. As early as February 23, 1521, soldiers under the command of Hernán Cortés had met with representatives of the Cazonci—led by the Cazonci's adopted brother, Don Pedro—at "Tajimaroa," a village on the border between the regions controlled by the Mexica and Purhépecha empires.[29] As a result of these and other contacts, the Cazonci and Don Pedro had journeyed to Mexico City by 1524 or 1525, where they were received by Cortés.[30] In 1525, Cortés sponsored the Cazonci in his baptism by Franciscan missionaries, and on June 7, 1525, the newly christened Don Francisco agreed that some male children of the indigenous elite should be educated by the Franciscans.[31]

It is difficult to state precisely when and where Spanish settlers tried to establish their presence in Michoacán, although a preliminary survey of the region was taken by Antonio de Caraval, who most probably arrived in

28. Two works that examine this potential for misunderstanding are Inga Clendinnen, *Ambivalent Conquests: Maya and Spaniard in Yucatán, 1517–1570* (Cambridge, England, 1987), and Vicente Rafael, *Contracting Colonialism* (Ithaca, N.Y., 1988).

29. Martínez, "Los inicios," in Florescano, *Historia general de Michoacán*, 2:16–30; Ross Hassig, *Mexico and the Spanish Conquest* (London, 1994), 33–34; Warren, *Conquest of Michoacán*, 29; López Sarrelangue, *La nobleza indígena de Pátzcuaro*, 51.

30. These meetings are described in Cortés, *Letters from Mexico*, 266, 271.

31. López Sarrelangue, *La nobleza indígena de Pátzcuaro*, 52; Warren, *Conquest of Michoacán*, 83–84.

Michoacán in mid-1523.[32] Spanish attempts at settlement can be noted as early as 1524, and missionaries arrived in the region during 1525.[33] Legal proceedings against the Cazonci, which provide tangible proof of the difficulties Spanish settlers faced in occupying the region, were initiated by Bernaldino de Albornoz between June 25 and 28, 1529.[34] Only five years passed between the Cazonci's baptism, perhaps the strongest evidence of his accommodation to colonial rule, and his execution, obviously a sign that things were not going well. How can we explain the incongruity between the Cazonci's well-established friendly relationship with Cortés and his execution by those Spaniards who attempted to settle in Michoacán?

The most plausible explanation is that the Cazonci did not consider his relationship with Cortés a total surrender to Spanish colonial rule, or even an acceptance of an extensive Spanish presence in Michoacán. Rather, the Cazonci struck an alliance with Cortés informed by his own political concerns and obligations. The Purhépecha had been one of the few indigenous peoples to maintain their independence from the Aztec empire during the prehispanic era, and a fierce rivalry had existed between them.[35] Thus the Cazonci had no reason to view the initial Spanish military victory as anything but a boon to his people, and no reason not to seek Cortés out as an ally. Of course, this is far removed from "craving the protection of invincible beings," or even accepting "Spanish sovereignty and the Christian faith."[36] The strength of the myth of the Cazonci's acceptance of Spanish colonial rule can be traced to the failure of successive generations of historians to come to grips with the indigenous past, or even to search for traces of the indigenous presence in colonial sources. After all, the strongest challenge to this myth comes from the testimonies of Spanish settlers themselves.

32. Warren, *Conquest of Michoacán*, 74.

33. Ibid., 74–75.

34. Scholes and Adams, *Proceso*, 37, 43.

35. See Pollard, *Taríacuri's Legacy*, 167–85; idem, "Ecological Variation and Economic Exchange in the Tarascan State," *American Ethnologist* 9, no. 2 (May 1982): 250–68; and idem, "Prehispanic Urbanism at Tzintzuntzán, Michoacán" (Ph.D. diss., Columbia University, 1972). Also of interest are Marcia Castro-Leal, Clara L. Díaz, and Ma. Teresa García, "Los tarascos," in Florescano, *Historia general de Michoacán*, 1:191–304; Ulises Beltrán, "Tarascan State and Society in Prehispanic Times: An Ethnohistorical Inquiry" (Ph.D. diss., University of Chicago, 1985), 1–6, 63–77; Otto B. Schondube, "Las exploraciones arqueológicas en el área tarasca," in *La cultura Purhé: II coloquio de antropología e historia regionales*, comp. Francisco Miranda (Zamora, Mexico, 1980), 16–30; and Austin, *Tarascos y Mexicas*.

36. Prescott, *History of the Conquest of Mexico*, 236; Warren, *Conquest of Michoacán*, xii.

While Todorov may believe that the conquest of Michoacán was "swift and complete: no battle, no victims on the side of the conquistadores," the Spanish participants in this conquest had a decidedly different view.[37] Francisco de Villegas charged that the Cazonci was responsible for "the deaths of Spaniards in quantity."[38] Another Spanish settler, Miguel de Mesa, testified that "it was very public and notorious that in this province of Michoacán many Spaniards have died." Miguel de Mesa believed that the Cazonci bore responsibility for the Spaniards killed in the region, because "without his order the Indians would not have dared to do it."[39] More detailed testimony came from Juan López Patiño, who noted that six Spaniards had been killed in Tacamboro and three in Uruapan, and that several others had disappeared. López Patiño claimed that the Indians "would not have killed Christians if the said Cazonci had not ordered it because the entire land does that which he commands." López Patiño also noted ominously that "because the said Spaniards have disappeared and because the Indians that killed them confessed it, they killed the said Indians justly."[40] One witness, Francisco de los Ríos, testified that "in this province many Spanish have died but I do not know who ordered them to be killed."[41] However, like Miguel de Mesa and Juan López Patiño most witnesses held the Cazonci responsible for Spanish deaths.[42] All of the testimonies contained in the trial record flatly contradict the image of Indian passivity during the conquest of Michoacán.

Despite the fact that the indigenous people of Michoacán killed some Spanish settlers, at least initially indigenous resistance involved a selective rather than complete rejection of colonial rule. Obviously, Spanish attempts at occupying the region met a hostile reception, which extended to a rejection of the basic institutions of Spanish colonialism. Spanish missionaries complained that the resistance they met during this period almost forced them to abandon their task, and Spanish attempts to establish colonial economic institutions fared poorly as well.[43] Nevertheless, at least some factions of Spaniards—namely, those who recognized the Cazonci's continued local

37. Todorov, *Conquest of America*, 97.
38. Scholes and Adams, *Proceso*, 12.
39. Ibid., 31.
40. Ibid., 17–18.
41. Ibid., 30.
42. Ibid., 19, 27, 34.
43. *La Relación de Michoacán*, 355.

authority, and had not yet attempted settlement in the region—fared better than others. Gonzalo López, a resident of the village of Tenuxtitan, testified that

> in most of the province in her villages I have seen silver and I have not seen any Indians give it to their masters but I have been four or five months in this region; and I have seen that the said Cazonci has given much abundance of gold and silver to Don Hernando Cortés and to the treasurer Alonso de Estrada and to others that have come as judges to this province. And that in this refer yourself to the books of the foundry, in which will not be found melted or paid duty on [at the rate of twenty percent] silver nor gold of any Spaniard of this province but only that which Don Hernando Cortés has paid duty on, and as is public and notorious, the Cazonci has collected all this silver and he collects it from the villages that are granted in *encomienda* to the Spaniards.[44]

This quotation corroborates the existence of an alliance between Cortés, his allies, and the Cazonci and reveals the frustration felt by Spanish settlers at the Cazonci's continued authority. By all accounts, this frustration had become quite profound by the time that Spanish settlers began compiling legal documents to be used against the Cazonci.

The Spanish testimonies contained in the trial record of the Cazonci's execution reveal that Michoacán's indigenous peoples quickly resisted Spanish attempts at colonial occupation, despite the Cazonci's baptism and the gold and silver he gave to Cortés. This resistance involved a number of strategies, including an attempt to accommodate at least one faction of conquistadores, a refusal to recognize the legitimacy of Spanish direct tribute claims, flight, and armed attacks that resulted in Spanish deaths.[45] This reality challenges dominant representations of the conquest of the region, which have emphasized Indian passivity and the rapid acceptance of Spanish colonial rule. This climate of resistance, and perceived political instability, also formed the context in which Spanish colonials executed the Cazonci. We cannot understand this execution unless we take into account the frustrations of the initial wave

44. Scholes and Adams, *Proceso*, 16.
45. Ibid., 12, 14, 16–19, 27–28, 31, 35, 39.

of Spanish settlers and their self-defined need to establish control over the region. To do so, they believed they had to remove the Cazonci from power, despite whatever alliances he may have forged. Thus the need to construct a particular image of the Cazonci, one that would justify the actions they intended to take.

The Construction of a Colonized "Other"

Spanish settlers, and their military ally Nuño de Guzmán, compiled their trial record in the hope of legitimizing an action they intended to take prior to the collection of testimonies—or, at the very least, prior to the time when Francisco de Villegas assembled his witnesses. As Villegas himself remarked in his introductory comments, before hearing witnesses respond to his questioning, "the said Cazonci . . . with his contrivances and with an abundance of gold and silver has freed himself from the punishments he has deserved."[46] Villegas, and the other Spaniards involved, believed that the Cazonci deserved punishment and saw the trial record as a way of demonstrating—to other Spanish settlers and royal authorities in Spain—that they had delivered it in a "legitimate" manner. Recognizing this basic reality should not be controversial. As is well known, the Spanish legal tradition of this era did not presume innocence.

The trial record is open to multiple readings. However, anyone reading it should recognize that the information obtained and recorded in each section of the document was shaped by the concerns of those devising the questions. The brief investigation by Bernaldino de Albornoz indicated rising Spanish frustration with indigenous challenges to the colonial presence, particularly their refusal to serve in the *encomienda* and the depopulation of the villages. More detailed information about similar charges is provided in the Villegas lawsuit. This section also contains information revealing a hardening of Spanish attitudes toward the Cazonci. At this point, we can note that some Spaniards began to conceive of the Cazonci not only as "other," but as a "perverse" and "murderous" other. This image of the Cazonci, notable in the Villegas lawsuit, pervades the section produced by Nuño de Guzmán. The final section, which details the Cazonci's trial and execution, focuses primarily on issues of military security, armed threats, and justifying the

46. Ibid., 12.

repressive measures Spanish colonials deemed necessary to curtail mounting indigenous rebellion.[47] Although each of these sections has a distinct identity, they are linked. When analyzed contextually, they provide glimpses into a historically specific instance of the construction of "otherness" for a particular purpose, in this case, the legitimization of the execution of the Cazonci.[48]

Although Bernaldino de Albornoz claimed that he would provide testimonies from nine Spaniards—whom he lists by name—and all the Indians who "could be brought forward profitably," in the end only five nearly identical Spanish testimonies were recorded in the version of the trial record that reached royal authorities. The profound similarity between these testimonies is not surprising, given that the five witnesses responded to a standardized set of questions prepared by Bernaldino de Albornoz. Spanish settlers in Michoacán certainly considered the information elicited by these questions as evidence of criminal wrongdoing, which is why they chose to insert a record of this investigation into the lawsuit compiled seven months later by Francisco de Villegas. Surprisingly, however, the primary targets of this earlier investigation were the Cazonci's adopted brother, Cuinierángari/ Don Pedro, and Nahuatl speakers identified as Francisco and Gonzalo Xuárez.[49] A more sustained attack on the Cazonci developed later, at the initiative of Francisco de Villegas.

Bernaldino de Albornoz completed his investigation on June 28, 1529. On January 26, 1530, Francisco de Villegas began collecting testimony. The questions asked by Villegas repeat and go beyond those asked by Albornoz. Like Albornoz, Villegas sought information about the continued rule of the Cazonci and the local indigenous elite, the refusal of Michoacán's indigenous peoples to participate in the *encomienda,* and the depopulation of the villages. He also inquired about silver mines the Cazonci allegedly had "in all the villages of this province." Villegas sought information about how the Cazonci encouraged the Indians to hide these mines from their Spanish masters, while also preventing them from giving silver to the Spaniards. On a

47. Ibid., 11–36, 36–44, 44–68.
48. On the finely grained ways in which the self/other dynamic is constructed in various historical contexts, see Steve J. Stern, *The Secret History of Gender* (Chapel Hill, N.C., 1995), 217–21, 226–27; Gruzinski, *Conquest of Mexico,* 79, 86; and James Lockhart, "Sightings: Initial Nahua Reactions to Spanish Culture," in *Implicit Understanding,* ed. Stuart B. Schwartz (Cambridge, England, 1994), 238–39.
49. Scholes and Adams, *Proceso,* 37, 36–42.

more ominous note, Villegas asked witnesses if they knew, had seen, or heard of an "abundance" of Spanish deaths in the province, all or most of which could be attributed to the Cazonci.[50] In total, the Villegas lawsuit contains the testimonies of thirteen Spanish witnesses, a confession from the Cazonci, a statement from a Spaniard appointed by Nuño de Guzmán to defend him, an interrogation of Don Pedro, and a record of the Albornoz investigation.

Villegas asked more questions of a greater number of Spanish witnesses than did Albornoz, and also recorded two indigenous accounts. He also sought information assigning responsibility for the killing of Spaniards—an issue not raised by Albornoz only seven months earlier—which implies that the situation had worsened. The sixth and seventh questions asked by Villegas were entirely new. The sixth refers to prior investigations against the Cazonci that allegedly produced evidence of "sodomy"—in this instance meaning male to male sexual intimacy, possibly with an adult/youth dimension, although the document is vague about specific practices—and the seventh concerns the aforementioned killing of Spaniards. According to Villegas, this led past investigators to conclude that the Cazonci merited death.[51] As the editors of the published version of the trial record point out, the only record of prior investigations included in the text is that of Albornoz.[52] In his questions, Villegas referred to these other past investigations, while Albornoz did not. Either they did not exist at the time of Albornoz's investigation, or he did not feel compelled to cite them. Villegas, on the other hand, included references to them in his questions because he wished to add an additional layer of legitimacy to the charges against the Cazonci, an intention probably related to the proximity of the Cazonci's execution. In this context, Villegas's attempt in the sixth question to elicit information concerning the Cazonci's alleged sodomy takes on added significance.

Any discussion of indigenous sexuality taken from Spanish colonial documents must begin by noting that colonizers utilized descriptions of indigenous sexuality as a means of justifying colonial rule.[53] Scholars who ignore

50. Ibid., 14.
51. Ibid., 14, 15.
52. Ibid., 24 n. 5.
53. Araceli Barbosa Sánchez, *Sexo y conquista* (Mexico City, 1994), 14, 54–70; Jonathan Goldberg, "Sodomy in the New World: Anthropologies Old and New," *Social Text* 29 (1991): 46–56; Ramón Gutiérrez, *When Jesus Came, the Corn Mothers Went Away* (Stanford, Calif., 1991), 73; Richard C. Trexler, *Sex and Conquest* (Ithaca, N.Y., 1995), 1–4.

this basic fact tend—perhaps unintentionally—to reproduce the biases of colonial documentation. This is especially the case when colonial discussions of indigenous sexuality are selectively cited. Frequently, this is done in a manner that also ignores the basic truth that many sexualities have been expressed, and repressed, in all historical epochs, and among all human cultures.[54] For example, based primarily on his reading of the trial record and perhaps other colonial sources, Warren concludes that "homosexuality was not uncommon among them."[55] He is referring, of course, to the indigenous peoples of Michoacán. While this may have been true, no mention is made of the fact that the same could have been said about European society, or that classifications of sexual behavior have shifted substantially over time.[56] Perhaps more important, there is no discussion of how the use of the charge of sodomy played a strategic role in justifying particular colonial actions, one of which was the execution of the Cazonci. Be that as it may, we can discern a pattern to the questions asked by Francisco de Villegas. Villegas included the question seeking information about the Cazonci's alleged sodomy immediately prior to the question aimed at establishing his responsibility for Spanish deaths. In this latter question, Villegas also sought confirmation that a previous investigator found that the Cazonci merited execution for his crimes.[57] Obviously, the stakes here were very high. Villegas almost certainly aimed at confirming the Cazonci's guilt—from a Spanish perspective—while demonstrating his "perversity," a factor that would facilitate his execution.

Surprisingly, given the extent to which future historians reproduced the charge of the Cazonci's alleged sodomy, the response of witnesses to this question contained considerable ambivalence. Of the thirteen Spanish witnesses questioned by Villegas, only one, Gonzalo López, responded entirely positively. He stated: "To the sixth question he said that . . . this witness had heard rumors about it and thus it is public and notorious."[58] Four Spanish

54. Peter Brown, *The Body and Society* (New York, 1988), 21–23; Alfredo López Austin, *The Human Body and Ideology*, trans. Thelma Ortiz de Montellano and Bernard Ortiz de Montellano (Salt Lake City, Utah, 1988), 1:235, 238, 244, 255, 290–312.

55. Warren, *Conquest of Michoacán*, 19.

56. Mary Elizabeth Perry, *Gender and Disorder in Early Modern Seville* (Princeton, 1990), esp. 118–36; Jeffrey Weeks, *Sexuality and Its Discontents* (London, 1985); Michel Foucault, *The History of Sexuality*, trans. Robert Hurley (New York, 1978).

57. Scholes and Adams, *Proceso*, 14–15.

58. Ibid., 16.

witnesses responded that they had heard these charges, but had not witnessed the alleged crimes. Three Spanish witnesses, questioned by Juan de la Peña but whose testimony was included in the Villegas lawsuit, were not asked about charges of sodomy.[59] The notary recorded that the remaining five testified that they knew nothing about it.[60]

For their part, the Cazonci and Cuinierángari either were not asked about, or denied, the charges of sodomy leveled by Villegas. Cuinierángari responded to the same set of questions the Spanish witnesses did, and said that he knew nothing about the charges of sodomy. However, his testimony does condemn the Cazonci, and is quite fascinating, particularly when we recognize that by the late 1530s Cuinierángari had utilized his contacts with Spaniards to become Don Pedro, the Spanish-appointed governor of Michoacán.[61] It is here that we can note the opportunism of Cuinierángari beginning to emerge, a tendency that would fully flower only after the execution of the Cazonci. In sum, although denying the charge of sodomy, Cuinierángari testified that local Indians continued to serve and pay tribute to the Cazonci, and that the Cazonci had ordered the deaths of four Spanish settlers.[62] These claims, because of their plausibility, provided compelling evidence in the campaign to execute the Cazonci. With hindsight, we can also see that the Cazonci's execution created a void in local indigenous political authority. By the time of the compilation of the *Relación de Michoacán*, Cuinierángari's alliance with the missionary faction of Spanish colonizers had enabled him to fill this void.

The Villegas lawsuit also contained a confession from the Cazonci, obtained by the conquistador Nuño de Guzmán. Apparently after hearing the first three Spanish witnesses, Nuño de Guzmán ordered the Cazonci taken into custody. According to the chief constable Juan de Burgos, the Cazonci had been kept "prisoner with shackles and chain" prior to January 27, 1530. On this date, Nuño de Guzmán and the translator Juan Pascual went to the prison where the Cazonci was being held to record his confession. At this point, Nuño de Guzmán did not display much concern with any sodomy charges, at least none that was recorded in the text. Rather, his questions centered on silver and gold. He also confronted the Cazonci about Spanish

59. Ibid., 42–43.
60. Ibid., 18, 27, 28, 29, 30.
61. *La Relación de Michoacán*, 296–99; Stone, "A Fragile Coalition," 172–81.
62. Scholes and Adams, *Proceso*, 35–36.

deaths and the refusal of Indians to serve in the *encomienda*. He asked the Cazonci about the silver and gold he had given to Hernán Cortés and Cristobal de Olid, and the Cazonci replied that it had been collected by his ancestors. He then questioned him about a silver mine in one of the villages, and the Cazonci replied that this mine had existed, but that the Spaniards had taken all the silver from it. The Cazonci also denied Spanish charges that he had ordered Spaniards killed, and that he took gold, silver, and other things belonging to the Spaniards.[63]

All three sections of the final document submitted to royal authorities paid close attention to legalism, that is, to the customary adherence to the protocol required in the Spanish legal tradition of this era. For Bernaldino de Albornoz, this attention to legalism can be noted in his compilation of a standardized list of questions presented to each witness, and in the care taken to identify when and where the testimonies were recorded. The Villegas lawsuit also contains a list of standardized questions. These were deemed of such importance that the Spanish notary carefully recorded them twice, once at the beginning of the lawsuit, and again following the insertion of the Cazonci's confession and a mandatory statement by his defender. In addition, the text of the Villegas lawsuit is permeated with standard references to the fact that the entire proceeding was being carried out in conformance to the norms and obligations of Spanish law. The terms "en forma de derecho" and "según derecho"—that is, "in the established practice of law" and "according to the law"—appear frequently, and each individual swore an oath before testifying.[64] This persistent emphasis on legalism demonstrates an intent to act with respect for the proper authorities, and in the proper manner, as defined by the Spaniards.

In terms of the raw exercise of power, Nuño de Guzmán's interrogation of the Cazonci and other indigenous witnesses is unsurpassed in the text, although undoubtedly he had the support and assistance of many, and probably all, the Spaniards who testified. Indeed, the manner in which information is collected in the portion of the text compiled under the direction of Nuño de Guzmán is the most revealing aspect of this entire affair. By the time that Nuño de Guzmán began his interrogation of the Cazonci and other indigenous witnesses—between February 5 and 14, 1530—his entire entourage had moved from Tzintzuntzan, the former center of the Purhépecha empire, to a

63. Ibid., 19–22.
64. Ibid., 11–15, 18–19, 20–23, 26–28, 30–32, 34–35, 37–38.

location alongside the Lerma river in west-central Mexico.[65] Here, Guzmán and his army remained poised—with the Cazonci presumably still held in chains—ready to embark on their invasion of lands to the north, soon to be called Nueva Galicia, and today known as Jalisco.

Invasions are risky business, and Nuño de Guzmán had ample reason to be jittery. The Spanish camp was rife with rumors—the Cazonci had "put many people of war in the village of Cuynao," the local indigenous population was bristling with "arms and projectiles and provisions," blood sacrifices had been made to pagan idols—and the Spaniards profoundly feared an Indian attack they believed to be imminent.[66] By moving into the region controlled by the Cazonci, Spanish settlers had initiated a period of intensifying conflicts. At this point, local Spaniards believed that the situation had become intolerable. Thus the Spanish settlers and Nuño de Guzmán perceived the need to demonstrate their authority, and believed that the humiliation— and ultimately the public execution—of the Cazonci provided the best vehicle for doing so.

Death as Public Spectacle:
Legalism, Torture, and Execution as Rituals of Power

Years later, in his memoirs, Nuño de Guzmán recalled that "the Cazonci, lord of Michoacán, had insulted and killed many Spaniards."[67] His selection of the term "insulted" was significant. By challenging Spanish colonial authority, failing to provide sufficient amounts of gold and silver, and possibly being responsible for Spanish deaths, the Cazonci had wounded Nuño de Guzmán's sense of honor. In this time and space, as in others, perceptions of wounded honor were highly gendered phenomena. Perceived attacks on an individual's honor tended to produce a violent response.[68] Unfortunately for the Cazonci, this reality, combined with Spanish fears of their own imminent destruction, proved to be an extremely volatile combination.

65. Ibid., 44.
66. Ibid.
67. Nuño de Guzmán, *Memoria de los servicios que había hecho Nuño de Guzmán, desde que fue nombrado gobernador de Pánuco en 1525,* edited and annotated by Manuel Carrera Stampa (Mexico City, 1955), 63–64.
68. On gender and conquest, see Louis Montrose, "The Work of Gender in the Discourse of Discovery," *Representations* 33 (Winter 1991): 1–41. On gender, political culture, and violence, see Stern, *Secret History of Gender,* esp. 151–88.

The section of the trial record attributed to Nuño de Guzmán does not contain a standardized list of questions, although the interrogation of witnesses followed a set pattern. Nuño de Guzmán questioned only Indian witnesses. This section of the document included—in the following order— interviews with two Indian witnesses; the questioning by torture of the Cazonci, Cuinierángari, and Indians identified as Don Alonso "in Tarascan called Vise," Gonzalo Xuárez, and Don Alonso de Avalos "known as Acanysante"; a post-torture statement from Don Pedro; two additional Indian testimonies; and a description of the sentencing and execution of the Cazonci. This section contains a graphic description of the tortures employed by Nuño de Guzmán. Although macabre, this description will be discussed in some detail, for the following reasons. We must recall, as Todorov indicates, that colonizing Spaniards constructed "receivable" accounts of their activities, an insight as valid for historical documents as it is for narrative chronicles.[69] This means that they believed, correctly, that the methods employed in this instance did not deviate from the standards of the era.[70] Nuño de Guzmán insisted that he interrogated his victims "in the accustomed form and manner," and it is appropriate to discuss precisely what he meant.[71] In addition, the experience of torture, public humiliation, and ultimately execution played a highly symbolic and essential role in the consolidation of a colonial order in the region. To state simply that the tortures were brutal does not adequately express the significance, or sufficiently describe the content, of what transpired.

Nuño de Guzmán began his investigation by questioning a witness identified as "Cuaraque, Tarascan Indian." He had two lines of inquiry, each intended to elicit information that would facilitate the Cazonci's execution. First, he sought to establish that an Indian attack was imminent; and second, he sought to further the construction—begun by other Spaniards—of an image of the Cazonci as a "perverse other." He asked Cuaraque "if he has heard to say or knew that the Cazonci has people of war in Cuynao, a village of Chichimecas." As recorded by the Spanish notary, aided by the translation

69. Todorov, *Conquest of America*, 54.
70. Michel Foucault, *Discipline and Punish*, trans. Alan Sheridan (New York, 1979), esp. 1–69. Ritual violence can be noted across cultures in this era. For examples relevant to Mexican history, see Inga Clendinnen, "The Cost of Courage in Aztec Society," *Past and Present* 107 (May, 1985): 44–89, and *The Aztecs* (Cambridge, England, 1991), esp. 236–63. Also see López Austin, *The Human Body and Ideology*, 1:375–82.
71. Scholes and Adams, *Proceso*, 48, 56, 60.

of Juan Pascual, the witness reportedly responded in the affirmative, noting that for six months "many people of war with their weapons from the entire province of Michoacán" had gathered there, some unwillingly and under the threat of death from the Cazonci. Cuaraque went on to testify that the Cazonci had planned an ambush with other Indians, and that the process of arming the Indians had continued, even after Nuño de Guzmán entered the region. Cuaraque also testified that the Cazonci had ordered Spaniards killed, as did Guanax, another Indian interviewed prior to the torture of the Cazonci.[72]

Nuño de Guzmán also sought information about religious and sexual practices the Spaniards considered abhorrent, and rhetorically useful for the condemnation of the Cazonci. He asked the witness "if he knew whether the said Cazonci has sacrificed any Indians to his idols and whether he has killed by [his] command any Spaniard."[73] Cuaraque responded that the Cazonci did sacrifice Indians, and that he had ordered five Christians killed, and sacrificed them to the idols Yoroacuse and Querendaro. According to the testimony of Cuaraque—as recorded in the final copy of the document presented to royal authorities—the Cazonci kept the skins with a "huge idol." Reportedly, he, Cuinierángari, and "Coyuze, a Nahuatl speaker who is already dead" occasionally dressed in these skins. No Spanish witnesses were asked about, and only one reported, such a scandalous and obviously useful event. As recorded by the Spanish notary, Pedro Muñoz—identified as a "teacher from Roa"—stated that he and one "Juan Xuárez" traveled to Pátzcuaro for the sole purpose of burning indigenous idols and the remains of sacrificial victims. Muñoz testified that Xuárez went to a place where the local Indians worshiped idols "to look for the skins of the Christians that they had killed there, that they had said to him that they have them there, but that he would burn them."[74] This is the only time this practice is mentioned in the entire text, in all of the Spanish testimonies, prior to the interrogations of Nuño de Guzmán. Nevertheless, Nuño de Guzmán extracted information "confirming" this charge with great vigor.

In addition, in response to Guzmán's question concerning the Cazonci's alleged sodomy, Cuaraque replied: "He has male Indians with whom he couples, that the one is called Juanico, who is in Pascuaro . . . , and another that

72. Ibid., 45–48.
73. Ibid., 46.
74. Ibid., 33.

he knew is a youth that is called Guysaquaro . . . and that it is notorious among the Indian servants of the said Cazonci, . . . that when the said Cazonci is drunk, he has seen him put his tongue in his mouth and kiss the said Juanillo, and since he was little the said Cazonci had them for that purpose."[75] Whatever the "truth" of this particular passage, we can note that its inclusion at this point in the trial, torture, and execution demonstrates the construction of an image of the Cazonci as a "perverse other" in the eyes of his Spanish interrogators. This was an essential step in creating the necessary distance, between victor and victim, for what was to ensue.

Humiliation plays an essential role in establishing, maintaining, and experiencing relationships of domination.[76] This important insight helps us understand the behavior of Nuño de Guzmán and others who seek to dominate, as well as the resistance their actions encounter. According to the trial record, Nuño de Guzmán began his torture of the Cazonci by stating that "to better know the truth" the Cazonci must be tortured "in the accustomed form and manner."[77]

Guzmán placed great emphasis on conformance to standard, even customary procedures, and on recording these proceedings in writing. As we shall see, he carried out the interrogation of these individuals with a technical proficiency long the hallmark of those engaged in professional torture.[78] Indeed, it is plausible that the strands of professionalism and adherence to protocol, combined with a hatred bred by distancing and the perception of an immediate physical threat, were intertwined in the thought and actions of Nuño de Guzmán.

On February 5, 1530, Guzmán ordered his sentence condemning the Cazonci to torture be carried out. He was careful to note that "if any injury, wound or death came to him, it is his fault" and not that of Guzmán's, since it was the Cazonci, and not he, who had refused to tell the truth.[79] At this point, the Spaniards seated the Cazonci on a ladder and tied his arms to it. In

75. Ibid., 47.
76. James C. Scott, *Domination and the Arts of Resistance* (New Haven, Conn., 1990), xii, 37, III; Gerald Sider, "When Parrots Learn to Talk and Why They Can't: Domination, Deception and Self-Deception in Indian-White Relations," *Comparative Studies in Society and History* 29 (1987): 21.
77. Scholes and Adams, *Proceso*, 48.
78. Foucault, *Discipline and Punish*, 34–35; A. J. Langguth, *Hidden Terrors* (New York, 1978).
79. Scholes and Adams, *Proceso*, 48.

reference to what happened next, Patricia de Fuentes—who translated and edited several eyewitness accounts of the Spanish Conquest, including one describing this incident—provides essential background information: "In the cord and water torture, a strong thin cord was tied around the victim's temples and the fleshy parts of the arms and legs. A heavy rod was placed under the cord next to the body, and turned so as to slowly tighten the cord, which cut deeper and deeper into the bleeding flesh. Then cold water was dropped onto the cord, making it contract and tighten further."[80] Nuño de Guzmán, and the Spaniards under his command, inflicted a variant of this, and additional tortures, on the Cazonci and the other indigenous victims during their interrogation.

The Spanish notary employed a straightforward narrative to record the tortures in the trial record. After being tied to the ladder, the Cazonci denied that he knew anything. Then, "his arms were tied with the cords and turned." At this point, the Cazonci admitted that the people of Cuynao and surrounding areas served him and gave him tribute. Guzmán then recited the full range of Spanish charges against the Cazonci—plotting an attack on Guzmán's army; killing Christians; sacrificing Christians and keeping their skins for what he believed were native rituals; worshiping idols; ordering indigenous villages created by the Spaniards to depopulate; and commanding that the Indians refuse service to their Spanish masters—and then stopped, possibly waiting for the Cazonci's response. The Cazonci sidestepped the charges, admitting that four Christians and possibly some indigenous nobles had been killed, but claiming this killing had not been at his command. Here the text indicates that the Spaniards waited for a while. In fact, periods of waiting are interspersed throughout the interrogation, following each cluster of questions and answers. These intervals allowed the cords to tighten, thus creating—for the Cazonci—an exhausting experience of intensifying pain. After some time, the Cazonci admitted that an indigenous lord from the village of Cuyseo, entrusted to Gonzalo López, had been discovered dead. This did not satisfy Guzmán, who ordered his legs tied as well, and repeated the rejoinder that the Cazonci, and not he, bore responsibility for the injuries that would result from this torture.[81]

80. Patricia de Fuentes, ed. and trans., *The Conquistadores: First-Person Accounts of the Conquest of Mexico* (New York, 1963), 243. A more sensationalist description of this torture can be found in López Portillo y Weber, *La conquista de la Nueva Galicia*, 159.

81. Scholes and Adams, *Proceso*, 48–49.

After another period of waiting, Guzmán decided to try additional measures. An unidentified Spaniard struck the Cazonci on the right arm with a club, once, then once again. Interestingly, the Spanish notary employed passive constructions to record the tortures and active ones to record the Cazonci's alleged crimes. The notary recorded that the Cazonci then stated "he has not done anything more than that which he has said." After an additional period of waiting, the Cazonci reportedly said that if the *alguaciles*, or constables—in this context undoubtedly referring to Nuño de Guzmán's assistants—went away, he would say the truth. At this point, he testified that he had continued to prepare for war after Nuño de Guzmán arrived, plotted an ambush in Cuynao, ordered Christians killed and kept their skins, and that he had continued to worship "idols." After this, Nuño de Guzmán ordered the torture stopped, although he noted that it could be resumed as necessary. Not quite an hour after his torture had ceased, the Cazonci "was read and made to understand his confession by the said Juan Pascual."[82] Apparently, he agreed that it was accurate. Having successfully forced the Cazonci to confirm the "truth" that he had constructed prior to the interrogation, Nuño de Guzmán turned his attention to the other Indians in custody.

In essence, the torture of these victims followed the same procedure as that applied to the Cazonci, although there were some variations. The most surprising aspect of Cuinierángari's testimony—which began on February 6, 1530, one day after that of the Cazonci—is that he readily conceded most of Guzmán's charges, but was tortured anyway. This demonstrates that Guzmán was not interested in mere information. He was also seeking to humiliate his victims, to establish total Spanish dominance and control. Cuinierángari actually received harsher treatment than the Cazonci. In addition to the cord and water torture, he received the cudgel seven times, with each blow separated by a sufficient interval to allow the cords to tighten. Cuinierángari also had "a red cloth" placed in his mouth. The Spaniards then poured a jar of water over this cloth, thus temporarily covering his mouth and nose.[83] At this point, Cuinierángari agreed that the charges of basing an ambush in Cuynao, of killing Christians, of dressing in Christian skins, of worshiping idols, and of planning to kill all the Christians in Guzmán's army

82. Ibid., 49–50.
83. Ibid., 53; Warren, *Conquest of Michoacán,* 230.

were true. The notary also recorded that he denied there were traps waiting for the Spaniards. Instead, he reportedly stated that "ten times eight hundred men" awaited the Christians.[84] In a manner identical to that of the Cazonci, Guzmán ordered Cuinierángari's torture stopped, while noting that the process could begin again as needed. Cuinierángari's interrogation also concludes with Juan Pascual reading the transcript of the confession to the torture victim, who at that point agreed it was the truth.[85]

The torture of the other Indians—Don Alonso/Vise, Gonzalo Xuárez, and Don Alonso de Avalos/Acanysante—followed the same pattern as the tortures of the Cazonci and Don Pedro/Cuinierángari.[86] However, their tortures were more intense, and in the case of the latter two involved a different and even more brutal torture, apparently because they steadfastly denied all Spanish charges. In addition to the cord and water torture and repeated clubbings, Vise did not confess until six jars of water had been poured over the cloth stuffed in his mouth.[87] Gonzalo Xuárez and Acanysante never confessed, although in the midst of his tortures Gonzalo Xuárez blamed the Cazonci and Cuinierángari for killing the Spaniards. This was despite the fact that they received the cord and water torture, garrotes, several jars of water poured over cloth stuffed in their mouths, and finally had their feet wetted, wrapped in cotton, and placed into braziers of red hot coals.[88]

Guzmán concluded his investigation by interviewing two more Indian witnesses who were not tortured, possibly because they readily confirmed that the Cazonci had ordered Christians killed and was planning an ambush, or perhaps because it had been a long day for the Spaniards and they weren't important enough to humiliate. On February 13, 1530, Nuño de Guzmán concluded his investigation by giving a copy of the confessions obtained to the Cazonci's defense counsel and demanding a response. Reportedly, the Cazonci did not respond to or say anything against this new information. On February 14, 1530, Nuño de Guzmán, having reviewed the available evidence and obtained additional proof, condemned the Cazonci to "be taken from the prison in which he is, his feet and hands tied, with a cord to his throat, and with the voice of a crier that makes known his crime be placed on a

84. Scholes and Adams, *Proceso*, 54.
85. Ibid., 55.
86. Ibid., 55–58, 59–61, 61–63.
87. Ibid., 56–58.
88. Ibid., 59–63.

pannier if it could be had, and tied to the tail of a nag to be brought round about from where camp is pitched and be carried conjoined to the passage of this river and there to be bound to a large piece of squared wood and burned in vigorous flames until he dies naturally and is made ashes."[89] Guzmán also ordered that if the Cazonci wanted to die as a Christian—since he had received "the water of baptism," although he had "returned to idolatry," as indicated by his confession—he be "given a garrote to the throat," or strangled, prior to being burned. In this way, according to Guzmán, the Cazonci would die and his "vital spirit" could be separated from his body, prior to his burning. He also commanded that the Cazonci's ashes be scattered into the river, so that the Indians would not worship his remains. Guzmán concluded by seizing the Cazonci's property, claiming that his estate would be applied to the costs of the trial, and ultimately revert to His Majesty.[90] After a last-minute appeal by the Cazonci's appointed defender, which was immediately rejected, the Spaniards carried out their sentence.[91] Thus ended the life of the Cazonci. So, too, ends the colonial document recording his trial, torture, and execution.

Reading this source "against the grain" allows us to uncover multiple truths obscured or only partially reflected in the conqueror's account; this process challenges the myth of Indian passivity and acquiescence to Spanish colonial rule during the conquest of Michoacán. As I have argued, Spanish settlers chose to execute the Cazonci because of frustration with his continuing authority and power following their occupation of the region. The Cazonci's alliance with Cortés proved useful to both during the initial phase of the Spanish Conquest. However, in the end this alliance could not protect him. Given the well-known rivalry between Cortés and Nuño de Guzmán, it is plausible to suggest that the Cazonci also may have been victimized by the factional politics of the conquerors themselves. In order to make the Cazonci's execution "receivable"—among themselves as well as among their Spanish colonial peers—Guzmán and his allies needed to construct an image of the Cazonci as a perverse and murderous "other." They did so by collecting testimony and by compiling a record demonstrating that the entire event had been conducted in compliance with Spanish colonial norms. Recognizing the "constructedness" of this historical document is the essential first step in evaluating the evidence it provides.

89. Ibid., 66.
90. Ibid., 66–67.
91. Ibid., 67.

The trial, torture, and public execution of the Cazonci also constructed a "receivable" message asserting Spanish dominance. This message was intended for the colonized. However, it was also intended for the colonizers, and was as much a response to their fears and doubts as a display of their strength. The Cazonci's executioners believed that their actions had substantial justification, and their beliefs derived from experience as well as fantasy. Power, as Foucault and others have noted, tends to create its own truths.[92] In fact, power creates its own illusions, delusions, and projections, and presents them as "truth." In the ambiguous and shifting circumstances of this early colonial encounter, it must have been difficult to know precisely where truth blurred into fiction. In the course of their investigation, Spanish interrogators uncovered and manufactured evidence of overt and subtle threats to their efforts at establishing colonial rule. These threats were real in the eyes of a settler population that had experienced such persistent difficulties in seizing indigenous wealth and establishing control.

In the end, however, the Spaniard's deepest fear never materialized, or at least did not materialize in this time and place. The attack by "ten times eight hundred men" never happened.[93] According to García del Pilar, a self-seeking ally of Nuño de Guzmán present during the trial, torture, and execution of the Cazonci:

> We left there after spending twenty-five days more or less, suffering hunger and want, and we took along Don Alonso, Don Pedro, and the Nahuatl interpreters, who were so disabled from the tortures inflicted on them that they could travel only in hammock litters. We followed the river downstream through uninhabited country for seven or eight days, until we reached a town called Cuynao, where we made war and burned the town, and all the people fled to the hills. From there we also made raids on the surrounding hills. After we had been in Cuynao about two weeks the people came to give themselves up peaceably, and we departed leaving it in peace.[94]

Thus ended the threat of Spanish annihilation.

92. Foucault, *Discipline and Punish*, 35–36, 49; Steven Best and Douglas Kellner, *Postmodern Theory* (New York, 1991).

93. Scholes and Adams, *Proceso*, 54.

94. García del Pilar, "The Chronicle of García de Pilar," in de Fuentes, *The Conquistadores*, 201.

Nuño de Guzmán in History

Juan Infante, despite the fact that he did not participate in the Spanish Conquest, emerged as the most powerful *encomendero* in Michoacán during the 1530s and 1540s.[95] He defended Nuño de Guzmán's execution of the Cazonci while testifying in a lawsuit filed by Hernán Cortés, Guzmán's rival for power during the first-generation political struggles among Spanish colonizers.[96] According to Infante, after the Cazonci was "burned," Michoacán had been reformed.[97] In his testimony, Infante recognized a basic truth, which is that there are no conquests without men like Nuño de Guzmán.

Although Nuño de Guzmán was brutal, it would be wrong to view him as exceptional. Similar scenarios were played out in many other sixteenth-century contexts. As Foucault has demonstrated, public and even ritual execution was a basic feature of European society during and after the era of Nuño de Guzmán.[98] The execution of the Inca emperor Atahualpa at Cajamarca in 1532—which established Spanish dominance in Peru—bears a strong resemblance to the execution of the Cazonci, as does the 1572 execution of the neo-Inca insurgent Tupac Amaru, under the direction of the Viceroy Francisco de Toledo. Indeed, Toledo so feared that indigenous peoples would worship the slain leader's remains that he violated standard procedure and commanded that Tupac Amaru's head not be displayed on a post. Toledo simultaneously ordered indigenous religious relics destroyed and launched a vicious persecution against Tupac Amaru's surviving

95. For information on Infante, see Carlos S. Paredes M., "El tributo indígena en la region del lago de Pátzcuaro," in Carlos S. Paredes Martínez, Marcela Irais Piñon Flores, Armando M. Escobar Olmedo, and María Trinidad Pulido Solis, *Michoacán en el siglo XVI* (Morelia, Mexico, 1984), 37–43; J. Benedict Warren, *La administración de los negocios de un encomendero en Michoacán* (Mexico City, 1984), and Fintan B. (J. Benedict) Warren, *Vasco de Quiroga*, 89–97; Robert Theron Himmerich, "The Encomenderos of New Spain, 1521–1555" (Ph.D. diss., University of California, Los Angeles, 1984), 331; and Martínez, "Los inicios," in Florescano, *Historia general de Michoacán*, 2:106–10.

96. These struggles have become legendary. They are frequently commented upon in the literature, a prime example being Peggy K. Liss, *Mexico Under Spain, 1521–1566* (Chicago, 1975), 51–52.

97. "Juicio seguido por Hernán Cortés contra los Lics. Matienzo y Delgadillo año 1531," *Boletín del Archivo General del al Nación* 9, no. 3 (July/August/September 1938), 357–58.

98. Foucault, *Discipline and Punish*, esp. 1–69. See especially 3–6 for an example of this sort of ritual violence in a European setting.

relatives, thus taking his crusade far beyond that of Nuño de Guzmán.[99] Public corporal punishment remained extremely common throughout the colonial period in Latin America. There is also the basic reality that the scope of these selective killings pale in comparison to the massive bloodletting involved in the major military confrontations of the initial conquest, such as the final Spanish overthrow of the Aztec empire at Tenochtitlán, in 1521.[100] All of these factors, then, argue against interpreting the execution of the Cazonci as a uniquely violent event.

Despite this, future generations of intellectuals did not defend Nuño de Guzmán, as Juan Infante had. In fact, throughout the centuries, representations of Guzmán as an exceptional figure, perhaps even a criminal deviant or psychopath, have appeared frequently. These images of Nuño de Guzmán are pervasive, even dominant, and they have their own ideological implications. As recently as 1993, Hugh Thomas wrote of Guzmán's "savageries," which made those of other conquistadors "look mild." In 1990, the Mexican novelist Herminio Martínez concluded his *Diario maldito de Nuño de Guzmán*—which translates as *The Accursed Diary of Nuño de Guzmán*— with the declaration "Nuño Beltrán de Guzmán, the cruelest case that one could speak of." Todorov, in *The Conquest of America* (1984), having immersed himself in the writings of Hernán Cortés, referred to Nuño de Guzmán as a "conquistador and tyrant." In *Motolinia's History of the Indians of New Spain*, Francis Borgia Steck declares that Nuño de Guzmán's "unsavory career in Pánuco, Mexico City and northwestern New Spain constitutes the blackest page of early Mexican history." In *The Spanish Empire in America* C. H. Haring describes Guzmán as "a rapacious and cruel tyrant." In *Many Mexicos* Lesley Byrd Simpson notes that "his capacity for hatred was only equaled by an apparent delight in sadistical orgies of burning, torture, and destruction." In *The Audiencia of New Galicia in the Sixteenth Century* J. H. Parry calls him "a natural gangster" whose "dominant characteristic was a sombre ferocity, a demonic energy which enabled him to command and hold together whole armies of lesser scoundrels." Parry argues that "the

99. Hemming, *Conquest of the Incas*, 72–85, 441–51, esp. 449–51. On the symbolic importance of executing the indigenous ruler in Peru, and subsequent representations of this event over time, see Raquel Chang-Rodríguez, "Cultural Resistance in the Andes and Its Depiction in *Atau Wallpaj P'uchukakuyninpa Wankan* or *Tragedy of Atahualpa's Death*," in Francisco Javier Cevallos-Candau et al., *Coded Encounters* (Amherst, Mass., 1994), 115–34.

100. For an account of this conflict, see Clendinnen, *Aztecs*, 267–73.

murder of Caltzontzín" occurred because he refused "to disclose the where-abouts of an imaginary treasure." Parry relied heavily on *La conquista de la Nueva Galicia* by José López Portillo y Weber, who describes Guzmán as "ferocious, greedy, cruel, lustful, cynical, avaricious and a slanderer." For good measure, he adds that Guzmán had "the frightful personality of a Lu-cifer, and like Lucifer he does not permit defenders." In his *History of the Conquest of Mexico* Prescott, an admirer of Cortés, cites the "oppressive con-duct of Guzmán, especially toward the Indians."[101]

Although these condemnations of Nuño de Guzmán were expressed in the nineteenth and twentieth centuries, they can be traced to colonial docu-ments. Indeed, when Herminio Martínez concluded his novel with the phrase "caso el más cruel que decirse puede," he reproduced the exact words found in the description of the execution of the Cazonci by the eighteenth-century Franciscan historian Pablo Beaumont. In turn, Beaumont based his account on the early-seventeenth-century Franciscan historian Torquemada, who based his account on several first-generation sources.[102] These images of Nuño de Guzmán—though containing elements of truth—present him as exceptionally violent, in a manner that obscures the essential violence inher-ent in founding a colonial order. This depiction of Nuño de Guzmán as aberrant is intimately linked to the power struggles of his day, which, as we shall see, he lost. This political defeat, more than the exceptional quality of his actions, explains his historical image.

We know that royal authorities appointed Nuño de Guzmán president of the First Audiencia—or high court and advisory body—of Mexico, specif-ically to act as a counterweight to the growing power of Hernán Cortés. His conflicts with Cortés, and Cortés's allies among the Franciscan order, are legendary.[103] One of the primary ways to discredit a rival during the

101. Thomas, *Conquest,* 558; Herminio Martínez, *Diario maldito de Nuño de Guzmán* (Mexico City, 1990), 237; Todorov, *Conquest of America,* 134; Francis Borgia Steck, O.F.M., *Motolinia's History of the Indians of New Spain* (Washington, D.C., 1951), 11; C. H. Haring, *The Spanish Empire in America* (Oxford, 1947), 78, 80; Lesley Byrd Simpson, *Many Mexicos* (1941; Berkeley, Calif., 1960), 33; Parry, *The Audiencia of New Galicia,* 19, 21; López Portillo y Weber, *La conquista de la Nueva Galicia,* 81; Prescott, *History of the Conquest of Mexico,* 325–26.

102. Fr. Pablo Beaumont, *Crónica de Michoacán* (ca. 1788; Mexico City, 1932), 2:183. See Juan de Torquemada, *Monarquía Indiana,* 7 vols., ed. Miguel León Portilla (Mexico City, 1977), vol. 1, bk. 3, chap. 43.

103. My definition of the term "Audiencia" was aided by the glossary in Mark A. Burk-holder and Lyman L. Johnson, *Colonial Latin America* (Oxford, 1990), 336. On power strug-gles among the first generation of conquistadores and settlers, see Liss, *Mexico Under Spain,*

founding of the Spanish colonial order—and perhaps in other eras—was to accuse him of being exceptionally abusive or violent. When the accuser was engaged in similar activities, this had the added benefit of creating distance between the accuser's own behavior and truly evil excess. The attacked figure provides a symbolic foil, an example of someone whose "deviant" behavior serves to legitimize less "excessive" actions. Many examples of this rhetorical strategy can be gleaned from early colonial writings. López de Gómara, the personal secretary of Cortés, authored a history of the Spanish Conquest extremely favorable to his patron. In it, he laments that Guzmán had burned "King Cazoncin, friend of Cortés, servant of Spaniards and vassal of the Emperor, and who was in peace." Despite his own participation in some of the bloodiest campaigns of the Spanish Conquest, Bernal Díaz del Castillo argued that the execution of the Cazonci—which he incorrectly believed had been carried out by hanging—"was one of the worst and ugliest things that a president or other people could do." In a similar vein, although referring to earlier incidents, the Franciscan Juan de Zumárraga—first bishop of Mexico and a close ally of Cortés—wrote to the king that Nuño de Guzmán needed to repent to the Church because of his slavetrading activities.[104] This was despite the fact that Zumárraga himself possessed both slaves and Indian vassals.[105] The written evidence left by these men has long served as the basis for our understanding of the conquest generation, and thus the politics of early Spanish colonialism has shaped subsequent representations of Nuño de Guzmán.

Successive generations of intellectuals have taken their cues from Nuño de Guzmán's political rivals. They have done so simply by reproducing the contents of the documents left behind and have frequently used his deviant image for their own purposes. Possibly the most influential of these was Bartolomé de Las Casas. In his *Brevísima relación de la destrucción de las Indias* (1552), Las Casas provides a detailed description of the execution of the

48–68; Warren, *Conquest of Michoacán*, 138–56; and C. Harvey Gardiner, *Martín López* (Lexington, Ky., 1958), 82–100.

104. López de Gómara, *Historia de la conquista de México* (1552; Caracas, 1979), 305; Bernal Díaz del Castillo, *Historia verdadera de la conquista de la Nueva España*, 5th ed., ed. Joaquin Ramírez Cabañas (Mexico City, 1960), 2:297; "Carta de Don Fray Juan de Zumárraga al Emperador-Valladolid, 1533," in P. Mariano Cuevas, S.J., *Documentos inéditos del siglo XVI para la historia de México* (1914; Mexico City, 1975), 17–46, esp. 29–30.

105. The classic treatment of this issue is Silvio Zavala, *Los esclavos indios en Nueva España* (Mexico City, 1967). See especially pages 16–20, 64.

Cazonci. Never one to avoid the use of hyperbole in a good cause, Las Casas stressed the Cazonci's kind and generous reception of Spanish settlers and Guzmán's cruelty and thirst for gold. According to Las Casas, the Cazonci's feet were attached to a block of wood and his body stretched out, with his hands tied to another piece. Then the conquistadores placed his feet in a brazier. A youth with a piece of linen—soaked in oil, placed on a stick, and lit on fire—roasted his skin, and all the while two men stood watch, one with a loaded crossbow and the other with a terrible and savage dog. According to Las Casas, several other Indians received the same treatment. This account, dog and all, passed into Fray Antonio Tello's *Crónica miscelanea de la sancta provincia de Xalisco,* composed in the mid-seventeenth century, and from there at least temporarily into the regional lore of the Conquest.[106]

Las Casas, perhaps uniquely, cited the execution of the Cazonci to facilitate his rejection—late in life—of the entire Spanish colonial venture.[107] In contrast, Tello sought to highlight what he considered to be the contributions made by Christian missionaries in the region. Most of the historical accounts after Las Casas reproduced this pattern of singling out Nuño de Guzmán's allegedly deviant behavior as a way of excusing, or even exalting, the activities of others. Thus Pablo Beaumont, in his *Crónica de Michoacán,* praises the activities of the first generation of Spanish Franciscan missionaries while condemning "this cruelest death." Another eighteenth-century historian, Juan José Moreno (in his *Fragmentos*) lamented the "atrocious and inhuman death" Nuño de Guzmán inflicted on the Cazonci. However, Moreno did so only to glorify the saintly behavior of Vasco de Quiroga, the first bishop of Michoacán, whose tenure followed Nuño de Guzmán's activities in the region. In his *History of Mexico* the nineteenth-century historian Hubert Howe Bancroft accuses Nuño de Guzmán of the "black crime of having foully and without provocation murdered the kind-hearted Cazonci," primarily to emphasize the superiority of North Atlantic and

106. Bartolomé de Las Casas, *Brevísima relación de la destrucción de las Indias,* ed. André Saint-Lu (1552; Madrid, 1984), 118; Fray Antonio Tello, *Crónica miscelanea de la sancta provincia de Xalisco* (1653?; Guadalajara, 1968), 6 (date of composition), 95–98 (execution of the Cazonci). For a rather harsh critique of Tello, which correctly notes the excessive influence his work has had on the subsequent historiography, see Donald D. Brand, "Ethnohistoric Synthesis of Western Mexico," *The Handbook of Middle American Indians* (Austin, Tex., 1971), 11:632–56, esp. 634, 644.

107. Gustavo Gutiérrez, *Las Casas,* trans. Robert R. Barr (Maryknoll, N.Y., 1993); Luis N. Rivera, *A Violent Evangelism* (Louisville, Ky., 1992), 48–62.

specifically Anglo-Protestant civilization. In the twentieth-century, the Jesuit historian Mariano Cuevas, in his *Historia de la Iglesia en México* (1921), condemns the cruelty of Nuño de Guzmán, but only to highlight the virtues of the Spanish court, and the good judgment of those who opposed him. This curious process of exalting Spain by condemning a Spaniard was taken to absurd lengths in the rabidly ethnocentric *El IV centenario de don Fray Juan de Zumárraga* of Constantino Bayle (1953), who describes Nuño de Guzmán as a "man of a black soul, cruel, cowardly," while praising Bishop Zumárraga, and specifically Zumárraga's burning of indigenous codices and religious symbols.[108]

The earliest trace of a countercritique that I have been able to find comes in the work of Arthur Scott Aiton. In his *Antonio de Mendoza: First Viceroy of New Spain* (1927), Aiton notes perceptively that what historians usually refer to as the Spanish Conquest would be more appropriately termed "the conquest of the Nahua Confederation." He argues that while Nuño de Guzmán engaged in brutal activities, his behavior was quite similar to that of the other conquistadores. Thus he did not deserve the particular opprobrium that had befallen his name.[109] More substantial revisionist attempts came from Donald E. Chipman (in *Nuño de Guzmán and the Province of Panuco in New Spain*) and J. Benedict Warren (in *The Conquest of Michoacán*), both former students of France V. Scholes.[110] Neatly dividing Nuño de Guzmán's brief career in New Spain into its constituent parts, Chipman examines his tenure as governor of Pánuco during 1527–28, while Warren focuses on his conquest of western Mexico, primarily during the years 1529 and 1530. Chipman and Warren demonstrate that Nuño de Guzmán's activities did not deviate from the standards of the day. However, they assumed that this fact permitted a recasting of the historical image of Nuño de Guzmán in a more benign light. At times, in their search for

108. Beaumont, *Crónica de Michoacán,* 2:183; Hubert Howe Bancroft, *History of Mexico,* vol. 2, *1521–1600* (San Francisco, 1886), 347; Juan José Moreno, *Fragmentos de la vida y virtudes del V. ILMO Y RMO. Sr. D. Vasco de Quiroga primer obispo de la santa catedral de Michoacán y fundador del real y primitivo colegio de S. Nicholas Obispo de Valladolid,* in *Don Vasco de Quiroga: Documentos,* ed. Rafael Aguayo Spencer (1722; Mexico City, 1940), 24; P. Mariano Cuevas, S.J., *Historia de la Iglesia en México,* vol. 1 (Mexico City, 1921), 148; Constantino Bayle, S.J., *El IV centenario de don Fray Juan de Zumárraga* (Madrid, 1953), 14, 57–58.

109. Arthur Scott Aiton, *Antonio de Mendoza* (Durham, N. C., 1927), 16, 20.

110. Donald E. Chipman, *Nuño de Guzmán and the Province of Panuco in New Spain* (Glendale, Calif., 1967); Warren, *Conquest of Michoacán.*

evidence to support their justifiable rejection of the so-called "black legend" of Spanish colonialism, these authors became rather extreme in putting the best possible "spin" onto the evidence they uncovered. For example, Chipman situates Guzmán's slave trading in context by noting that "due to his contacts in the Caribbean Isles, where there was a terrific demand for slaves, Guzmán could upgrade the value of an Indian; fifteen slaves at four gold pesos each would probably buy a better horse there than would eighty slaves at one silver peso each in Mexico City. Be that as it may, his contacts outside New Spain were beneficial to the province, for the settlers received a 661 per cent increase in the value of every slave."[111] Beneficial to whom? Certainly not to the recently enslaved indigenous peoples. Chipman, while presenting an "objective" reconstruction of the economic logic that certainly motivated Guzmán, does not even ask this question. Thus his conceptual framework excludes a discussion of the treatment of those newly defined as "Indians," at the very least a salient—and arguably the most important—issue.

Warren, to his credit, makes an effort to understand indigenous perceptions and realities. However, he too was unable to break out of the either/or dichotomy of the "black" and "white" legends of Spanish colonialism. Thus, perhaps his major conclusion—coming after two hundred and forty detailed pages, and a direct response to the work of Hubert Howe Bancroft—was that "the evidence now available, however, indicates that neither was the Cazonci as kind-hearted nor was Guzmán's crime as black as was supposed."[112] This rather timid statement evades all of the fundamental issues raised by this event, such as the relationship between social power and what becomes defined as truth, the legitimacy of Spanish law in the context of the initial expropriation of Indian lands, or even a recognition of Spanish responsibility for the abuses of colonial power that did occur. It serves simply to move the various images of Nuño de Guzmán and the Cazonci a bit further along—in either direction—on the grid of "black" and "white" legends. Also, while there is nothing inherently wrong with the struggle for a humane "objectivity"—if by this is meant the effort to rise above narrowly defined self-interest—at times Warren's pursuit of "objectivity" results in contorted logic. For example, in an effort to provide a "balanced" view of Nuño de Guzmán, he argues that "the Cazonci must have shown sufficient repentance

111. Chipman, *Nuño de Guzmán*, 205.
112. Warren, *Conquest of Michoacán*, 241.

to satisfy Guzmán, because he was given the garrote before he was burned. The odium that attached to Guzmán's name, however, would not even give him credit for this small humanity."[113] Small indeed. Warren even ended up resorting to the method responsible for Guzmán's widespread infamy, namely finding a deviant to excuse deplorable behavior. According to Warren, it was the virtually unknown *encomendero* Alonso de Mata, and not Guzmán, who was "the kind of sociopath upon whose actions the 'Black Legend' was based."[114]

Alas, the obscure Mata knows no defenders. However, those who seek to revise the image of Nuño de Guzmán, or condemn him, must confront several important realities. Nuño de Guzmán's actions were extremely functional for the founding of Spanish colonialism in Michoacán and cannot be understood simply as the acts of a deviant individual. As I shall argue in the next chapter, the Cazonci's execution symbolically demonstrated Spanish dominance of the region and created a context in which indigenes would benefit from seeking an alliance with factions of colonizers to improve their position within an emerging colonial state. Thus, ironically, Nuño de Guzmán's campaign provided a more receptive space among the local indigenous population for representatives of the early colonial Church, especially Guzmán's critics—the Franciscans, allied to Cortés and the bishop Vasco de Quiroga. Guzmán did not act alone in executing the Cazonci, but rather fulfilled the aspirations of most—probably all—of the Spanish settlers in the region. These settlers had experienced substantial resistance in their attempts to occupy Michoacán, proving that they and Cortés had misunderstood the nature of their alliance with the Cazonci.

Indigenous resistance, occurring in multiple ways with varying degrees of subtlety, challenges the myth of passivity in response to the Spanish Conquest. We can also note that as the balance of power in Michoacán shifted, internal divisions and even opportunism among the indigenous population took new forms. These divisions facilitated the Cazonci's execution, but did not cause it. It is possible that the condemnation of Guzmán, rooted in Spanish political conflicts and reproduced in subsequent historiography, has also assuaged indigenous humiliation resulting from the Conquest. And so, through the complex and at times contradictory process referred to as "the

113. Ibid., 234.
114. Ibid., 194.

construction of hegemony," political antagonists in Michoacán together created a relationship of dominance that effectively subordinated indigenes.[115]

Epilogue: *Sic Transit Gloria Mundi*

Nuño de Guzmán died as he had lived, rigorously observing the conventions of his time and place. For many Spaniards, the discovery and conquest of the Americas symbolized the possibility of fulfilling great utopian desires. In sixteenth-century New Spain among Spanish colonists, yearnings for a reformed and purified Christian order mingled with, and at times confronted, dreams of wealth and enhanced social status. The allure of these visions can be traced, at least in part, to the fact that they promised escape from the limited possibilities and oppressive social conditions of Spanish feudalism in decline, or perhaps painful transformation.[116] As the sixteenth century progressed, the realities of New Spain proved cruel to most Spanish utopias. By the 1550s, as Nuño de Guzmán composed his final words, disillusioned churchmen and impoverished former conquistadors were the norm.[117] Once again, he proved no exception.

Nuño de Guzmán spent his final years a bitter and sickly man, one of the great losers in the battles that occurred as the Spaniards fought over their newly seized wealth. Ironically, Guzmán—unlike Juan Infante, and possibly Francisco de Villegas, Bernaldino de Albornoz, and other Spaniards—gained no lasting benefit from the execution of the Cazonci, or any other acts of pillage and plunder. In 1536, colonial authorities forced him to return to Mexico City. Initially, he lived in the house of Viceroy Antonio de Mendoza, until his 1537 arrest and incarceration in the public jail in Mexico City. Apparently, he found this to be a disagreeable experience. In his memoirs, he complained about the "eighteen months and eighteen days" he spent there and made deprecating remarks about the ethnicity and occupations of his fellow prisoners.[118] In 1538, royal authorities recalled him to Spain. There, in deference to his aristocratic status, he endured a form of house arrest until his

115. Kellogg, "Hegemony Out of Conquest," 27–46.
116. Stern, "Paradigms of Conquest," 7–9.
117. Based on Guzmán's will, Palomino y Cañedo claims the date of Guzmán's death was October 26, 1558. See the *Testamento de Nuño Beltrán de Guzmán*, ed. Jorge Palomino y Cañedo (Mexico City, 1973), 13, 55, for the will. Martínez, "Los inicios," in Florescano, *Historia general de Michoacán*, 2:73, gives the year of death as 1550.
118. Guzmán, *Memoria*, 86.

death.[119] Nuño de Guzmán was to recall bitterly that his experience had been "for one year of presidency, ten years of residency."[120]

In his will, composed shortly before his death, he complained of being ill in mind and body, and unjustly deprived of the wealth and honor he had won "at my cost and with my blood and sweat." Guzmán resentfully complained about the ministers who "against all justice and reason and fairness" had convinced the king to take away the Indian vassals he had earned through his role in the Conquest. According to Guzmán, this was grossly unfair. He argued that the king would be served by restoring "all my Indian vassals with the fruits and rents from them from the day they took them from me," a request that went unheeded. Among Nuño de Guzmán's final recorded words were "thus I have been plundered of my service and work and sweat and destroyed in a hospital."[121]

And so died Nuño de Guzmán. Juan Infante had gratefully testified in his defense, claiming that the killing of the Cazonci had "reformed" Michoacán.[122] In fact, Infante's statement reveals only part of the truth. The trial, torture, and execution of the Cazonci demonstrated Spanish colonial power. However, the consolidation of a new social order in Michoacán went beyond the actions of soldiers and settlers. In addition, it can be traced to another, linked dimension of colonization, the sixteenth-century Castilian Catholic evangelization of the region. As we shall see, the sixteenth-century missionary presence in Michoacán resulted in a complicated dynamic of conflict, alliance, and opportunism that generated its own documents, marked by their own exclusions and content.

119. Warren, *Conquest of Michoacán*, 242.
120. Guzmán, *Memoria*, 88.
121. Guzmán, *Testamento*, 62.
122. "Juicio seguido," 358.

2

ALTERITY, ALLIANCE, AND THE
RELACIÓN DE MICHOACÁN [1541]

> The *Relación de Michoacán,* incomplete like the Venus de
> Milo, is our classical monument, our Iliad and Odyssey.
> —Luis González y González,
> *La vuelta a Michoacán en 500 libros*

> The early history of Latin America, as well as the first fictions
> of and about Latin America, are told in the rhetorical modes
> furnished by the notarial arts.
> —Roberto González Echevarría, *Myth and Archive*

> Why don't all winners tell the same story?
> —Michel-Rolph Trouillot, *Silencing the Past*

The *Relación de las ceremonias y ritos y población y gobernación de los indios de la provincia de Michoacán* is a complex and beautiful text.[1] It has long been considered the single most important source of information about Michoacán's indigenous peoples

---

1. *La Relación de Michoacán.* For a complete survey and critique of the manuscript forms and various published editions of the *Relación de Michoacán,* as well as debates over authorship and the estimated dates of compilation, see Stone, "A Fragile Coalition," ix–18. Our knowledge of all aspects of the *Relación* will be enhanced with the publication of Stone's book (forthcoming from the University of Oklahoma Press). Several editions of the *Relación* have been published, including a facsimile edition by José Tudela. *The Chronicles of Michoacán,* ed. and trans. Eugene R. Craine and Reginald C. Reindorp (Norman, Okla., 1970), may prove useful to the English-speaking reader, although it is seriously limited in certain regards. Also see Miranda, "Estudio preliminar," in *La Relación de Michoacán,* xix–xlv, and Pollard, *Taríacuri's Legacy,* 17.

during the preconquest and conquest eras. However, as we shall see, it reveals as much about the political contests and social struggles of the era in which it was produced as the indigenous past it claims to represent. The *Relación* was completed in 1541, eleven years after the *Proceso*. Taken together, the *Relación* and the *Proceso* hint at realities more complex than are represented in either one and heighten awareness of how each was produced.

It would be a mistake to define the *Relación* as authentically indigenous in any way that the *Proceso* is not. To be sure, the *Proceso* privileges the statements of settlers and soldiers, and the *Relación* is based on the accounts of elite male indigenes, as transcribed, translated, and edited by a Franciscan missionary author. However, despite their differences, both documents are best considered as artifacts of the same process of conquest and colonization. Rather than allowing us to recover "Indian" and "Spanish" views, each source reveals a colonizing gaze, one capable of making distinctive uses of the image of the Indian. Recognizing this reality ought not to exclude a discussion of indigenous influences in these texts, since these are demonstrably evident. Instead, it should shift attention to how relationships of power constrained the descriptions preserved in written form.[2]

The notion of a powerful and stable Purhépecha/Tarascan empire, with historical roots reaching back centuries, is in large part traceable to the *Relación*. It is true that there was a dominant indigenous polity in the region at the time of the Spanish invasion. However, scholars now acknowledge that our understanding of its emergence and consolidation remains "in the realm of myth and legend," and that much work remains to be done to determine its precise scope and functioning.[3] Much also remains unknown about the era of conquest, and even about the composition of the *Relación*. The *Relación* itself confirms that the author was a Franciscan missionary, and that it was composed at the request of Viceroy Antonio de Mendoza, the highest-ranking colonial official in Mexico. The missionary most probably was Fray Jerónimo de Alcalá, although we cannot be entirely certain of

2. Max Harris, "Disguised Reconciliations: Indigenous Voices in Early Franciscan Missionary Drama in Mexico," *Radical History Review* 53 (1992): 13–25. Theoretical background can be gained from Roland Barthes, "Historical Discourse," trans. Peter Wexler, *Social Science Information* (International Social Science Council) 6, no. 4 (August 1967): 145–55, and "What is Criticism," in *Critical Essays*, trans. Richard Howard (Evanston, Ill., 1972), 255–60. Terry Eagleton, *Literary Theory* (Minneapolis, 1983), 194–222.

3. Pollard, *Taríacuri's Legacy*, xv, 14, 17–19; Rodrigo Martínez, "Reorientaciones," in Florescano, *Historia general de Michoacán*, 2:78.

this.[4] The testimonies were collected between 1538 and 1541, although we do not know precisely when, or how. The informants, with one exception, are also unknown.[5] These uncertainties indicate important gaps in our knowledge and lend a provisional quality to interpretive claims based on this source.

Since our knowledge about the *Relación*'s authorship and composition is limited, situating it in historical context can provide us with a means for discerning some of its meanings. The *Relación* contains important references to the indigenous past. However, these were memories of a bygone era, recalled as the survivors of conquest struggled over the terms of their incorporation into a newly emerging colonial order. An alliance between missionaries and a faction of elite male indigenes was a necessary precondition for the compiling of the text. As we shall see, this alliance temporarily worked against anyone who was not a member of it, whether Spanish or indigenous. Nevertheless, this was a tenuous relationship, marked by an overall context of colonial domination as well as individual power dynamics. At times, the *Relación* challenges the abuses of soldiers and settlers. However, it also demonstrates the paternalism and ethnocidal assumptions of the missionaries and the political opportunism and social inequality of the informants. In the end, the *Relación* provides a lens into the sixteenth-century missionary and Indian encounter in Michoacán.[6] As we shall see, it was constructed to fit the requirements of the time, as defined by those who controlled its composition.

4. A considerable amount of scholarly effort has been expended to determine who wrote *La Relación de Michoacán*. Fray Jerónimo de Alcalá is the most plausible candidate, for a variety of reasons, although limitations in the existing evidence prevent establishing his authorship beyond a shadow of a doubt. Nevertheless, the series of illustrations that accompanied the original manuscript clearly indicate that the missionary presenting the text to the viceroy was a Franciscan. See J. Benedict Warren, "Fray Jerónimo de Alcalá: Author of the *Relación de Michoacán*?" *The Americas* 27, no. 3 (January 1971): 307–26; and Miranda, "Estudio preliminar," in *La Relación de Michoacán*, xxiii–xxv. Georges Baudot, *History and Utopia in Mexico*, trans. Bernard de Montellano and Thelma Ortiz de Montellano (1980; Niwot, Colo., 1995), 399–446, misidentifies the author of the *Relación* but provides an interesting discussion of sixteenth-century Franciscan writings as a genre. See also José Rabasa, "Writing and Evangelization in Sixteenth-Century Mexico," in *Early Images of the Americas*, ed. Jerry M. Williams and Robert E. Lewis (Tucson, Ariz., 1993), 64–92.
    5. Stone, "A Fragile Coalition," 20–67. On dates of compilation, see ix–x.
    6. Interesting comparative materials can be found in Erick Langer and Robert H. Jackson, eds., *The New Latin American Mission History* (Lincoln, Nebr., 1995); Clendinnen, *Ambivalent Conquests;* and Sabine MacCormack, *Religion in the Andes* (Princeton, 1991) and "The Heart Has Its Reasons: Predicaments of Missionary Christianity in Early Colonial Peru," *Hispanic*

On Executions

According to the *Proceso,* the execution of the Cazonci was as follows:

> The said chief constable [Juan de Burgos] in compliance of that mentioned previously, brought a mat of the local style made to the form of a pannier and on this he [the Cazonci] was placed and his feet tied to the tail of a horse, and by the proclamation of Pedro Martín, crier of this army saying, "This is the justice which the Emperor and Queen our lords and the very excellent señor Nuño de Guzmán, president of New Spain and Captain-General of the army in their name, command to be done to this man as an idolatrous traitor, and because he has killed many Spaniards, he commands him to be dragged around and burned for it. Let he who does such pay such." And later he was brought round about from the camp and brought to the said passage [of the river] and given a garrote and suffocated and burned.[7]

However, the notion of a justified execution, carried out according to the Spanish legal norms, does not appear in the *Relación.* In this document, Cuinierángari—or Don Pedro Panza, the Cazonci's adopted brother—stated that it took place in the following way

> Guzmán sentenced the Cazonci to be dragged along live by a horse's tail and to be burned. They bound him to a mat and tied him to a horse's tail and he was burned. A Spaniard rode the horse and a crier went about shouting to everyone: —"Look, look people at he who was such a rogue that he wanted to kill us. We have already interrogated him and therefore pronounced a sentence against him who is

American Historical Review 67 (1985): 443–66. Standard though dated works include John Leddy Phelan, *The Millennial Kingdom of the Franciscans in the New World* (Berkeley, Calif., 1956); Pedro Borges, *Métodos misionales en la cristianización de America* (Madrid, 1958); and Ricard, *Spiritual Conquest of Mexico.* See also Jonathan D. Spence, *The Memory Palace of Matteo Ricci* (New York, 1983); Jerry H. Bentley, *Old World Encounters* (New York, 1993); and Steven Kaplan, ed., *Indigenous Responses to Western Christianity* (New York, 1995).

7. Scholes and Adams, *Proceso,* 67–68. I have used the translation of the *pregonero*'s statement found in Warren's *Conquest of Michoacán,* 234, although with some very slight alterations. I translated the term "alguacil mayor" as "chief constable," following the suggestion made by A. R. Pagden in the glossary of Cortés, *Letters from México,* 527.

dragged about. Look and pay heed, look you lowly people who are all rogues!"[8]

As historians, we are presented with two eyewitness accounts that vary on at least one crucial detail. Which statement did the Spanish crier Pedro Martín call out following the execution of the Cazonci?

It is impossible to provide a definitive answer to this question. Indeed, the Spanish crier may have "said," or at least communicated, both messages. To understand how this could be, we must evaluate these conflicting testimonies contextually, as the products of specific historical moments.[9] Cuinierángari recalled the execution of the Cazonci for the Franciscan missionary several years after the event. Together, they portrayed the incident as a humiliating one, calculated to demonstrate the dominance of Spanish colonial forces. The public nature of the execution—that is, its ritual and even didactic quality—seems to support Cuinierángari's interpretation.[10] After all, Spanish colonial forces could have simply executed the Cazonci if their sole desire had been to punish him for the various crimes he was accused of committing. Despite this, it is probable that Cuinierángari's version misquotes the Spanish crier. Given the Spanish attachment to legalism, a deeply rooted cultural reflex in this era, it is highly unlikely that Nuño de Guzmán and his allies incorporated a false version of the Spanish crier's statement into their text.[11]

Although Cuinierángari may have heard a boastful attempt to intimidate newly subjugated "Indians," the Spanish crier almost certainly stressed that the execution had been carried out by the proper authorities and was a

8. *La Relación de Michoacán,* 353.

9. On the relationship between text, context, and interpretation, see Edward Said, *The World, The Text, and the Critic* (Cambridge, Mass., 1983), 1–53, and Mignolo, *The Darker Side of the Renaissance,* 1–25.

10. For an analysis of public execution as ritual intimately bound up with power, see Foucault, *Discipline and Punish,* esp. 23–25, and Chang-Rodríguez, "Cultural Resistance in the Andes and Its Depiction in *Atau Wallpaj P'uchukakuyninpa Wankan* or *Tragedy of Atahualpa's Death,*" in Cevallos-Candau et al., *Coded Encounters,* 115–34.

11. On Spanish legalism, and legal/political institutions as applied in colonial contexts, see Patricia Seed, *Ceremonies of Possession in Europe's Conquest of the New World, 1492–1640* (Cambridge, England, 1995), 69–99; Steve J. Stern, *Peru's Indian Peoples and the Challenge of Spanish Conquest: Huamanga to 1640* (Madison, Wis., 1982), 114–37; Colin M. MacLachlan, *Spain's Empire in the New World* (Berkeley, Calif., 1988), 21–44, 58–65; Liss, *Mexico Under Spain,* 46–68; Charles Gibson, *Spain in America* (New York, 1966), 90–111; and Mario Góngora, *El estado en el derecho indiano* (Santiago, 1951).

measured response to serious provocation. Thus if we limited our investigation to a literal reading of the documents, the portrayal of the Cazonci's execution found in the trial record would be the more accurate one. At least, this would be the case in the sense of presenting the words actually called out by the Spanish crier. However, to do so would marginalize the meaning assigned to the event by Cuinierángari, and implicitly to accept Spanish definitions of this early colonial encounter.[12] We can begin to construct a more historically accurate reading of this source, and understanding of this event, by recognizing that in this time and place Spanish legalism facilitated and confirmed the consolidation of colonial authority. This was a new social reality that many indigenes—especially among the former ruling elite—must have found humiliating. When we situate these accounts in historical context, we can see that while Cuinierángari's testimony may have been inaccurate, in one sense at least it was true.

The conflicting eyewitness accounts of the Spanish crier's utterance serve as what Hulme calls a key location laying bare the workings of colonial discourse.[13] These two textual representations contradict each other and hint at complex realities imperfectly reflected in the written sources that refer to them. Cuinierángari's discussion of the Cazonci's execution forms only a small part of the *Relación*, and as we shall see, he had his own concerns and motivations. Nevertheless, the depiction he put forth, as reported by the missionary author, challenged the accounts of the executioners found in the *Proceso*. This challenge was real, although a sustained interrogation of the *Relación* argues against defining this resistance in exclusively heroic terms.

The Authors of the Text:
Missionary and Native Elite in a Colonial Context

According to the missionary author, the *Relación de Michoacán* was compiled because the first viceroy of Mexico, Don Antonio de Mendoza, repeatedly requested information that might prove useful in ruling over his new subjects. In particular, the viceroy wanted "something about the governing of these peoples," that is, how they ruled themselves.[14] The missionary

12. See Warren, *Conquest of Michoacán*, 211–36, esp. 233–34. For a discussion of the strategic utility of blaming the victims in relationships of domination, see Sider, "When Parrots Learn to Talk," 3–23, esp. 7.

13. Hulme, *Colonial Encounters*, 12.

14. *La Relación de Michoacán*, 4.

clearly performed the task of writing in the service of the colonial state and took advantage of the opportunity to advise the viceroy on how best to utilize the new information. His instructions were straightforward. After assuming the modest posture befitting a Franciscan missionary, the writer stressed that the viceroy, having been chosen by God to be the Crown's representative, now had the obligation to use his authority "to have peace for all, to maintain justice for everyone, to hear the humble as well as the powerful, to make amends to the injured."[15]

Perhaps abstract conviction led the missionary to believe that the viceroy's zeal in implanting the Christian faith, combined with benevolent and prudent rule, would be essential if the Spanish were to "sustentar y conservar lo conquistado," that is, consolidate and maintain control over the conquered lands. He felt that this new task required a different approach, based on different and better human qualities. After all, the Conquest had been relatively brief, a "work of a few days," while what lay ahead, the building of the Spanish colonial order, was a "work of many years." In order to be successful, the viceroy needed to substitute kindness for the courage so highly prized during the Conquest.[16]

However, it was the missionary's experience of Conquest which convinced him that, at times, prudence would have to temper the viceroy's benevolence. The missionary was not a fool and had spent years working with the Indians of Michoacán. He could testify firsthand about their stubborn reluctance to give up drunkenness, idolatry, and pagan rituals. In fact, they resisted Christianity so intensely that the missionaries almost abandoned their task, not once, but two or three times. In the end—with the help of God, he must have reasoned—there had been successes, despite the stubbornness of the Indians.[17] As he warned, the viceroy must rule without "losing the authority and seriousness that the office requires," if he were to continue to inspire the "love and fear and respect" necessary for a successful administration.[18]

If the *Relación* consisted solely of a report by the missionary to the viceroy, it would provide a fascinating opportunity to explore this paternalistic vision, and the seemingly contradictory egalitarian and authoritarian tendencies which it incorporated. However, it contains substantially more than

15. Ibid., 5.
16. Ibid., 4–5.
17. Ricard, *Spiritual Conquest of Mexico*, 79; *La Relación de Michoacán*, 355.
18. *La Relación de Michoacán*, 5.

the missionary's reflections. The missionary author writes as himself only infrequently, in the short prologue and a few scattered comments throughout the work. The bulk of this lengthy document consists of statements by the local indigenous elite. Indeed, the Franciscan introduces the text to the viceroy by stating that "the elders of this city of Michoacán present to Your Lordship this writing and *relación,* and I also in their name, not as author but rather as an interpreter of them."[19] Although the influence of the missionary as translator, transcriber, and editor permeates the entire compilation, his self-definition as an interpreter qualifies his presence in important ways. The result goes well beyond a missionary worldview.

It is relevant to note that virtually the entire first section of the text was destroyed, quite possibly because it contained a representation of indigenous religious practices deemed overly graphic by colonial authorities.[20] This does not mean that the Franciscan missionary succeeded in presenting a reconstruction of indigenous religious beliefs that would be considered to be "objective," or even respectful, by late-twentieth-century standards. However, it does indicate that he strove in some way to make accessible that which was different, to render the "other" more intelligible and authentic, even if only for the purposes of colonial administration and Christian evangelization.[21] His relative success apparently troubled many of his Spanish contemporaries. This attempt to explain the "other" gave the indigenous elders a space, however constrained, in which they could express themselves and claim their history. They used it to struggle for recognition, legitimacy, and—at least in the case of Cuinierángari—personal advancement.

After the execution of the Cazonci, recorded in the *Proceso* and challenged in the *Relación,* the indigenes of Michoacán undoubtedly discussed and contemplated their history, assessing its significance in light of recent events. Their experiences and narrations would be imperfectly recorded in the *Relación.*[22] Its description emphasizes the symbolic importance of the Cazonci's execution, while condemning the cruelty of Nuño de Guzmán. By

19. Ibid., 6.

20. Stone, "A Fragile Coalition," esp. 66–67, 96; Warren, "Fray Jerónimo de Alcalá," 307; Miranda, "Estudio preliminar," in *La Relación de Michoacán,* xxv; Ricard, *Spiritual Conquest of Mexico,* 58. See also Baudot, *History and Utopia in Mexico,* 491–524.

21. Stone, "A Fragile Coalition," 72, for a compelling critique of Baudot; Rabasa, "Writing and Evangelization," esp. 77–85.

22. On the production of archives and sources, see Trouillot, *Silencing the Past,* 50–52; Gruzinski, *Conquest of Mexico,* 6–69; and Florescano, *Memory, Myth and Time in Mexico,* 65–99.

stressing the origins, history, and impressive extent of the Purhépecha empire, and thus making a claim for the legitimacy of the indigenous nobility in its "historical present," the *Relación* also provided a version of the past that challenged the humiliation of conquest in important ways.

Nuño de Guzmán and the Trauma of Conquest

> And Guzmán sentenced the Cazonci to be dragged along live by a horse's tail and to be burned. They bound him to a mat and tied him to a horse's tail and he was burned. A Spaniard rode the horse and a crier went about shouting to everyone: "Look, look people at he who was such a rogue that he wanted to kill us. We have already interrogated him and therefore pronounced a sentence against he who is dragged about. Look and pay heed, look you lowly peoples that are all rogues!"[23]

These are powerful words. They graphically portray the violence that is an essential feature of imperialist domination, a reality that transcends the example of Michoacán, colonial Mexico, and the Spanish empire. All conquests have Nuño de Guzmáns and moments that require crude displays of force.

The death of the Cazonci on February 14, 1530, demonstrated—indeed, performed and enacted—the consolidation of Spanish colonial power in Michoacán.[24] This event had profound implications for all those involved in Michoacán's colonial equation. For the indigenes of Michoacán, the trial, torture, and execution of the Cazonci signified the end of an era and the establishment of a Spanish-dominated colonial order. For the Spanish, it represented a major transition in a process that had begun with their "discovery" of a "new" world.[25]

We know that the Franciscan missionary began the *Relación de Michoacán* in 1539, since the prologue refers to Viceroy Antonio de Mendoza's request for information during his first visit to the region. The viceroy received the report when he returned around 1541, a trip related to the Mixton

---

23. *La Relación de Michoacán*, 353.
24. Warren, *Conquest of Michoacán*, 287.
25. Stone, "Rewriting Indigenous Traditions"; Shirley Gorenstein, "Introduction," in Pollard, *Taríacuri's Legacy*, xiv.

war, a result of Spanish colonial expansion to the north.[26] Thus it was only a few short years after the Cazonci's death that Cuinierángari recalled his execution. His account of this event took place within a fairly explicit criticism of the behavior of the Spanish conquerors.[27] "Don Pedro," the only indigenous elder mentioned by name in the text, had been at the Cazonci's side during his torture and execution, and he described in detail the excesses of Nuño de Guzmán and his entourage. The missionary not only provided a space for Cuinierángari to air complaints, but also verified that his arms still bore marks from torture.[28] What compelled the missionary author to accord Cuinierángari and the other indigenous elders so much space in the text?

The brutality of Nuño de Guzmán's campaign, and its impact on missionary attempts to colonize the region, had both immediate and longer-term consequences. In the short run, Nuño de Guzmán and his allies clearly angered the missionary author, perhaps building upon previous hostilities. Prior to his campaign, Guzmán had been denounced by Franciscans in Mexico City.[29] In Michoacán, his excesses further strained relationships. It is apparent that considerable animosity existed between the Franciscans, generally viewed as allies of Hernán Cortés in early colonial intra-Spanish rivalries, and Nuño de Guzmán, a fierce opponent of Cortés.[30] At one level, then, the missionary promotion of the "Indian view" in the *Relación de Michoacán* indicates an attempt to gain a political advantage over another faction of colonizing Spaniards. The author made his appeal to the viceroy at a time when the Crown was considering measures, such as the New Laws, which were intended to rein in the first generation of conquistadores and prevent the establishment of a New World landed aristocracy. The missionary's motives may have been less than pure in this. Even scholars partisan to the missionary cause admit to powerful currents of paternalism in missionary practice, and it is not difficult to imagine power struggles within the Spanish community over the control of the Indian population.[31]

26. Miranda, "Estudio preliminar," in *La Relación de Michoacán*, xxiii; Warren, "Fray Jerónimo de Alcalá," 309. For a thorough discussion of the influences of the Mixton War on the *Relación*, see Stone, "A Fragile Coalition," 74–86.

27. *La Relación de Michoacán*, 339–56, esp. 353; Warren, "Fray Jerónimo de Alcalá," 307.

28. *La Relación de Michoacán*, 351–52.

29. Warren, *Conquest of Michoacán*, 86.

30. Parry, *The Audiencia of New Galicia*, 20.

31. Borges, *Métodos*, 94–98; Ricard, *Spiritual Conquest of Mexico*, 52; David Sweet, "The Ibero-American Frontier Mission in Native American History," in Langer and Jackson, *The New Latin American Mission History*, 1–48.

In order to understand the longer-term implications of the execution of the Cazonci, we need to examine, briefly, the establishing of the missionary presence in Michoacán, and the impact that Nuño de Guzmán's activities had on their efforts at evangelization. The Franciscan Martín de la Coruña arrived in Michoacán in 1525, four short years after conquistadores first came into contact with Michoacán's indigenous population. There, he reportedly destroyed all the temples and idols in Tzintzuntzan, the major Purhépecha urban and religious center. The *Relación* contains descriptions of this initial contact with missionaries, although it does not describe the activity of Fray Martín de la Coruña, or indeed any evangelizing activity, outside a few very limited comments. Perhaps these descriptions were lost when the first section was destroyed, or maybe our missionary author did not feel compelled to probe too deeply into the missionary past.[32] In 1526, the Franciscans established a monastery in Tzintzuntzan and began their work in earnest. These were difficult years, according to our author, marked by the stubbornness of the Indian peoples and their resistance to the Franciscans.[33] It seems obvious that a tremendous gulf separated the missionaries from the indigenous population during this period.

The increasing hostilities that developed as Spanish settlers moved into the region escalated in the years leading up to the Cazonci's execution. In this sense, the expedition of Nuño de Guzmán played a crucial role in consolidating the conditions that permitted a temporary and partial alliance between missionaries and at least some of the indigenous male elite. Rather than a profound cultural revolution imposed from above, a temporary political alliance forged from below—in response to local pressures, including power conflicts within indigenous communities, and global trends, such as Iberian expansion—left us the *Relación* as an artifact. With the death of the Cazonci, the old order slipped irrevocably into the past. From that point on, the issue facing the indigenous population of Michoacán was no longer how to avoid Spanish colonization, but rather the terms of their integration into colonial society.

Apparently, at least some found the missionaries' terms more acceptable than those of the conquistadores, although it would be wrong to view this as an all-or-nothing decision. It is plausible to suggest that the Franciscans, by

---

32. Warren, *Conquest of Michoacán,* 51; Ricard, *Spiritual Conquest of Mexico,* 37; *La Relación de Michoacán,* 307–11.

33. *La Relación de Michoacán,* 335.

opposing and even forcefully confronting Nuño de Guzmán and other soldiers and settlers, gained a certain moral standing in the eyes of Michoacán's indigenous population. For example, during his testimony Cuinierángari recalled how Nuño de Guzmán bitterly opposed the attempts of Fray Martín (de la Coruña?) to intervene in the torture and execution of the Cazonci.[34] Ultimately, Michoacán became one of the major centers of missionary activity throughout the sixteenth century, a complex process that generated its own dynamic of social and political conflict, as well as alliance. However, the initial acceptance of the missionaries within the indigenous communities, not only as a physical presence but also as possible allies, resulted from the shifting political circumstances of the early colonial period. This process reached a decisive turning point with the execution of the Cazonci by Nuño de Guzmán.[35]

In the 1530s the Church, as a representative of colonial authority, carried out a sweeping campaign of *reducciones* in Michoacán. This was a strategy intended to enhance colonial surveillance and missionary control by resettling scattered indigenous populations into Spanish-style villages.[36] This campaign of *reducciones* had a powerful impact on local society, and therefore on the indigenous "voice" in the *Relación*. This was the context within which the indigenous elite recalled their history, and the text's focus on elite lineage can be interpreted as a response to the demands of this era. If the execution of the Cazonci served to demonstrate, irrefutably, Spanish colonial authority in Michoacán, then the local elites would have had a powerful incentive to establish their "nobility" in the eyes of the Spaniards. Missionaries clearly directed their efforts at the leadership of local communities, and the preservation of elite status and authority could provide indigenous people with tangible benefits in the rapidly changing context of the post-conquest period.[37] The way to establish oneself as a member of the natural aristocracy, in the eyes of the Spanish, was through lineage. Lineage was also a pervasive concern of the elite in Purhépecha society, thus creating the distinct possibility of a convergence of viewpoint between the two cultures on this specific issue.[38]

34. Ibid., 349.
35. On the fragility of such convergences, see Sabine MacCormack, "Pachacuti: Miracles, Punishments, and Last Judgments: Visionary Past and Prophetic Future in Early Colonial Peru," *American Historical Review* 93, no. 4 (October 1988): 960–1006.
36. Ricard, *Spiritual Conquest of Mexico*, 135–44.
37. José María Kobayashi, *La educación como conquista (empresa franciscana en México)* (Mexico City, 1974), esp. 171–407.
38. Pollard, Taríacuri's Legacy, esp. 87–92; Ulises Beltrán, "Estado y sociedad tarascos," in

The Emphasis on Lineage

One of the very few times that the Franciscan missionary comments explicitly on the content of the *Relación* comes at the end of a chapter discussing the transference of authority from the mythical politico-religious figure who is attributed with founding the ruling lineage, Taríacuri, to two of his offspring, Hirepan and Tangaxoan. He states: "The Cazonci held the entire past chapter in great reverence and he made the priest who knew that history tell it many times. He said that this chapter was the creed of the nobility and it was advised that Taríacuri had given it to everyone."[39] This transfer of authority, through lineage, from Taríacuri to Hirepan and Tangaxoan, and through them to the conquest-era indigenous nobility, plays a crucial role within the text.

In the *Relación*, Taríacuri appears as an intensely devout man whose austere lifestyle in some regards corresponds to the Franciscan missionary ideal. He derived his authority from profound devotion to the god Curicaueri, whom he served through hard physical labor, primarily the collecting of wood to be burned in the temples, and material deprivation. The extent of Taríacuri's devotion is measured by the frequency of his ritual observations, which were intimately integrated into his daily life. The transition of authority from Taríacuri to Hirepan and Tangaxoan, although political, was conceived of as a transfer of religious authority, legitimated by the daily renewal of the relationship with Curicaueri.[40]

The authors placed great emphasis on the significance of this event. Thirty-four chapters of the second part of the text, in which the region's history prior to the Spanish invasion is presented, examine this single transition period from Taríacuri to Hirepan and Tangaxoan. The final two chapters of this second section describe the transmission of the lineage up until the Spanish colonial presence; this latter period actually included at least three generations. This is a testimony, on the one hand, to the rapidity of the turnover in indigenous leadership immediately prior to and during the Spanish Conquest. For example, Zuanga, the father of the Cazonci executed by Nuño de Guzmán, died of smallpox shortly before the physical arrival of the

---

La sociedad indígena en el centro y occidente de México, ed. Pedro Carrasco et al. (Zamora, Mexico, 1986), 49–54; Ralph L. Beals, "The Tarascans," in The Handbook of Middle American Indians (Austin, Tex., 1969), 8:727.

39. *La Relación de Michoacán*, 148.

40. Ibid., 154.

Spanish in Michoacán.[41] However, this also represents the author's attempt to document the lineage of the local nobility, with a particular emphasis placed on the deeply rooted nature of indigenous elite legitimacy.

The proper lineage of Michoacán's indigenous nobility was an important matter to both the Franciscan missionary and his informants, so much so that a lineage chart was included among the illustrations that accompanied the original text.[42] It is impossible to say whether the presence of this chart should be attributed more to the Franciscan missionary, or the indigenous elite. However, it is possible to state that lineage, and elite status, had tangible and important benefits for the indigenous nobility of colonial Michoacán, as it did throughout the Spanish colonial empire. All missionaries, including the Franciscans, made important distinctions between the indigenous elite and the common people. This tendency derived from preexisting Spanish notions of a hierarchical, yet organic social order, and a pragmatic recognition that the conversion of the ruling class provided the most practical route to a rapid, although perhaps superficial, conversion of the subject populations.[43]

Francisco Miranda has suggested that throughout time, the various Cazoncis had an explicit interest in convincing their peoples to accept a particular version of their own history. The Cazoncis' power and wealth depended upon their association with the ancestors and deities of the local peoples, and it is precisely this relationship which the oral histories recorded by the Franciscan missionary emphasized, particularly when they described the prehispanic past.[44] My own interpretation of the *Relación de Michoacán* has been influenced by Miranda's insight, which explains the importance that the Cazonci placed on this specific section. However, when we interpret this text in terms of the politics of the moment, the relevant issue is not the Cazonci's use of history to legitimize his rule in the eyes of his subjects. Rather, we need to ask what was the purpose of Cuinierángari and the other indigenous

41. Ibid., 213–14, 307–10.

42. Miranda, "Estudio preliminar," in *La Relación de Michoacán*, ix, xli.

43. On Spanish notions of social order, see Richard Morse, "The Heritage of Latin America," in *The Founding of New Societies,* ed. Louis Hartz et al. (New York, 1964), 123–77, and "Towards a Theory of Spanish American Government," *Journal of the History of Ideas* 15, no. 1 (January 1954): 71–93. On missionary conversion strategies, see Borges, *Métodos,* 377–81; Ricard, *Spiritual Conquest of Mexico,* 135–42; Kobayashi, *La educación;* and Adam Versényi, *Theatre in Latin America* (Cambridge, England, 1993), 1–35.

44. Miranda, "Estudio preliminar," in *La Relación de Michoacán,* xxxvii.

elites in recalling this history for the missionary author and, through him, the Spanish colonial state?

One possibility is that they wanted to establish themselves as a legitimate aristocracy in Spanish eyes, so as to obtain a status prized among the colonials themselves. It is evident that the indigenous people of Michoacán had a conception of status, transmitted through lineage, prior to the Spanish presence. Thus the indigenous nobility did not assimilate, in a wholesale manner, a definition of noble status from the Spanish cultural tradition. Rather, the selective reconstruction of their own history by the male elite during this early colonial moment emphasized those elements of the local cultural heritage which would work most effectively to establish the legitimacy of the indigenous aristocracy in the eyes of the colonial state.

The treatment of marriage in the text is important in this regard, since marriage assumes an extremely important role in societies placing great value on lineage.[45] An examination of marriage practices begins in section 3, chapter 12, which the missionary author entitles "On The Manner In Which the Lords Marry [Here is placed how Don Pedro, who is now ruler, married, because in this way all (lords) married]."[46] The description of the marriage of Cuinierángari, in conjunction with his dominant position in the text, is particularly revealing. Cuinierángari obviously had an intimate relationship with the Franciscan missionary, since he is the only informant named. As an adopted brother, he did not possess the status of the dead Cazonci, and thus could only succeed him in a qualified way. Nevertheless, he had obviously obtained a significant amount of status by the time of the *Relación,* most probably due to his ability to adapt to the new situation created by Spanish settlement, including the presence of colonial missionaries.

Thus it is interesting to note that both authors are careful to distinguish Cuinierángari's marriage from that of the "gente baja," or common people. Cuinierángari is presented as monogamous, which would be unexpected in most Mesoamerican cultural contexts. This indicates a response to or gesture toward missionary norms. His partner comes from a suitable social stratum. The participants at the ceremony are amply provided for in terms of food and gifts, and the relatively lavish ritual is mediated by a priest. The vows

45. Ramón Gutiérrez, "Honor Ideology, Marriage Negotiation, and Class-Gender Domination in New Mexico, 1690–1846," *Latin American Perspectives* 44 (Winter 1985): 81, 91–93.

46. *La Relación de Michoacán,* 260; see 260–73 for a discussion of marriage. See also Pollard, *Taríacuri's Legacy,* 178–79, and Stone, "A Fragile Coalition," 134–43.

contained statements that imply acquiescence to Spanish control. In fact, during the ceremony Cuinierángari states that he and his spouse would be vassals of the Spaniards, and would work hard for them as their servants.[47] Thus, at one level he is clearly accepting Spanish dominance, and his marriage indicates an attempt to conform to Spanish norms.

However, his marriage also works to add to Cuinierángari's prestige, despite his vassal status. While Cuinierángari's acceptance of Spanish control may seem servile, his status is actually enhanced, at least in the eyes of the Spanish missionary. Not only does he accept monogamy and Spanish rule, but he also gains control over a vassal. During the ceremony, Cuinierángari states: "Here is a woman that is our daughter and a true lady. How is she given us as a woman? She is not given as a woman, but only for us to raise her as her tutors."[48] Thus Cuinierángari's vision of marriage includes male dominance, a pattern that would certainly conform to Spanish and, quite possibly, indigenous expectations. His status is also enhanced within both communities by the contrast between his marriage and the marriage customs of the "gente baja," or common people.

According to our authors, the "gente baja" marriage ritual consisted of a lecture from the father of the bride to his daughter that she should not commit adultery. If she did so and disgraced the family, the father warned, she would be killed. The sharp contrasts in marriage practices between the "gente baja" and "Don Pedro," and the way in which these practices are juxtaposed in the text, indicate an effort to establish a higher grade of status for the indigenous nobility, and particularly Cuinierángari. For example, the "gente baja" often do not marry, and when they do, it can be messy, at least according to missionary norms. The text states of the "gente baja" that some "took the mother-in-law first, the daughter being very young, and after she became an adolescent, they left the mother-in-law and took the daughter, with whom they married. Others married with their in-laws after their spouses died. Others with their relatives, as is said. And they left them and took others when they did not make them blankets or when they had committed adultery."[49] This comment is intriguing, because it indicates a

47. *La Relación de Michoacán*, 261.
48. Ibid.
49. Ibid., 267. Also see Pedro Carrasco, "Parentesco y regulación del matrimonio entre los indios del antiguo Michoacán, México," *Revista Española de Antropología Americana* 4 (1969): 219–22, and Jose Tudela De La Orden, "La pena de adulterio en los pueblos precortesianos,"

similar pattern of male dominance while highlighting the elevated status of Cuinierángari. After all, it is the men who are choosing the partners in this example, and the ones who are leaving when adultery is committed or blankets are not made.

For a member of the indigenous elite it was extremely important, given the treatment generally accorded to the male elite by missionaries, to present the Franciscan missionary with a version of history establishing a noble lineage deeply rooted in the past. For the missionary, it was important to show the Crown that these were people with some merit, who, although pagan and clearly not the equal of Spaniards, enjoyed the possibility of salvation. Thus one can suggest that there was a convergence of the voices in the text to establish the indigenous lineage, so as to convince the Crown to pursue an Indian policy that placed control over the Indian population in missionary hands. This convergence directly challenged another sector of the Spanish colonial order, the settlers who depended upon the Indian communities as a source of labor.[50] A related struggle, profoundly gendered, was waged to recoup a sense of honor lost in the humiliation of Conquest.

Honor, Images of Masculinity and Femininity, and Their Relationship to the Conquest

The *Relación de Michoacán* records the following statement made to representatives of the Cazonci, as they journeyed toward Tenochtitlán for their first formal meeting with the Spaniards. "You are welcome, Chichimecas of Michoacán. Now we have seen ourselves anew, we do not know who these gods are that have destroyed us and have conquered us. Look at this city of Mexico named for our god Zinzuiquixo, which is totally destroyed! They have put women's underskirts on all of us! How they have left us!"[51] The shifting power relationships, and subsequent gendered sense of humiliation apparent in the greeting cited above, dramatically illustrates the point that gender is "a primary way of signifying relationships of power."[52] The con-

Revista de Indias 31, no. 123–24 (January–July 1971): 377–88, esp. 380–85.

50. Borges, *Métodos;* Clendinnen, *Ambivalent Conquests,* esp. 54–92; Phelan, *Millennial Kingdom,* esp. 76–87; Ricard, *Spiritual Conquest of Mexico,* esp. 239–64.

51. *La Relación de Michoacán,* 326.

52. Joan Wallach Scott, "Gender: A Useful Category of Historical Analysis," in *Gender and the Politics of History* (New York, 1988), 48.

quest of Mexico initiated intense struggles for power among both colonizing and colonized populations, within an overall context of Spanish domination. As we shall see, these struggles were frequently expressed in gendered terms.

It is fascinating to note that much of the initial conversation between Nuño de Guzmán and the Cazonci, as recalled by Cuinierángari, was phrased in terms of honor, and above all else, manliness. An example of this comes at the point in the text where the Cazonci has been transported to Mexico City, and is being questioned by Nuño de Guzmán, recently appointed as president of the First Audiencia.[53] There, they engaged in a dialogue over the failure of the Cazonci to provide as much gold as Nuño de Guzmán had requested:

> *Guzmán:* Why do you bring so little? Are you a boy? Send for more!. . .
> *Cazonci* (to the *principales,* or indigenous elders, who had accompanied him): Go again to my brother Don Pedro and say to him: What do I have to do? What, am I not a man? That they keep me like this! That he should bring more gold!

Later, after the Cazonci, whom Nuño de Guzmán was holding prisoner, had received more gold, Nuño de Guzmán made the following remarks: "Why do you bring so little? Do you not have shame? What, am I not a lord?" And after the Cazonci protested that there was no more gold, Nuño de Guzmán, quite possibly enraged and screaming in a loud voice, stated:

> There is a lot! What are you, a little man [señor pequeño]? If you do not bring it to me, I will treat you as you deserve because you are a rogue and fleece the Christians. Well, knowing and having seen how I have treated you, why do you want the gold? Bring it all because the Christians are all furious against you. They say that you rob from them the tributes of the villages and that you rob the villages as well. They say that I should kill you for the grief that you give them. I do not believe them, why do you not believe this that I say to you? Do you want to die, perhaps?[54]

53. Warren, *Conquest of Michoacán,* 136–37.
54. *La Relación de Michoacán,* 344–45.

This dialogue, and its aftermath, reveal several of the important political dynamics of the Conquest and immediate post-Conquest period, dynamics which elite male indigenes responded to as they recalled their history for the Franciscan missionary.

As we know, Nuño de Guzmán did indeed kill the Cazonci. The immediate event which triggered the Cazonci's public humiliation and execution was his refusal or inability to provide gold. Nuño de Guzmán also suspected the Cazonci of maintaining an autonomous power base, which fed the conquistadores' omnipresent fear of indigenous attack.[55] The Spanish had a passion for gold, and killed for it, because it was a universal equivalent, and thus could be exchanged for all things. However, it is not accurate to say that gold was their sole motivation. For men like Nuño de Guzmán gold was important as the means to an end. Gold was the difference between being a powerful lord (*señor grande*) or a little man (*señor pequeño*), a man (*hombre*) or a boy (*muchacho*). In short, gold was the basis of power, and a powerful man had honor, which was gained, demonstrated, and renewed by assertion.[56]

Nuño de Guzmán gained honor through the humiliation and dishonoring of the Indian population, and especially the Cazonci. If this were not the case, it would have been sufficient simply to kill the Cazonci, or to punish him with some restraint for the various crimes that he was accused of committing. Instead, he was publicly tortured, humiliated, and disgraced. In addition, this dishonor extended to the entire Indian population. Why else would Cuinierángari have heard the Spaniard following the Cazonci's burnt body, as it was dragged behind a horse, call out: "Look and pay heed, look you lowly people who are all rogues!"[57]

Michoacán's indigenous population as a whole endured the devastation and disgrace of the Conquest. However, after the Spanish invasion, the elite male indigenes adapted preexisting patriarchal norms for a new purpose and attempted to recoup the honor that had been lost.[58] This attempt to recoup lost honor becomes evident when we analyze the text as a whole. One of the recurrent themes throughout the *Relación de Michoacán* is the prevalence of

55. Ibid., 350–52.
56. Ibid., 344–45; Gutiérrez, "Honor Ideology," 86–89.
57. *La Relación de Michoacán*, 353.
58. Pollard, *Taríacuri's Legacy*, 175, 179–84, provides a sophisticated discussion of "prehispanic" gender and state formation in Michoacán.

male domination within local indigenous society, a pattern that predates the Conquest. The point is tentative, but it appears that the emphasis placed on male domination by the indigenous elite, as they transmitted their oral history to the Franciscan missionary, stemmed from the humiliation of Conquest. This humiliation was particularly harsh during the immediate post-Conquest period, and particularly challenging to their sense of masculine honor. As they recounted, even their own women challenged their valor after the Conquest, when they proved unable to keep the Spaniards from looting the Cazonci's ceremonial gold and silver.[59]

In emphasizing male dominance, the indigenous elites drew on an established patriarchal tradition whose particular features bore a strong resemblance to elite patriarchal norms within the invading culture. For example, they told the missionary that when one of their own (an elite) was killed in war, part of the burial ritual was to tell his wife, as consolation, that she should not slander her husband by her behavior. If she were a bad woman, she would disgrace him, and this would be unacceptable, given her husband's prominence. They spoke explicitly in this regard, and concluded by reminding her that "by him you are known."[60] This practice reinforced the notion of an indigenous aristocracy, in a way that resonated strongly with the existing ideals of an "honorable man" in Spanish culture. Recall, too, Cuinierángari's assertion of dominance over his wife.

This tendency to emphasize male dominance is also pronounced in those segments of the *Relación* dealing with Taríacuri, the founder of Purhépecha society, and the origin of the lineage. The initial conflict between Taríacuri and his neighbors, which developed into a series of wars ultimately resolved by Taríacuri's victory and the establishment of an indigenous state on the shores of Lake Pátzcuaro, began because Taríacuri had an adulterous wife. It was her lies and sexual impropriety that finally led Taríacuri to attack her kin. The language the indigenous elite chose to assign this "mala mujer," or bad woman, as she lies to her brothers about Taríacuri, is significant: "He said that he is a valiant man and took an arrow in his hand and he showed it to me saying: Look, look woman, with these I have enough to kill all your brothers and relatives! How, are they valiant men? They are lightweights! . . . Are they strong men? No, they are women!"[61] Later, after a series of

59. *La Relación de Michoacán*, 324.
60. Ibid., 251.
61. Ibid., 90.

incidents with his adulterous wife, Taríacuri, aided by his god Curicaueri, has his revenge. The people of Coringuaro, his wife's home village, had surrounded Taríacuri in the hope of killing him, but instead Curicaueri made them extremely ill. As they fell to the ground, old women picked them up and carried them into the temple, where they were sacrificed and their heads placed on poles.

Again, the language assigned, this time to Taríacuri, is extremely significant. In triumph, he cries out: "If my woman, the daughter of the lord of Coringuaro, were a man, she would be a very valiant man. Now, as a woman, she has caused the killing of her brothers and uncles and her grandfather. She has given to the gods on this feast day, and to them she has appeased their stomachs. My woman has been a valiant man!"[62] As the *Relación* explains, what Taríacuri meant was that his wife had started the war, and thus had caused these deaths. Thus we have the very origins of the indigenous peoples of Michoacán presented as a reassertion of lost honor, a presentation shaped in many ways by the regional experience of Spanish conquest.

Conclusion

In the end, the *Relación* is an intricate text, one that permits only a tenuous critique. The main unifying feature of this work is that it had one transcriber and editor, the Franciscan missionary. However, other influences are also notable. The specific history of early colonialism in Michoacán did not preclude a limited and temporary convergence between missionaries and indigenes once the colonial order had been established, particularly when the missionaries acted against powerful interests like the soldiers and settlers allied to Nuño de Guzmán. In this sense, then, we can speak of the *Relación* as an early colonial artifact, produced by a political alliance that temporarily brought together some indigenous male elders with missionary representatives of the early colonial state.

The *Relación* presents the execution of the Cazonci as a crucial symbolic moment in an ongoing process of consolidating and re-creating colonial power. This process began in 1522, when an expedition headed by Cristobal de Olid first "discovered" "Tarascan" civilization.[63] It was to continue throughout the centuries of colonial rule and into the neocolonial nine-

---

62. Ibid., 112.
63. Warren, *Conquest of Michoacán*, 42.

teenth and twentieth centuries. As Helen Perlstein Pollard, one of the most knowledgeable scholars of Michoacán's precolonial past, perceptively notes, "In the centuries following European contact, the political conquest, completed by 1530, was accompanied by a cultural conquest that continues to this day."[64] The execution of the Cazonci in 1530 brought one era to a close, but the inability to complete the "cultural conquest," and its persistence into the present, demonstrates indigenous creativity, autonomy, and survival. As we shall see throughout this book, struggles over power, culture, and the meaning of the past have remained part of successive "historical presents."

Sabine MacCormack has noted that the convergence between missionary Christians and indigenes in Peru has always been "riddled throughout by tensions and conflicts that are still alive today."[65] These tensions and conflicts raged in Michoacán as well and were responsible for the fragile and historically specific nature of the alliance between missionaries and the male indigenous elite in the 1530s. In Michoacán and Mexico during the centuries that followed, no other issue would be so hotly contested as the role of the Catholic Church in political life.[66] The seeds of these disputes were planted in the moments after the conquest. It is here that we see the attempts at domination, violent repression, assertions of honor, and bitter disputes over the control of the local population that were to mark political culture for the remainder of the sixteenth century and beyond.

Over the centuries, there have been moments when representatives of the Catholic Church enhanced their moral standing and gained a degree of legitimacy in the eyes of the local population in Michoacán, despite frequent outbursts of hostility at the abuses of clerical power. This is the only way to explain the consistent loyalty of a significant portion of the region's population to Catholicism, a pattern that has extended into contemporary times, alongside anticlerical sentiment and the recent spread of evangelical Protestantism. If we return to the sixteenth-century origins of this relationship in Michoacán, and use the *Relación* as a guide, we can state that

64. Pollard, *Taríacuri's Legacy*, 3.

65. MacCormack, "Pachacuti," 960. For an example of conflict leading to intensely violent repression of indigenes by missionaries, see Clendinnen, *Ambivalent Conquests*, 72–92.

66. Roderic Ai Camp, *Crossing Swords* (New York, 1997); Jennie Purnell, *Popular Movements and State Formation in Revolutionary Mexico* (Durham, N.C., 1999); Becker, *Setting the Virgin on Fire*.

the least tenuous moments in the convergence between missionaries and indigenes came about when they launched political challenges against powerful interests in ways that benefited both. That they defined these challenges according to their own realities should not be allowed to obscure this point.

3

THE WRITINGS OF VASCO DE QUIROGA

> What motive other than preaching the gospel ideals im-
> pelled so many missionaries to denounce the abuses com-
> mitted against the *Indios* with the arrival of the conquista-
> dors? To demonstrate this we have the apostolic activity
> and the writings of intrepid Spanish evangelists like
> Bartolomé de Las Casas, Fray Antonio de Montesinos,
> Vasco de Quiroga, Juan del Valle, Julián Garces, José de
> Anchieta, Manuel de Nóbrega.
> —Pope John Paul II, Santo Domingo, October 12, 1992

In this chapter I seek to understand Vasco de Quiroga, *oidor* or
judge in the Second Audiencia (1528–36) and first bishop of
Michoacán (1538–65), in terms of his own historical context, to
the extent that this can be determined by a close reading of his
writings.[1] The traces of experience preserved in these documents
demonstrate the links between his religious beliefs and political actions, indicate the contours of his famous utopian vision,
and hint at his conceptions of self and other during the first-

1. I am not certain precisely when Vasco de Quiroga's term as *oidor* began or
ended. Although appointed *oidor* in 1528, Quiroga did not reach New Spain until
1530. In addition, he became a bishop-elect in December 1536, although he did not
officially assume these duties until January 14, 1539, after his ordination to the
priesthood. See Warren, *Vasco de Quiroga*, 4, 26, 85–88; José Bravo Ugarte, *Dioce-
sis y obispos de la iglesia mexicana (1519–1965)* (Mexico City, 1941), 68; Miranda,
Don Vasco de Quiroga; Carlos Herrejón, ed., *Humanismo y ciencia en la formación de México* (Zamora, Mexico, 1984); Vasco de Quiroga, *La Información en
Derecho,* ed. Carlos Herrejón (1535; Mexico City, 1985), 9–26 (unless otherwise indicated, all references to *La Información en Derecho* are to this edition); Julio Cesar
Moran Alvarez, *El pensamiento de Vasco de Quiroga* (Morelia, Mexico, 1990); and

generation missionary-Indian "encounter" in Mexico.[2] They also provide insights into an era of profound historical significance, since Vasco de Quiroga's term as bishop coincided with the consolidation of the regional colonial Church and state, and thus the end of the initial Spanish conquest of Michoacán.

As the quotation above indicates, Vasco de Quiroga lives on in historical memory as the founder of communal villages among the Indians of Michoacán, an act that restored the harmony that had been shattered by Spanish settlement, the initial failures of Franciscan evangelization, and the execution of the Cazonci. Perhaps surprisingly, however, given Vasco de Quiroga's well-established place in the contemporary pantheon of early colo-nial heroes, knowledge of his sixteenth-century vision is based on relatively few documents: the "Carta al Consejo de Indias" (1531); the *Información en Derecho* (1535), his most substantive work; the *Reglas y ordenanzas*—the by-laws for the communities he is credited with establishing among the indigenes of Michoacán—known only by the incomplete version copied and published by Juan José Moreno in 1760, although produced sometime prior to his death in 1565; and the *Testamento* (1565), his will, composed at the end of his life.[3]

Rodrigo Martínez, "Reorientaciones," in Florescano, *Historia general de Michoacán*, 2:76–122. There is an enormous and still growing secondary literature on Vasco de Quiroga, much of which is quite repetitive. A useful starting point is Francisco Miranda, "Bibliografía de Vasco de Quiroga," in *Vasco de Quiroga: Educador de adultos,* comp. Francisco Miranda and Gabriela Briseño (Pátzcuaro, Mexico, 1984), 181–94.

2. Recent scholarship successfully argues that More's influence on Quiroga has been over-stated. See Verastíque, *Michoacán and Eden,* xiv, 96.

3. Vasco de Quiroga, "Carta al Consejo de Indias (14 de agosto de 1531)," in Rafael Aguayo Spencer, *Don Vasco de Quiroga* (Mexico City, 1970), 78; idem, *La Información en Derecho,* ed. Carlos Herrejón; idem, *Reglas y ordenanzas para el gobierno de los hospitales de Santa Fe de México y de Michoacán,*" in Aguayo Spencer, *Don Vasco de Quiroga: Taumaturgo de la organización social,* 242–69; idem, "Testamento de Don Vasco de Quiroga Primer Obispo de Michoacán, 24 de enero de 1565," in Miranda, *Don Vasco de Quiroga,* 281–303. On the probable date of the *Reglas,* see Silvio Zavala, "Vasco de Quiroga ante las comunidades de indios," in Herrejón, *Humanismo y ciencia,* 34. I have excluded an examination of *De debellendis indis,* although various editions of this treatise have at times been attributed to Vasco de Quiroga, because the author-ship and authenticity of existing versions remains in dispute, and the main currents of his thought are clearly established in these other sources. On *De debellendis indis,* see Paz Serrano Gassent, "Introducción," in Vasco de Quiroga, *La utopía en América,* ed. Paz Serrano Gassent (Madrid, 1992), 44; René Acuña, *Vasco de Quiroga. De Debellendis Indis. Un tratado desconocido* (Mexico City, 1988); Benno Biermann, O.P., "Don Vasco de Quiroga y su tratado "De Debel-lendis Indis (II)," *Historia Mexicana* 18, no. 4 (April-June 1969): 615–22; and Silvio Zavala, "En torno del tratado "De Debellendis Indis" de Vasco de Quiroga," ibid., 623–26.

On Elites, Milieu, and History

This chapter is a cultural history "from above." Although inspired by scholarship that tries to recover fragments of the socially mediated beliefs, ideas, and attitudes—in short, mentalités—of subaltern groups or dominated individuals, the subject here is one of the more influential members of the new colonial administration.[4] Vasco de Quiroga had power and social standing, and he used these resources to pursue his dream of a reformed and purified Christian social order. His status did not preclude responding to—and, at a distance, in his writings, reflecting—the indigenous presence in early colonial Mexico. The sometimes subtle interactions between dominant and dominated social actors shapes the real experience, as well as the representation, of relationships of power. Thus, traces of Vasco de Quiroga's interactions with the indigenes are hinted at in the texts he constructed, and understandings of his experience deepen when these are taken into consideration.

I seek here to draw nearer to Vasco de Quiroga's world, rather than to demonstrate his intellectual lineage. Since the pioneering studies of Silvio Zavala, the corpus of Quirogian texts has been scrutinized meticulously by an array of scholars seeking to discover his intellectual precursors. Thus, we can now state that his thought displays multiple influences. These include figures from antiquity, such as Aristotle, Plato, and Lucian; intellectuals from early Christianity, such as Ambrose, Augustine, Basil, Athanasius, Cyril, and Chrysostom; and more recent thinkers, such as Antonine, Innocent III, Alexander VI, Cajeton, Johann Faber, John Gerson, Guillamé Budé, Sebastian Brandt, Thomas More, and Erasmus.[5] There is no longer a need to search for the intellectual antecedents of Don Vasco's thought, in part because the task has already been done. In addition, as Roger Chartier suggests, the historian's tendency to classify intellectuals or trends as

4. Serge Gruzinski, *Man-Gods in the Mexican Highlands,* trans. Eileen Corrigan (Stanford, Calif., 1989), 5. A pioneering effort is Carlo Ginzberg, *The Cheese and the Worms,* trans. John Tedeschi and Anne Tedeschi (Baltimore, 1980). See also Carlo Ginzberg, *Clues, Myths, and the Historical Method,* trans. John Tedeschi and Anne Tedeschi (Baltimore, 1989), and Eric Van Young, "Conclusions," in *Indian-Religious Relations in Colonial Spanish America,* ed. Susan E. Ramírez (Syracuse, N.Y., 1989), 87–97.

5. Herrejón, "Introducción," in Quiroga, *La Información en Derecho,* 19–21. See also Warren, *Vasco de Quiroga,* 12; Moran Alvarez, *El pensamiento,* 143–60, 175–91; Anthony Pagden, *The Fall of Natural Man* (Cambridge, England, 1982), 27–56, esp. 35; and Silvio Zavala, *Recuerdo de Vasco de Quiroga* (Mexico City, 1965).

"renaissance, humanism, reformation and the like" is misleading, because it imposes a simplified coherence on complicated, and at times contradictory, processes and patterns.[6]

In the case of existing scholarship on Vasco de Quiroga, the pattern has been to classify him as an early modern Christian humanist, and to assume that this designation refers to a static set of beliefs. This has led to a systematic denial of the importance of the Spanish colonial context in creating the space where his intervention would take on its first meanings, and also to the neglect of the specificity of his thought.[7] It is not necessary, or desirable, to reopen the entire debate on "white" and "black" legends of Spanish colonialism, the problematic nature of which extends far beyond the racist imagery of the terms themselves.[8] Nor is it useful to condemn Vasco de Quiroga anachronistically, for failing to adhere to twenty-first century norms, themselves subject to contention and debate. Rather, what is needed is to understand how his thought carried the imprint of a specific era, while also demonstrating multiple and even ambiguous responses to existing social processes. Vasco de Quiroga's writings, and particularly the complex blend of authoritarian paternalism and moral obligation they manifest, reflect—at times, uniquely—the milieu that created and was reinforced by the *encomienda*, the first colonial institution developed to regulate indigenous labor in order to extract economic surplus in a sustained and ongoing way.[9]

The *encomienda* granted access to the labor of conquered people as a reward for successful colonization. It worked, at least in part and for a while,

6. Roger Chartier, "Intellectual History or Sociocultural History? The French Trajectories," in *Modern European Intellectual History,* ed. Dominick LaCapra and Steven Kaplan (Ithaca, N.Y., 1982), 16. See also Dominick LaCapra, "Rethinking Intellectual History and Reading Texts," in LaCapra and Kaplan, *Modern European Intellectual History,* 54, and Giovanni Levi, "On Microhistory," in *New Perspectives on Historical Writing,* ed. Peter Burke (University Park, Pa., 1992), 93–113.

7. Pagden, "The Humanism of Vasco de Quiroga's *Información en derecho,*" in *Uncertainties of Empire,* 133–42; Mignolo, *The Darker Side of the Renaissance,* xi.

8. Stern, "Paradigms of Conquest." See also Edmundo O'Gorman, "Lewis Hanke on the Spanish Struggle for Justice in the Conquest of America," *Hispanic American Historical Review* 29 (1949): 563–71; Benjamin Keen, "The Black Legend Revisited: Assumptions and Realities," *Hispanic American Historical Review* 49, no. 2 (February 1969): 703–19; and Lewis Hanke, "A Modest Proposal for a Moratorium on Grand Generalizations: Some Thoughts on the Black Legend," *Hispanic American Historical Review* 51, no. 1 (1971): 112–27.

9. A concise discussion of the *encomienda* can be found in Benjamin Keen, *A History of Latin America,* 5th ed. (Boston, 1996), 81–86. Classic monographs include José Miranda, *El tributo indígena en la Nueva España durante el siglo XVI* (Mexico City, 1952), and Leslie Byrd Simpson, *The Encomienda in New Spain* (Berkeley, Calif., 1950).

because it absorbed and redefined preexisting labor systems in an incipient global market economy. Thus, it can be considered to be a colonial hybrid, one that brought together the feudal institutions of medieval Spain with the political and labor traditions of the indigenous world. Over time, it played a role in creating an enduring Latin American pattern by fusing forced labor with the profit principle.[10] At the ideological level, access to labor in the *encomienda*—from the Spanish verb *encomendar*, "to entrust"—was legitimated by the obligation to attend to the spiritual and material needs of one's chattels. Theoretically, then, ties of mutual obligation within a clearly defined "natural" hierarchy legitimated the *encomienda*, and this principle was recognized in Spanish law. Of course, law and reality were two different things, and the abuses of the *encomienda* soon provoked controversy, debate, and calls for reform and even abolition. Vasco de Quiroga emerged as a critic of the *encomienda* as it existed in New Spain, although—unlike Las Casas and the more "radical" of his contemporaries—he favored improving the institution rather than ending it.[11] It is precisely Vasco de Quiroga's self-definition as a reformer, and as a champion of the "native people"—whom he viewed as a "very soft wax" yet to receive any impression, "good metal" out of which to fashion a true Church—that makes him especially valuable for an examination of the workings of power in sixteenth-century Mexico.[12]

Sightings and Definitions

From the perspective of Don Vasco, the newness of it all, and the potential of so many souls to save, must have been stunning. We can almost feel his awe in a letter that he sent to the Council of the Indies in 1531. In reference to the indigenes of New Spain he reported that "there are so many that it seems like they are as the stars in the sky and grains of sand in the sea, that have no count." He continued by noting that "the multitude of these native Indians would not be believed," and—in a passage that reveals a colonizing gaze—observed that "their manner of living is chaos and confusion."[13]

Don Vasco's comments here and in his other writings reveal beautiful hopes for New Spain. However, they also point toward less heroic impulses

---

10. Enrique Semo, *Historia del capitalismo en México* (Mexico City, 1973).
11. Pagden, "The Humanism of Vasco de Quiroga's *Información en Derecho*," in *Uncertainties of Empire*, 136; Verastíque, *Michoacán and Eden*, 112–17.
12. Quiroga, *La Información en Derecho*, 175.
13. Quiroga, "Carta al Consejo de Indias," 78.

in his relationship to the people he intended to save. For example, his thought was marked by an authoritarian desire to impose "order" on patterns of indigenous life he perceived as unruly, from gender and sexual relationships to dispersed settlement patterns. Thus, he proposed a thorough reconstruction of indigenous society from the household to the community levels. To twenty-first-century eyes, his understanding of the peoples newly defined as "Indians" appears contradictory, and perhaps ambiguous, since he both exalted and condemned them. He saw indigenes as morally superior to corrupt and greedy Europeans, but also prone to "idolatry" and relapses into "barbarism." This latter flaw justified vigilance and firm guidance.[14] These pervasive descriptions indicate an authoritarian paternalism permeated by patriarchal assumptions and an early modern "racialism" that has been largely ignored in existing historiography. Before proceeding to a more sustained interrogation, a few brief definitions are necessary.

By "paternalism," I mean a set of social relations in which a dominant group or individual is linked to subordinates by ties of mutual obligation or hierarchical reciprocity. Paternalism has an innately authoritarian tendency, which frequently results in violence when one or both parties consider the terms of the relationship unfulfilled.[15] Although historically based on patriarchal definitions of the father—in which the eldest male controls the resources of the household, including biological and daily reproductive capacities—paternalistic social relationships have proven flexible enough to surface in multiple contexts.[16] I use the term "racialism" to refer to a hierarchical and prejudicial classification of peoples, in which religious ethnocentrism and lineage descent play very important roles, along with racial prejudice and contempt. This type of classification is different in important ways from modern racism, with its pretensions to scientific credibility and claims of innate genetic value, but it is a form of racial reasoning nonetheless.[17]

14. Ibid., 78–79 (order, chaos and confusion, barbarism). Quiroga, *La Información en Derecho*, 74, 170 (order/chaos); 79, 81, 92, 94, 129–30, 135, (barbarism); 175, 188, 197–99 (moral superiority). Idem, *Reglas y ordenanzas*, 251–54, 258, 260.

15. For a historically specific analysis of paternalism in the encounter between missionaries and the indigenous population of New Spain, see Clendinnen, *Ambivalent Conquests,* esp. 113.

16. For an ambitious attempt to situate the emergence of patriarchy historically, see Gerda Lerner, *The Creation of Patriarchy* (Oxford, 1986), esp. 231–43, for succinct definitions of terms such as "patriarchy," "paternalism," and "male dominance"; Elaine Pagels, *Adam, Eve and the Serpent* (New York, 1988), 25, 29, 78–97; Brown, *The Body and Society;* and Ute Ranke-Heinemann, *Eunuchs for the Kingdom of Heaven,* trans. Peter Heinegg (New York, 1990).

17. A sense for racial hierarchies and thought past and present can be drawn from Trouillot, *Silencing the Past,* 77–78; Ann Laura Stoler, "Rethinking Colonial Categories: European Com-

The sense of awe expressed in the "Carta," and the persistent allure of utopianism, undoubtedly explains much of Vasco de Quiroga's attractiveness to subsequent generations. In the end, however, appreciation of his significance is heightened when we confront the domination, as well as cherish the hope, expressed in his contradictory vision. Many of the most oppressive aspects of his thought reflect the sixteenth-century context in which they were elaborated, a terrain marked by imperial expansion, dramatic and unprecedented social change, and severe political conflict.

Politics

In a letter to the Crown written around 1551, long after infighting and jurisdictional disputes had caused deep divisions among the ecclesiastical authorities of New Spain,[18] Francisco de Mena—commissary general of the Franciscan order in the Indies—made the following complaint against Vasco de Quiroga.

> It would be well to advise the bishop of Michoacán to attend to his calling, because of a truth, he has not done anything pertaining to his office since the time he was consecrated. Most of the time he spends in Mexico in lawsuits. There are numerous complaints against him, and, no doubt, he will have many accounts to settle. During the fifteen years he has been a bishop, he has ordained no one, has never preached, nor has he heard confessions, baptized or confirmed the Indians.[19]

Given its hostile tone, it is perhaps surprising to recall that Vasco de Quiroga and the Franciscan missionaries who participated in the initial colonization

---

munities and the Boundaries of Rule," in *Colonialism and Culture,* ed. Nicholas B. Dirks (Ann Arbor, Mich., 1992), 319–52, esp. 322; and Nancy Leys Stepan, *The Hour of Eugenics* (Ithaca, N.Y., 1991).

18. Miranda, *Don Vasco de Quiroga,* 83–87; Ricard, *Spiritual Conquest of Mexico.* On the institution of the Church at all levels, see John Frederick Schwaller, *The Church and Clergy in Sixteenth-Century Mexico* (Albuquerque, 1987).

19. Fray Francisco de Mena, cited and translated in M. M. Lacas, "A Social Welfare Organizer in Sixteenth-Century New Spain: Don Vasco de Quiroga, First Bishop of Michoacán," *The Americas* 14 (1957–58): 66. Lacas cites Diego Basalenque, O.S.A., *Historia de la provincia de San Nicolás de Tolentino de Michoacán del orden de N. P. S. San Agustín* (Mexico City, 1673), 449. A Spanish version of this quotation can be found in *Documentos ineditos referentes al ilustrísimo señor Don Vasco de Quiroga,* comp. Nicolás León (Mexico City, 1940), viii.

of Mexico once shared similar dreams, and even worked together.[20] The mid-sixteenth-century decline of missionary utopianism, in part due to the maturing of the colonial system and also reflecting generational change, was accompanied by fierce struggles for control of institutional space. The attempt to build parish structures, called for in 1539 and begun in earnest after 1555, started what Miranda terms an "open war" between the bishops and members of the religious orders.[21]

In 1561, Archbishop Montúfar and Vasco de Quiroga filed a lawsuit against the Franciscans, Augustinians, and Dominicans for violating their jurisdiction and abusing Indians.[22] Maturino Gilberti, a Franciscan and gifted linguist, filed a similar complaint against Vasco de Quiroga on February 4, 1563. Gilberti charged him with abusing Indian labor during the initial construction of a cathedral that Don Vasco hoped to build in Pátzcuaro.[23] Quiroga had become furious earlier because Gilberti had refused to translate his catechism for the Indians, *Diálogo de doctrina christiana en lengua de Michoacán,* into Spanish, thereby preventing him and other Spanish churchmen from reviewing it. On December 3, 1559, Vasco de Quiroga requested that Archbishop Montúfar remove the book from circulation, and ultimately he succeeded in his efforts to censor Gilberti.[24] Hostilities developed to the point that Vasco de Quiroga accused the missionary orders of dismantling churches he had built, and there were even reported incidents of "regulars" burning the houses of "seculars."[25] At the time, it was widely recognized that Vasco de Quiroga had hired a "war captain" named Pérez Gordillo Negrón, who in 1560 destroyed the baptismal font of the Franciscan monastery in Pátzcuaro. Negrón was also accused of burning down an Augustinian monastery, of confiscating ornaments and chalices for saying mass, and of moving bodies from an Augustinian to a diocesan cemetery.[26]

20. Silvio Zavala points out that Vasco de Quiroga did not belong to any religious order, and thus served as a "secular" priest. Zavala, "El humanismo de Vasco de Quiroga," in *Recuerdo,* 60. Nevertheless, he shared the hope for a reformed and purified Christianity normally attributed to the Franciscans of his era. See Phelan, *Millennial Kingdom,* 44.

21. Miranda, *Don Vasco de Quiroga,* 85.

22. Ricard, *Spiritual Conquest of Mexico,* 244, also 246–51.

23. Mina Ramírez Montes, *La catedral de Vasco de Quiroga* (Zamora, Mexico, 1986), 82, 85, 100, 166–67.

24. On the entire Gilberti and Quiroga conflict, see Martínez, "Reorientaciones," 113–18.

25. Ricard, *Spiritual Conquest of Mexico,* 249–51.

26. Martínez, "Reorientaciones," 119–21; Verastíque, *Michoacán and Eden,* 107–9.

Rather than an aberration, this ability to engage in what might generously be termed "realpolitik" amidst the collapse of reformist visions is best understood as a constitutive part of Vasco de Quiroga's experience. After all, Don Vasco initially served as an *oidor,* or judge, in the Second Audiencia, a civil position with the colonial state. Later, as his career developed, he obtained an appointment as the bishop of Michoacán, prior to entering the priesthood. This demonstrates the unity of civil and ecclesiastical authority under Spanish colonialism, and the inherently political nature of obtaining a position of authority within the colonial Church.[27] Indeed, the link between religion and politics remained an enduring feature of Latin American life through several centuries.[28] Vasco de Quiroga was intimately acquainted with the workings of political power, and utilized his formidable skills throughout his time in New Spain.

Unfortunately, our analysis of his life is limited to the era after he arrived in the colony. Despite the best efforts of several skilled researchers, we know little about his previous existence in Spain. We do know that he was born in Madrigal de las Altas Torres, as Warren notes, "on the plain of Castilla la Vieja."[29] Legend has it that he was sixty-one years old when he arrived in Mexico, but it is more likely that he was in his early fifties, which places his birth sometime in the 1470s.[30] By the time he arrived in Mexico City on January 9, 1531, he had already obtained a powerful position as an *oidor* or judge of the Second Audiencia, although we do not know precisely how.[31] We lack specific evidence concerning his intellectual training in Spain, although his writings suggest that he was well educated. His life prior to arriving in early colonial Mexico remains something of a mystery.

The most important task of the Second Audiencia, assembled in Spain in 1529–30, was to repair the disastrous rule of the First Audiencia, which had

27. Warren, *Vasco de Quiroga,* 85–88; Miranda, *Don Vasco de Quiroga,* 126; Moran Alvarez, *El pensamiento,* 42. The emphasis on the political nature of this appointment is mine.

28. Thomas A. Kselman, "Ambivalence and Assumption in the Concept of Popular Religion," in *Religion and Political Conflict,* ed. Daniel Levine (Chapel Hill, N. C., 1981), 32; Daniel H. Levine, "Conflict and Renewal," in ibid., 237–38; Clodomiro Siller, "La iglesia en el medio indígena," in *Religión y política en México,* ed. Martín de la Rosa and Charles A. Reilly (Mexico City, 1985), 213–39; Ai Camp, *Crossing Swords.*

29. Moran Alvarez, *El pensamiento,* 28; Warren, *Vasco de Quiroga,* 8.

30. Carlos Herrejón, "Dos obras señaladas de Don Vasco de Quiroga," in *Don Vasco de Quiroga y Arzobispado de Morelia* (Mexico City, 1965), 65; Warren, *Vasco de Quiroga,* 8.

31. Warren, *Vasco de Quiroga,* 26.

been appointed toward the end of 1527.[32] The First Audiencia presided over a tumultuous era that began with the arrival in Mexico of Hernán Cortés and his soldiers in 1519, and continued through the Spanish military victory at Tenochtitlán. Intense infighting broke out almost immediately among the newly victorious invading forces. The corruption and brutality of the First Audiencia, under the leadership of its president, Nuño de Guzmán, exacerbated the conflicts of the new colony. Perhaps the most ominous trend was an increase in the rebelliousness of the indigenous population. By 1528 many indigenous revolts had occurred, even in regions—like Michoacán—where the Spaniards had made alliances to facilitate and secure their initial military victories.[33]

Prior to their departure from Spain, royal authorities assigned the Second Audiencia the task of reviewing the First Audiencia. Vasco de Quiroga first visited Michoacán in 1533, accompanied by the translator Francisco Castilleja, because his duties as *oidor* had required him to investigate the abuses of Nuño de Guzmán and other Spanish settlers.[34] These included the execution of the Cazonci.[35] As a result of these efforts, colonial authorities ultimately returned Nuño de Guzmán to Spain in 1538, where he was placed under house arrest for the rest of his life.[36] Thus, Vasco de Quiroga and the other *oidores* of the Second Audiencia had power, and knew how to use it effectively. They arrived in the colony during a major crisis, at a time when reformist efforts might be seriously considered, and even promoted by the colonial state.

On August 14, 1531, Vasco de Quiroga wrote a letter to the Council of the Indies.[37] Although brief, it is very revealing concerning his initial attitudes toward the peoples and problems he faced in New Spain. The conflicts between the Second Audiencia, Nuño de Guzmán, and other conquistadores, most probably influenced Vasco de Quiroga's observation that "to send a knight for president is no more suitable than to send a conflagration, because

---

32. P. Ramón López Lara, "El Oidor," in *Don Vasco de Quiroga y Arzobispado de Morelia*, 13–14; Warren, *Vasco de Quiroga*, 3–4, 26.

33. Gibson, *Spain in America*, 24–48; Warren, *Vasco de Quiroga*, 4; Zavala, *Los esclavos indios*, 16, 20; López Sarrelangue, *La nobleza indígena de Pátzcuaro*, 53.

34. Martínez, "Reorientaciones," 89; Warren, *Vasco de Quiroga*, 84.

35. Warren, *Vasco de Quiroga*, 79–82; López Sarrelangue, *La nobleza indígena de Pátzcuaro*, 56.

36. Zavala, *Los esclavos indios*, 51; Warren, *Vasco de Quiroga*, 3–7, 74–84.

37. Quiroga, "Carta al Consejo de Indias," 78–79.

here there is nothing lacking for things of war." It would be better, he continued, to send an educated person, preferably an experienced man with a moral sense.[38] In addition, because the newly discovered lands were so large, Vasco de Quiroga saw a need for many more religious workers. He was especially interested in obtaining additional Franciscans, who had worked particularly hard at educating the young sons of the indigenous elite. Vasco de Quiroga believed this work among elite male Indian children to be "the most successful route" for obtaining conversions. He hoped that these religious workers would live and work among the Indians, as Apostles had lived among the early Christians. Vasco de Quiroga dreamed of creating in this new environment Christians like those of the early Church.[39]

His early recommendations also demonstrate the "othering" so common in colonial encounters. According to Don Vasco, the diverse peoples of New Spain, recently defined collectively as Indians, "naturally have innate the humility, obedience, and poverty and contempt of the world" necessary to build a purified Church. Because of these innate qualities, however, they were simple, unrefined people, who lived in "nudity, walking shoeless with long hair and heads uncovered." In the end, Vasco de Quiroga considered Indians as a "clean slate" and a "very soft wax," capable of being formed into good Christians if they were kept under strict supervision, but also innately untrustworthy.[40] For this reason, he strongly supported Franciscan efforts to separate indigenous children from their parents. He deeply feared the possibility that these young people, if returned to their families, would return to their old beliefs.[41]

If colonial authorities allowed this to happen, continued Vasco de Quiroga, it would be "no small fault of negligence" on all sides, and the good work of the initial missionary generation might be lost.[42] His words appear to be unusually harsh, even when one concedes the distance of our twenty-first-century perspectives from his early modern world. He wrote: "And if the boys that they have raised and they raise in the monasteries were

38. Ibid., 77.
39. Ibid., 82–83.
40. "Porque naturalmente tienen ynata la humylldad, obediencia y pobreza y menosprecio del mundo y desnudez, andando descalzos con el cabello largo syn cosa alguna en la cabeza." Ibid., 79. I am indebted to Roberto Castillo-Sandoval for help with this translation.
41. Warren, *Vasco de Quiroga*, 28–29. This practice was widespread in New Spain. See Ricard, *Spiritual Conquest of Mexico*, 97–99.
42. Quiroga, "Carta al Consejo de Indias," 79.

to return to this vomit, confusion, and danger that they left, and to the bad and dangerous conversation of their parents . . . they would pervert themselves, returning themselves to their nature."[43] The solution, in addition to keeping children under missionary control, was to form closely supervised communities, with "holy and good and Catholic by-laws," where indigenous peoples would be formed into ideal Christians.[44] The desire to establish a place for children raised in the monasteries, who would serve as the basis for future evangelization efforts, led Vasco de Quiroga to found his first village-hospital, Santa Fe de México, in Mexico City, in 1532.[45]

One result of Vasco de Quiroga's 1533 investigative journey through Michoacán was the founding of the village-hospital of Santa Fe de Michoacán, which Vasco de Quiroga began building in 1535 near Tzintzuntzan, the former imperial center of the Purhépecha kingdom.[46] In 1536, he was designated bishop-elect, although he did not assume this position until 1539, after his ordination and consecration.[47] He served as bishop of Michoacán until his death in 1565, and during these years conflicts continued and intensified. In 1537, he became involved in a massive lawsuit with Archbishop Zumárraga over the geographical boundaries of the adjacent dioceses of Michoacán and México, and also over the implementation and distribution of tithe collection. In 1538, his apparently unilateral decision to make Pátzcuaro the diocesan seat, shifting regional administration from the established indigenous center of Tzintzuntzan, was opposed by the sons of the Cazonci, the last pre-Spanish indigenous ruler. However, this choice was supported by Cu128ierángari, the Cazonci's adopted brother and a newly established leader of the region's indigenes. Although Cuinierángari initially sold Vasco de Quiroga lands to support the village-hospital, they also would have land disputes in 1538, when Quiroga sought to expand his holdings.[48]

Vasco de Quiroga waged a prolonged legal and extralegal battle with the *encomendero* Juan Infante over control of several indigenous communities

43. Ibid., 79.

44. Ibid., 78–79.

45. Warren, *Vasco de Quiroga*, 51; Josefina Muriel, *Hospitales de La Nueva España* (Mexico City, 1956), 1:58.

46. Moran Alvarez, *El pensamiento*, 197–99; Muriel, *Hospitales de La Nueva España*, 1:64–65; Warren, *Vasco de Quiroga*, 74–84.

47. Miranda, *Don Vasco de Quiroga*, 126, 181; Warren, *Vasco de Quiroga*, 85–88, 106–15; Muriel, *Hospitales de La Nueva España*, 1:107; Moran Alvarez, *El pensamiento*, 42, 44.

48. Martínez, "Reorientaciones," 99–100, 105–6, 110.

located along the shores of Lake Pátzcuaro. This struggle, which at times included Don Vasco's threats of violence and even arming supportive factions of indigenes, began in 1539 and lasted through the 1540s.[49] His decision to locate ecclesiastical administration in Pátzcuaro also caused a long-lasting conflict with Spanish settlers in Michoacán. As early as 1537, Viceroy Mendoza—reputedly angry because Quiroga had not consulted him while making his decision—began to conspire with Don Vasco's opponents to establish a new site at Guayangareo (present-day Morelia). This move, which Vasco de Quiroga opposed for his entire life, did not take place until 1580.[50] There were numerous other disputes with various settlers in Michoacán and México, including one with the son of Hernán Cortés that began in 1563, when Don Vasco had allegedly reached ninety-three years of age.[51] Thus, the intense internecine disputes notable by the 1550s among former allies in the missionary cause conformed to widespread patterns during the early colonial period.

All of these conflicts created spaces that indigenes could appropriate for their own ends.

Vasco de Quiroga and the Debate over the Enslavement of Indigenous Peoples

While Vasco de Quiroga entered into many political conflicts, perhaps the best known was his opposition to the practice of enslaving "Indians" and the brisk early colonial slave trade in indigenous peoples. This position earned him the enmity of many powerful figures.[52] He argued that the long-established Western tradition of slaveholding and trading—a fundamental aspect of life in ancient Greece, under the Roman empire, and in European history until relatively recently—could not morally and legally be applied to the indigenous peoples of New Spain. "They are," declared Don Vasco, "no more slaves than I."[53] This bold statement challenged many of the intellectuals of

49. Warren, *Vasco de Quiroga*, 55–63; Paredes Martínez, "El tributo indígena, " 30–31; Moran Alvarez, *El pensamiento*, 197.
50. Martínez, "Reorientaciones," 110–12.
51. Warren, *Vasco de Quiroga*, 55–73, 85–105; Paredes M., "El tributo indígena," 43, 80.
52. Zavala, *Los esclavos indios*, 30–34, 42. Two important studies of slavery in Mexico, which contain some information on this early period, are Colin Palmer, *Slaves of the White God: Blacks in Mexico, 1570–1650* (Cambridge, Mass., 1976), 1–36; Gonzalo Aguirre Beltrán, *La población negra de México* (1946; Mexico City, 1972), 19–194, esp. 158.
53. Quiroga, *La Información en Derecho*, 84.

his day, and perhaps more importantly indicates the bluntness with which Don Vasco confronted those in New Spain who profited from enslaving indigenous people.[54]

Referring to the results of Nuño de Guzmán's invasion of Nueva Galicia, modern-day Jalisco, Vasco de Quiroga decried the violence and disruption of indigenous life that occurred as a result of slavery. In a passage intended to show that the conquistadores had gone far beyond the privileges granted to them by royal authorities, he stated that "in a province of Nueva Galicia . . . they have made and they make slaves even the women with children of three or four months at the breasts of the mothers, and all branded with the iron that says 'del Rey.'"[55] During this era, the brutal abuses associated with slavery and the slave trade proliferated throughout the colony.[56] In the *Información*, Don Vasco argued against the 1534 royal decision reinstating Indian slavery in cases of just war (*esclavos de guerra*, slaves of war), or where indigenous peoples had been enslaved prior to the arrival of the Spanish (*esclavos de rescate*, slaves of commerce or trade, that is, trafficking in already enslaved peoples).[57]

He did so for moral reasons, because he feared that the immorality of the Indian slave trade would undermine the divine legitimacy of Spanish colonialism. If these new provisions allowing slavery were not overturned, warned Don Vasco, a disastrous situation would continue. "It is customary to value a dog more than a man, and to sell at one peso and at two pesos and at three pesos a man (in truth free) as a slave to the Spaniards; and as they cost him so little, neither does he give them much until they are finished in the mines, where few last three years, even fewer five."[58] Vasco de Quiroga spoke out forcefully against the practice of branding the faces of indigenous peoples. In a famous statement, he castigated the Spanish for this practice, noting that "the face of man which was created in the image of God, has been transformed in this land, by our sins, into paper."[59] This is a rhetoric of

54. For a discussion of debates about slavery among sixteenth-century Spanish and European intellectuals, see Pagden, *Fall of Natural Man*, 27–56, and Robin Blackburn, *The Making of New World Slavery* (London, 1997), 15–156.

55. Quiroga, *La Información en Derecho*, 155–56.

56. Zavala, *La esclavos indios*, 1–105.

57. Warren, *Vasco de Quiroga*, 30–31; Moran Alvarez, *El pensamiento*, 48; Zavala, *Los esclavos indios*, 31, 46.

58. Quiroga, *La Información en Derecho*, 186.

59. Ibid., 162.

liberation, which squarely confronts the injustices of Indian slavery as practiced by the initial generation of Spanish colonial forces in New Spain.

In the *Información,* Vasco de Quiroga criticized those Spaniards who, since their arrival in New Spain, had spent their time "robbing and destroying persons, properties and lives, houses, children and women."[60] He believed that these individuals had prevented Spain from fulfilling its obligation to evangelize the Indians, as stated in the papal bull of Alexander VI (1493).[61] For Don Vasco, this duty legitimized Spanish authority over the lands and peoples of New Spain.[62] The failure of the Spanish missionary endeavor would call into question the legitimacy of the Spanish presence in the Americas. Obviously, this was a grave concern. At least in the eyes of Vasco de Quiroga, it had to be addressed immediately. According to Don Vasco, the greed and violence of certain Spaniards had led to the failure of missionary evangelization in New Spain.

He criticized his fellow colonists sharply, noting that in their relations to indigenous peoples "there is more place for their desire which is this to populate the mines: violent robberies, thefts, forceful acts, seizures, and assaults, seizing them, cutting them down and devouring them and destroying them."[63] Vasco de Quiroga's condemnation of the behavior of many Spaniards during the initial years of the Spanish colonial presence at times became quite extraordinary. He went so far as to claim, not once but several times, that the behavior of Spanish colonists justified the resistance of the Indians, which ranged from "the arms of the rabbit" ("las armas del conejo," i.e. flight) to armed conflicts resulting in Spanish deaths.[64] This is a remarkable position in any colonial context, and especially noteworthy since Vasco de Quiroga was writing during an era of heightened conflict. One current of Vasco de Quiroga's thought, then, is a powerful critique of Spanish colonialism, at least as it had occurred prior to 1535. This is a reality not always acknowledged in the existing historiography, especially among those partisan to the missionary cause. For example, Pedro Borges correctly notes that Vasco de Quiroga did not oppose the use of military force in the Spanish

60. Ibid., 59–60.
61. For a detailed discussion of these bulls, and the politics which produced them, see Gibson, *Spain in America,* 15–17, and Pagden, *Fall of Natural Man,* 29.
62. Quiroga, *La Información en Derecho,* 20, 52, 152.
63. Ibid., 94.
64. Ibid., 55, 59–61, 95, 155.

colonization effort under certain circumstances. However, he does not seriously engage Vasco de Quiroga's criticism of the actual practice of Spanish colonialism, or his rejection of the actually existing violence of Spanish conquistadores and settlers, evident in his defense of indigenous resistance throughout the *Información*.[65]

Despite his criticisms of elements of the colonial social order, however, we must also recognize Vasco de Quiroga's writings as a product of the colonial social relations that he intended to reform. He hoped to save the Indians, not only from the brutality of the conquistadores, but also from the "savage and bestial life" he believed they endured prior to his arrival. He considered the peoples of New Spain, with whom he was barely acquainted, to have a "poorly ordered," "miserable," and "wild" existence.[66] The use of these terms suggests that Vasco de Quiroga defined the indigenous peoples of New Spain as uncivilized. While he believed that they were human—which was more than many of his contemporaries believed—he did not consider them to be very far removed from other forms of life "discovered" in New Spain.[67] Vasco de Quiroga hoped to found his village-hospitals as an alternative colonization strategy, one that would fulfill the obligation to evangelize and prevent the genocide that had resulted from the Spanish presence in the Caribbean.[68] This was a commendable goal, given the possible alternatives for indigenous peoples. However, we should harbor no illusions about his intentions. In no way did Vasco de Quiroga desire to challenge the power relationships of colonialism itself.[69]

Despite Vasco de Quiroga's strong criticism of the Spanish practice of enslaving indigenes, his opposition to slavery was much more nuanced and limited than has been generally recognized. He did not oppose the institution of slavery itself, but only the practice of enslaving indigenous peoples as a result of a "just war," or because they were already enslaved peoples "rescued" by their new Christian masters.[70] Notwithstanding this opposition, Don Vasco

65. Pedro Borges, "Vasco de Quiroga en el ambiente misionero de la Nueva España," *Missionalia Hispanica* 67 (1966): 313; Quiroga, *La Información en Derecho*, 79 and 55, 59–61, 95, 155.

66. Quiroga, *La Información en Derecho*, 92.

67. For a discussion of "wild men," or "sylvestres homines," in the European intellectual traditions of Quiroga's era, see Pagden, *Fall of Natural Man*, 20–21.

68. Quiroga, *La Información en Derecho*, 82–83.

69. Pagden, *Fall of Natural Man*, 35. Pagden's position is developed further in "The Humanism of Vasco de Quiroga's *Información en derecho*," in *Uncertainties of Empire*, 133–42.

70. Quiroga, *La Información en Derecho*, 55, 59–60, 68, 111–12, 116–24, 136, 138, 156, 160–68.

at least initially accepted, and even promoted, forced labor for indigenous peoples as a legitimate punishment in criminal cases.[71] Moreover, in the *Información,* he repeatedly stated that enslavement as a result of just war was legitimate, but not applicable to the Indians of New Spain.[72] Of course, it was possible to enslave the survivors of a "good and just war against Turks and Moors, who are not only infidels, but also enemies of our holy Catholic faith and Christian religion."[73] For Vasco de Quiroga, those "infidels who occupy lands of Christians" could legitimately be repressed, including if necessary through the use of military force. However, he argued that in other cases—where infidels had not been subjects of the Roman empire or Christian princes, or lived in lands never called Christian—the Spanish could not legitimately engage in forceful conversion, and especially slavery.

Vasco de Quiroga believed this to be precisely the situation for the indigenes of New Spain, and argued that in this case the continued use of force would prevent the Spanish from becoming "legitimate lords" over them.[74] His desire to reduce the Spanish use of force, and abolish the practice of slavery, did not extend to all the inhabitants of New Spain. While condemning the Indian slave trade, Vasco de Quiroga apparently supported African slavery, a position also held by Queen Isabella, the early Bartolomé de Las Casas, and others.[75] Vasco de Quiroga's will confirms that he held slaves. One of his last acts was to grant them freedom. He stated: "I declare and it is my desire that all the slaves that I have, men and women, be free without any addition because this is my desire."[76] These slaves were most probably African, given Don Vasco's well-established position on the enslavement of Indians, although the document does not specify their ethnicity.

If we are to make sense of Vasco de Quiroga's seemingly contradictory positions, we must briefly examine Aristotle's views on slavery, which

71. Zavala, *Los esclavos indios,* 32.
72. Quiroga, *La Información en Derecho,* 70–71, 163.
73. Ibid., 163.
74. Ibid., 70–71.
75. Pagden, *Fall of Natural Man,* 32. See also Lewis Hanke, *Aristotle and the American Indians* (Chicago, 1959), 9, and Siller, "La iglesia," 221. The issues of Isabella's support of African slavery, her complicity in the expulsion of the Moors and Jews from the emerging Spanish nation-state, and her role in the conquest of the Americas remains a painful and politically charged issue on both sides of the Atlantic. See "Sainthood Bid for Queen Isabella Stirs Debate," *New York Times,* December 28, 1990, A5, and Peter Hebblethwaite, "Bid to Beatify Isabella Will Ignite Furor," *National Catholic Reporter,* January 18, 1991, 10.
76. Quiroga, "Testamento," 300.

profoundly influenced Vasco de Quiroga's own thoughts on this issue. Based on his understanding of Greek society, Aristotle argued for two categories of slave, civil and natural. For Aristotle, civil slavery involved depriving humans—who were like all other humans—of their civil liberties, for reasons such as punishment for a criminal act or capture in a just war. Natural slavery, on the other hand, referred to a specific type of human, whose deficient psychological state naturally resulted in servitude. He wrote, "The lower sort are by nature slaves, and it is better for them as for all inferiors that they should be under the rule of a master."[77] According to Anthony Pagden, "Aristotle's natural slave is clearly a man (*Pol.* 1254b 16, 1259b 27–28) but he is a man whose intellect has, for some reason, failed to achieve proper mastery over his passions."[78] Pagden notes that Aristotle's theory of natural slavery had some support in the ancient world, although its sixteenth-century influence owed much to its thirteenth-century revival by Aquinas.[79]

Of course, this was not an exclusively Spanish debate, but rather one that lay at the core of many European intellectual traditions. Pagden attributes the original late medieval / early Renaissance linking of political authority over slaves and "barbarians," with Aristotle's theory of natural slavery, to the Scottish theologian John Mair of the Collège de Montaigu in Paris, whose work was influential in the late fifteenth and early sixteenth centuries.[80] As we shall see, Vasco de Quiroga's position on the enslavement of the Indians derived more from a particular reading of Aristotle's theory of natural slavery, than from a rejection of it.[81] Moreover, this position, when fully understood, reveals much about Vasco de Quiroga's thinking on other issues, such as his support for the institution of *encomienda*, and his conception of the proper places for women and children in the emerging colonial society. Aristotle's thought, as interpreted by Mair and many sixteenth-century Spanish intellectuals, legitimized a particularly profound paternalistic dynamic, in which a "superior" individual controlled his "inferiors" by divine right, in exchange for Christian guidance and also the material security he provided.

77. Aristotle, *The Politics,* ed. Stephan Everson (Cambridge, England, 1988), 7; Pagden, *Fall of Natural Man,* 27–56.

78. Pagden, *Fall of Natural Man,* 42.

79. Ibid., 41.

80. Ibid., 39.

81. This reality contradicts the famous interpretation of sixteenth-century Spanish reformism by Lewis Hanke, at least for the case of Vasco de Quiroga. See Hanke, *Aristotle,* 79.

This deeply rooted conception of paternalistic authority was the fundamental lens through which Vasco de Quiroga interpreted all of his experience in New Spain.

There is no doubt that Don Vasco accepted what Aristotle would have termed civil slavery as a legitimate and divinely sanctioned social relationship. His defense of enslavement due to "just war" in contexts other than New Spain, his acceptance of forced labor in criminal cases, and his possession of slaves all indicate with certainty that he considered certain forms of slavery to be just. In addition, if we accept Pagden's definition of Aristotle's natural slaves, cited above, as humans whose deficient intellect had not enabled them to master their passions, it is evident that Vasco de Quiroga placed Indians in a category very similar to that of natural slaves. More than some other European intellectuals, Don Vasco recognized the humanity of the peoples of New Spain. Nevertheless, he firmly believed that their "poorly ordered and barbarous" existence, and "savage and bestial life," prevented them from controlling their passions and becoming truly civilized, which for Don Vasco included embracing Christianity. Thus, he proposed a pattern of colonization based on the formation of village-hospitals, "to join them together, to order them, to guide them, and give them laws and rules and ordinances in which they live in good and Catholic order and conversation."[82] Vasco de Quiroga conceived of his village-hospitals as an alternative to slavery, one with the potential of lifting the Indian out of what he considered to be a degraded status.

In his definition of Indians as human beings capable of improving if social circumstances were reformed, Vasco de Quiroga's early Renaissance views perhaps moved beyond Aristotle. However, his perceptions of Indians at the time of first contact clearly designated them as inferior beings, and bears a strong Aristotelian imprint. Don Vasco stated that the indigenous peoples of New Spain "were barbarous and tyrannical, and people without law, until the time that they were subjected to your Catholic Majesty, and simple and ignorant."[83] He commented that "they were among themselves cruel, barbarous, ferocious, and still are barbarous nations."[84] The only solution for these people, "barbarous and ignorant and without law," was a strictly regulated community life that would allow them to flourish as

82. Quiroga, *La Información en Derecho*, 91.
83. Ibid., 129.
84. Ibid., 72.

Christians.[85] For Don Vasco, it was not simply a matter of placing them under Spanish control. Many Spaniards wanted to order indigenous life in such a way as to leave "the subjects remaining miserable, wild, barbarous divided and spread out, ignorant, savage as before . . . as beasts and animals without reason."[86] Vasco de Quiroga argued that this type of rule, was obviously unacceptable, and must be replaced with a "good and Catholic ordering" if the Indians are to be lifted out of their "bestiality and corrupt customs."[87] According to Don Vasco, it was "a thing of great shame" for a "people so docile and able" as the Indians "to live so savagely and spread out and miserable and bestial."[88]

In this context, Vasco de Quiroga's characterization of the evangelization of the indigenous peoples of New Spain as "not war, but [a] hunt in which the bait of good works is more suitable," carries important implications.[89] Vasco de Quiroga recognized the humanity of the indigenous peoples, and he opposed their enslavement. Nevertheless, his writings indicate that he also considered them inferior beings, who lived in an almost animal state. In an argument that appears paradoxical to the twenty-first-century reader, Vasco de Quiroga repeatedly referred to what he considered to be the innately inferior quality of indigenous civilizations, while also producing a discourse exalting the vastly superior qualities of Indians, when compared to most colonizing Spaniards. The Indians, declared Don Vasco, "live in so much liberty of souls, with contempt and carelessness of our finery and pomp, in this wretched century, with uncovered heads and almost in the nudity of their flesh, and barefoot, without handling money among themselves and with great scorn of gold and of silver."[90] According to him, indigenous peoples were "the simplest, absolutely meekest, most humble, most obedient" of human beings, "the best and most apt for our Christian religion."[91] Although Vasco de Quiroga considered indigenous civilizations to be inferior, individual Indians clearly possessed superior qualities when compared to

---

85. Ibid., 132. References to indigenous peoples as savage, barbaric, without law, without reason, etc., abound in the *Información*. See 72, 74, 81–82, 91, 92, 129, 132. On the significance of these designations, see Pagden, *Fall of Natural Man,* 15–26.

86. Quiroga, *La Información en Derecho,* 81.

87. Ibid., 82, 77.

88. Ibid., 82.

89. Ibid., 157.

90. Ibid., 197.

91. Ibid., 197, 188.

most Spaniards. Indeed, he utilizes most extreme language when he condemns those Spaniards whom he believed threatened the Indians, and especially the revitalized Christian Church that he hoped to found among the peoples of New Spain. These individuals, he complained bitterly, "are worse than infidels."[92]

Vasco de Quiroga's struggle to define the other while intervening in the debate over indigenous slavery thus reveals the most profound tension in his thought. It is here that Don Vasco tried to reconcile the imperatives of Spanish colonialism, which he believed to be divinely sanctioned, with his understanding of the peoples of New Spain. This attempt at definition raised an important problem for him. If indigenous peoples possessed superior traits to the Spanish, who lived in "every extreme of wickedness and corruption," how could the Spanish presence in New Spain be justified, particularly in a divinely sanctioned position of authority over Indians?[93] The answer, in short, was a paternalism situated at the crossroads of a feudal past and colonial future, expressed as the obligation of true Christians to civilize the barbarians of the New World. In this way, the "soft wax" of the Indians, could be fashioned into a pure and reformed version of Christianity, similar to that of the early Church.[94]

As we have seen, Vasco de Quiroga argued against the legality of enslaving indigenous peoples on the basis of a just war by noting that the behavior of the Spanish themselves had justified the resistance of indigenous peoples.[95] He also contested the notion that Spaniards could buy and sell Indians that had been previously enslaved. He remarked ironically that to call trafficking in indigenous slaves commerce is like calling "the black Juan white," a literary flourish which may have deeper significance, given Vasco de Quiroga's acceptance of African slavery.[96] Don Vasco claimed that indigenous people did not understand what the Spanish meant by slavery, as "there is no proper word for this" in their languages.[97] Thus, they might incorrectly respond to an inquiring Spanish official that they had been slaves previously. However, according to Don Vasco, these statements were incorrect, and meant only

92. Ibid., 167, 201.
93. Ibid., 199.
94. On Indians as "wax," see Quiroga, "Carta al Consejo de Indias," 79, and *La Información en Derecho*, 166. On the early church, see *La Información en Derecho*, 166–68, 198–99.
95. Quiroga, *La Información en Derecho*, 55, 59–61, 95, 155.
96. Ibid., 85.
97. Ibid., 133.

that Indians were "most simple."[98] To enslave such people, he argued, defied "all three laws, divine, natural, and human."[99]

He also tried to demonstrate that those whom indigenous peoples might incorrectly believe to be "slaves" had never actually been so, according to Spanish definitions, and thus they could not be "rescued" from previous slave owners. Although Don Vasco believed that a form of servitude existed in indigenous societies, these individuals were more like rented people, although sometimes "rented in perpetuity."[100] According to Vasco de Quiroga, subordinated peoples in a state of indigenous servitude behaved in ways simply not available to slaves in the Spanish tradition, at least by the sixteenth century. For example, intermarriage between slaves and masters frequently occurred, a pattern of social relations that profoundly confused the class and gender roles clearly established under Spanish slavery. Don Vasco believed that indigenous "slaves" married "the men with their [female] masters and the women with their [male] masters or with their sons or daughters or with their brothers and sisters of their masters, like free people."[101] He also claimed that under indigenous servitude individuals "retain their liberty and family and house and children and woman and property and household furnishings," and thus could not be considered "slaves" as the Spanish defined the term.[102] Whether or not Vasco de Quiroga's argument was correct, or ethnographically accurate, is less important than what his discussion about the enslavement of indigenous peoples reveals about prevailing European definitions of slavery and freedom. In a very precise way, we can state that Vasco de Quiroga viewed the ability to exercise control over women and children, both conceived of in similar terms, as one sign of free status, or at least of someone who was not a slave.[103] Moreover, his view of free persons excluded those he conceived of as justly enslaved, namely believers in Islam, and under the proper circumstances African and Jewish peoples as well.

Vasco de Quiroga's view of the native peoples, although not as cruel as that of many of his contemporaries, was permeated by a paternalism that

98. Ibid., 134.
99. Ibid., 136.
100. Ibid., 84.
101. Ibid., 106.
102. Ibid., 138.
103. Vasco de Quiroga's thought corresponds to Aristotle's in this regard as well. As Pagden notes, Aristotle considered women and children as incomplete men, who could reason but lacked authority. Pagden, *Fall of Natural Man,* 43–44.

blended with racial hierarchy: a classification of peoples as superior and inferior by virtue of their innate abilities, and by virtue of their cultural experience (their adoption, rejection, or innocent ignorance of Christianity). This was not the racism of callous labor masters, or of a later era of "scientific racism," but instead a racialism that blended evaluation of the innate with evaluation of the cultural and the religious. Thus, Vasco de Quiroga could exalt the Christian-like innocence and simplicity of the indigenes, and see them as the potential cornerstones of an ideal Christian community if brought under proper tutelage. However, he also believed that they remained susceptible to the barbarism of their natural state, especially when left untutored or subjected to the caprice of evil masters.

In sum, all of Vasco de Quiroga's thought was enmeshed in a deeply rooted paternalistic ethos. Thus, he could proclaim that if the Indians were given "time and space" for Christianity, as they were in his village-hospitals, they would live in peace, "according to their great humility and obedience and docility and good simplicity, and even kneeling would they come kissing the earth that the Spanish Christians trample underfoot."[104]

For Don Vasco, the evangelization of the Indians was not a war but a hunt, and the most effective lure was the "bait of good works."

Patriarchy, Paternalism, and Utopia

The sole source providing information about the internal ordering of the communal village-hospitals attributed to Don Vasco's efforts is the *Reglas y ordenanzas,* preserved only in the incomplete copy reproduced two centuries later by Juan José Moreno. What can we imagine about these communities based on this document, and what does it reveal about Vasco de Quiroga's sixteenth century? Moreno was the first historian to use the *Reglas* in an effort to recover the contours of daily life in these communities. Many others have followed in his steps, sometimes drawing on Don Vasco's other writings and additional sources, but always basing their discussion on Moreno's version of the *Reglas.* There is no way of knowing whether or not the *Reglas* were implemented, or how indigenes responded to them in practice. Rather than a transparent guide to actual practice, this source is most useful for what it reveals about Quiroga's inspirations and hopes. Given its wide circulation,

104. Quiroga, *La Información en Derecho,* 95.

there is no need to reproduce all of the information it contains.[105] Instead, I will focus on a few particularly relevant passages, whose significance has been noted, although perhaps underestimated, by other investigators.

The fact that Vasco de Quiroga sought to impose a patriarchal model of social relationships within his utopian communities is beyond dispute. As he stated:

> And thus in this way each group of relatives will live in their family as is said, and the oldest grandfather will be he who presides in it, and whom the entire family must respect and obey, and the women will serve their husbands, and the descendants the ancestors, fathers and grandfathers and great-grandfathers, and in sum, those of lesser age and the youngest, the oldest, because thus it is possible to avoid, mainly [the matter] of male servants and female servants and other retainers, who are customarily expensive and very annoying to their masters.[106]

Indeed, he proposed to build a new social order within the confines of Spanish colonialism, from the household up to the community level. In this social order, the distribution of power was based on gender and age, and presided over by dominant male authority at each level. The patriarchal currents in Vasco de Quiroga's thought, as well as his similarity in this regard to Thomas More, have been neglected in historical scholarship.[107] In part, this is because a predominantly male profession has tended to overlook the obvious until relatively recently.[108] The fact that Vasco de Quiroga discussed women and their role in his utopian communities only briefly, particularly when compared to the depth of his argument concerning indigenous slavery, is

105. For a recent discussion of the contents of the *Reglas,* see Verastíque, *Michoacán and Eden,* 124–40.

106. Quiroga, *Reglas y ordenanzas,* 252–53.

107. Many scholars note that males were dominant figures in Vasco de Quiroga's utopian communities, but none of the scholarship on Vasco de Quiroga that I am aware of seriously subjects his thought to a gender analysis. On patriarchy and utopian thinkers, see Elaine Hoffman Baruch, "Women in Men's Utopias," in *Women in Search of Utopia: Mavericks and Mythmakers,* ed. Ruby Rohrlich and Elaine Hoffman Baruch (New York, 1984), 209–19, esp. 211. See also Timothy Kenyon, *Utopian Communism and Political Thought in Early Modern England* (London, 1988), 87–93, and St. Thomas More, *Utopia,* ed. Edward Surtz, S.J. (New Haven, Conn., 1964), 24, 61, 69, 75, 80.

108. Joan Scott, "Women's History," in Burke, *New Perspectives,* 42–66.

also relevant. The general lack of women's voices in the documents of early Spanish colonialism stands as mute testimony to the power of male privilege in the social order under consideration.

When Vasco de Quiroga expressed opinions concerning the status and proper place for women in New Spain, and tried to implement these notions in his utopian communities, he drew on a deeply entrenched pattern of male authority. Ultimately, this tradition was rooted in patriarchy, or the control of all household resources, by a dominant male. The European versions of patriarchy and male dominance, which Vasco de Quiroga attempted to recreate in New Spain, varied in important ways from the social organization of indigenous communities prior to the arrival of the Spanish. As Pagden notes, Don Vasco organized his village-hospitals around artificial "families," based on a single lineage through the male line.[109] Vasco de Quiroga's imposition of this model altered the indigenous social order in the Lake Pátzcuaro region. Specifically, it led to a heightened emphasis on male lineage, replacing what appears to have been a more fragmented, less consolidated pattern of male dominance that included polygamy, joint-residence patterns, and, unsurprisingly, arranged marriages.[110] Don Vasco also incorporated a carefully defined sexual division of labor into the design for his village-hospitals, and attempted to transform indigenous sexuality. As one would expect, he promoted specific types of sexual unions, which he believed to be divinely sanctioned, and tried to impose "decent" standards of dress on Indian women. He also expressed dismay at a group of young Indian males, whom he referred to as "los telpuchetles," whose traditional function was "to corrupt virgin girls before they marry."[111] Outside these areas, however, Don Vasco's references to women, gender, and sexuality are quite meager.

Vasco de Quiroga's writings do not grapple with these issues to the same extent as others, such as the debate over indigenous slavery, or the practical aspects of organizing utopian communities. Given the fragmentary quality of the evidence available, it is impossible to tell if this indicates priorities within Don Vasco's thought, or if it reflects the assumption that a proper order of gender and family was so "obvious" that it required little comment. Nevertheless, we do know that he hoped to transform the sexual behavior of both

109. Pagden, *Fall of Natural Man*, 35; Quiroga, *Reglas y ordenanzas*, 258.
110. López Sarrelangue, *La nobleza indígena de Pátzcuaro*, 105; Pollard, *Tariacuri's Legacy*, 178–79.
111. Quiroga, *La Información en Derecho*, 135.

men and women. In his village-hospitals, he implemented specific regulations for indigenous sexual unions. He believed that the fathers and mothers of each family had the right to arrange the marriages of their children at a "legitimate age," which for males began at the age of fourteen, and for females at twelve. Preferably, parents would arrange these marriages with members of the same village-hospital, or, if this were impossible, with a neighboring community. He hoped that these unions would not be clandestine, but rather performed with the knowledge and good will of the mothers and fathers, and the families of the young couple.[112]

Don Vasco also had specific notions about how indigenous women should dress. He believed it best to inspire modesty, and thus required that "the women wear their white headdresses of cotton with which they cover the head and most of the body, over the other clothing they customarily wear and without pictures nor works of color."[113] The obligation to wear this headdress did not extend to young, unmarried women, so as to facilitate the differentiation between those who were married, and those who were not.

His thinking about gender relationships, as much as his struggle to define indigenous peoples, are particularly revealing of the extent to which his views corresponded with prevailing standards of domination in European society. Pagden cites the famous example of the Spanish king Philip II, who proclaimed "that in every case, two Indians or three women presented as witnesses are worth one Spanish man."[114] We have no way of knowing whether Don Vasco accepted this precise formula. Nevertheless, his writings consistently demonstrate an aristocratic belief in the innate inferiority of subordinated peoples, whatever his intentions for reform. In the context of an emerging colonial order, this meant a subaltern status for indigenous peoples. It also meant an attempt to impose European patterns of male dominance, which to a certain extent corresponded to prevailing norms in indigenous societies. Vasco de Quiroga tried to realize these notions of "proper" gender relationships and patterns of sexual behavior in his utopian communities.

In the village-hospitals, gender-specific education began early in childhood. Boys were taught to work in the fields, while girls learned "women's

112. Quiroga, *Reglas y ordenanzas*, 251. For a detailed discussion of the social importance of marriage, and associated rituals, in the Catholic tradition, see Gutiérrez, *When Jesus Came, the Corn Mothers Went Away*, 241–70.
113. Quiroga, *Reglas y ordenanzas*, 259.
114. Pagden, *Fall of Natural Man*, 44.

jobs," which included weaving and other domestic labors.[115] This sexual division of labor probably did not vary significantly from that of the region's indigenous societies prior to the Spanish Conquest, although incorporation into the colonial economic system over time would substantially transform the role of women in production.[116] Recent scholarship examining the transformation of gendered labor patterns and sexual relationships by European colonialism has demonstrated a decline in the frequently substantial authority and economic power that indigenous women enjoyed prior to their incorporation into European-dominated colonial states.[117] However, similarities in the gender division of labor in Spanish and Indian cultures, combined with the rapid adaptation of at least elite indigenous males to Spanish patriarchal norms, suggest that indigenous societies had developed fairly extensive patterns of male dominance prior to European contact.

Missionaries continued to complain about the persistence of polygamy within indigenous communities, and about the sexual misconduct of the Spanish colonial population, throughout the sixteenth century. However, at least in public testimonies, indigenous elite males responded with enthusiasm to Vasco de Quiroga's attempts to order the social roles and sexual behavior of indigenous women according to professed Spanish norms. Thus, in a document dated May 19, 1536, Ramiro, a *principal* or indigenous elite figure from the village of Pátzcuaro, credited Vasco de Quiroga with the fact that Indians now "marry with only one woman and not with many as they did before." According to Ramiro, many Indians were now going to mass and saying prayers. In addition, Indian women had begun to behave in a different, more honorable way. "The women covered themselves with their shawls around their heads . . . before they wore their underskirts to their knees and now they go to the ankle by which they go decently and those who are married are known."[118] According to the few public testimonies we have, Indian men professed a belief in these new sexual values, and claimed

---

115. Quiroga, *Reglas y ordenanzas,* 251–53.

116. For an interesting article examining this process in the central valley of México, see Margaret A. Villanueva, "From Calpixqui to Corregidor: Appropriation of Women's Cotton Textile Production in Early Colonial Mexico," *Latin American Perspectives* 44 (Winter 1985): 17–40.

117. See Irene Silverblatt, "Interpreting Women in States: New Feminist Ethnohistory," in *Gender at the Crossroads of Knowledge,* ed. Micaela di Leonardo (Berkeley, Calif., 1991), 140–71, and Perry, *Gender and Disorder.*

118. "Residencia del Señor Quiroga," in León, *Documentos ineditos,* 62–63.

to have changed their lives. This was the case for Cuinierángari, the leader of the indigenous peoples of the Lake Pátzcuaro region during the era of Don Vasco. Cuinierángari had taken advantage of the turmoil surrounding the Spanish Conquest to succeed the Cazonci, after his brutal execution. He reportedly gave up several of his women, and remained with only one.[119] This may not have been simply a way for Cuinierángari to demonstrate his newfound faith. According to Alonso Rodríguez, a priest, Cuinierángari had "three or four women and mistresses" until one of the women complained to Don Vasco. At this point Don Vasco intervened, causing Cuinierángari to leave his other women, and marry the one who had complained, "with the consent of both."[120]

Other men, both Indian and Spanish, praised Don Vasco for the changes he had brought to Indian lives, particularly in terms of sexuality, and noted that he had succeeded where others had failed. According to an indigenous witness, somewhat ironically named Don Francisco, the Franciscan missionaries who initially evangelized the region had beaten the Indians, and treated them poorly. Thanks to Don Vasco, however, this treatment had stopped. Now, the Indians did not have "more than one woman," and followed God, not the devil. Alonso de Avalos, another Indian from Michoacán, agreed, pointing out that Indians had stopped worshiping idols and getting drunk because of Vasco de Quiroga's influence.[121]

Many Spanish male witnesses also testified to the significance of the changes brought by Don Vasco. Diego de Rivera, a *corregidor* or Crown official from Mexico City, testified that he had "seen many natives marry each other" in Michoacán. Because of Don Vasco, many Indians were hearing the word of God, attending mass, and being baptized. Moreover, Rivera noted, he had visited the village-hospitals of Michoacán, and had not found any "other dishonesty except for the husband to sleep with his woman."[122] Francisco Castilleja, most probably a Franciscan, since he is listed as a translator and resident of the "ciudad de Mechuacán"—at this time Tzintzuntzan—noted that the Indians "began to marry and not to have more than one woman and they had been accustomed to have ten and fifteen." Francisco also noted that before Don Vasco arrived, the Indians "did

119. López Sarrelangue, *La nobleza indígena de Pátzcuaro*, 56.
120. "Residencia del Señor Quiroga," in León, *Documentos ineditos*, 80.
121. Ibid., 60–64.
122. Ibid., 53–55.

not serve well."[123] Suero Esturiano testified that "before the aforementioned licentiate Quiroga went to the aforementioned province of Michoacán, the natives from there were very bestial and ignorant in the service of God." Now that many had been baptized and were going to mass, Suero could report that "he has seen how the women go about [with] their heads covered and in their very honest dresses."[124]

Interestingly, although no Spanish or Indian men commented on this, Don Vasco also expected indigenous males to dress austerely, although without the headdress, in clothes "of cotton and wool, white, clean and decent, without pictures, without other expensive works." In this way, thought Vasco de Quiroga, indigenous peoples would be protected from the cold and heat by clothes that were inexpensive, durable, and clean. Perhaps more important, by having conformity in dress between all members of the village-hospitals, it would be possible to avoid "the envy and pomp to go dressed and outstanding some more and better than others, of which is habitually born envy among vain and imprudent men, and dissension and discord."[125]

There are many other Spanish testimonies in this *residencia,* or administrative survey to assess how Don Vasco had performed his duties as *oidor.* They all praised his abilities in leading the Indians to conversion, and in successfully implementing a Christian lifestyle. Most noted Don Vasco's concern for the poor, his many baptisms, and the increase in Indians attending mass. In addition, many looked favorably on his attempt to introduce strict patterns of monogamy into the region. It is crucial that we not take these condemnations of past indigenous sexual practices, or claims of conformance to new sexual norms, at face value. In terms of the prehispanic past, we must note that all societies have had culturally specific rules governing sexual activity.[126] Scholars must begin their evaluations of claims of sexual excess, or of the free play of unbridled sexual desire in specific cultural groups, by asking what rhetorical purpose these claims served.[127] For Vasco de Quiroga, as for generations of Christian missionaries, a belief in the sexual impropriety of subordinated peoples served the political function of legitimizing the

123. Ibid., 55–56.
124. Ibid., 57.
125. Quiroga, *Reglas y ordenanzas,* 259.
126. Brown, *The Body and Society,* 21–23; Gutiérrez, *When Jesus Came, the Corn Mothers Went Away,* 73.
127. Gutiérrez, *When Jesus Came, the Corn Mothers Went Away,* 73. See also Weeks, *Sexuality and Its Discontents,* 17–21.

sexually repressive regime they had implemented.[128] These considerations, then, force us to evaluate Spanish condemnations of indigenous sexual practices with skepticism, or at least to view them as produced within a framework that served to legitimize the Spanish presence in New Spain.

There is also considerable evidence that the norms of behavior praised by the Spanish and Indian witnesses, in the residencia of Vasco de Quiroga, did not enjoy complete, perhaps even general, acceptance in the actual practice of either group. Scholars have only recently started the task of examining the richness and complexity of the social organization of gender, an issue intimately linked to human sexual practice. Nevertheless, we know that many sexualities were expressed, and frequently repressed, in sixteenth-century Spain.[129] From the evidence available, we know that the indigenous ruler Don Pedro had maintained relations with several women well into the era of the Spanish colonial presence, as did many other elite indigenous men. It is only logical to assume that these practices continued, at least to some extent. In addition, we need to consider Don Vasco's bitter condemnation of his fellow Spaniards, who requested "beautiful Indian women by the dozen and half dozen, and to have them in their houses recently having given birth and pregnant."[130] The behavior of male Spanish settlers did not necessarily conform to their public or religious pronouncements. It is also evident, at least in some cases, that the sixteenth-century clergy was not always beyond temptation.[131] Why, then, this seeming unanimity among Spanish and Indian male elites in praising Don Vasco's attempt to regulate indigenous sexuality?

It is plausible to argue that this unanimity represented more than the usual distance between publicly promoted sexual norms and actual sexual practices. The consolidation of authoritarian regimes has always been accompanied by sharp concern with restraining the sexual and social behavior of women.[132] The agreement between at least some indigenous male elites, and many Spanish colonists, on the legitimacy of Don Vasco's attempt to regulate Indian sexuality, particularly as these attempts pertained to Indian women, could indicate a broader process of convergence between Spanish

128. Gutiérrez, *When Jesus Came, the Corn Mothers Went Away*, 73.

129. Perry, *Gender and Disorder*, esp. 46–52, 118–36, 137–52. For interesting comparative materials, see Guido Ruggiero, *The Boundaries of Eros* (Oxford, 1985).

130. Quiroga, *La Información en Derecho*, 164–65.

131. Miranda, *Don Vasco de Quiroga*, 80. See also Asunción Lavrin, ed., *Sexuality and Marriage in Colonial Latin America* (Lincoln, Nebr., 1989).

132. Scott, *Gender and the Politics of History*, 47–48.

and Indian males. The evidence indicates that this convergence was an essential part of the consolidation of Spanish colonialism in sixteenth-century Mexico.

Moreno described Vasco de Quiroga as "most addicted" to the teachings of Saint Ambrose.[133] Moreno may have been correct, at least in part.[134] Vasco de Quiroga's thinking on sexuality, and the designated roles for women in his utopian communities, in some ways shared Saint Ambrose's "austere anti-sexuality," marked by "sharp antithesis" and "harsh boundaries," which set the correct, divinely ordained patterns of behavior for men and women.[135] Although Vasco de Quiroga's writings on gender-related issues are quite brief, we can state that he attempted to impose a patriarchal model of gender relations on the indigenous communities of New Spain. In this regard, Don Vasco's attitudes reflected powerful currents of thought concerning gender roles and sexuality that emerged quite early in the historical development of the Latin Church, and had become firmly established by the fourth century after the death of Christ.[136] Indeed, much of the paternalism of Vasco de Quiroga, who conceived of himself as "the first husband of so poor and so needy a Church," can be traced to a deeply rooted European tradition of patriarchal social organization.[137]

It would be a mistake to believe that the village-hospitals simply reflected European traditions. Vasco de Quiroga based the internal sociopolitical organization of the village-hospitals on what he understood to be democratic practices originating within the indigenous communities. Although his frustrations with Europe and familiarity with Thomas More may have predisposed him to favor aspects of indigenous social organization, some of his inspiration came from the natives themselves. In his own words, condemnation mingles with admiration: "By that which I have seen and understood of the things of these lands, I am almost certain that among them there was no

133. Moreno, *Fragmentos*, 54.
134. Ibid., 155. A careful reading of Moreno indicates that he placed much greater emphasis on sexuality than did Quiroga, and also spoke to a greater extent on the prominence of the worship of the figure of the Virgin. This may have been part of broader cultural transformations in Spain and New Spain in the seventeenth and eighteenth centuries. See Patricia Seed, *To Love, Honor and Obey in Colonial Mexico* (Stanford, Calif., 1988), 17–31, 32, and Perry, *Gender and Disorder*, 33–52, 99.
135. Brown, *The Body and Society*, 341–65, esp. 346–47, 352.
136. Ibid., 341–427; Pagels, *Adam, Eve and the Serpent*, 25, 29, 78–97.
137. "Sobre curas de mechuacán. Los ponga para que administren el culto. Y respuesta del obispo" (1545), 8–13; in León, *Documentos ineditos*, 10.

kingdom nor lordship nor succession nor legitimate, nor reasonable possession, but tyranny; and that which there was, for the most part was by the
elective route, and thus it appears that [this elective route] did not harm
them; so too the order [I designed] goes also by this elective route very
similar to theirs."[138] It is here, in his response to indigenous peoples, that we
can find an explanation for the appeal and centuries-long persistence of the
village-hospital, whether it originated with Vasco de Quiroga, or Franciscan
missionaries, or in the indigenous communities themselves.[139] Perhaps Don
Vasco had to veil his admiration for even the limited form of local democracy
he discerned in indigenous society, and criticize the lack of a royal succession—which he defined as rational and legitimate—because he knew his
recommendations had to be receivable by an absolutist monarchy. His criticism of past tyranny, but praise for the democratic ordering of local village
life, definitely corresponded to his well-known condemnation of the indigenous elite, and stated preference for poor, common folk.[140]

In spite of all the changes, the deepening intrusion of Spanish colonial
authority, and the success of Don Vasco's urbanizing strategy, indigenous peoples could maintain a certain limited control over their lives. In the
village-hospitals, the important posts filled by Indians—who were barred by
their race from the priesthood—were all elective.[141] Thus, families regularly
elected their "padre de familia," that is, the dominant male of each kinship
group. In addition, elections were held between the "padres de familias" to
fill important posts at the community level. While it would be naive to ignore
the internal power dynamics and conflicts within indigenous communities,
divided along lines of age, gender, and status, we can recognize a degree of
local control in this system. Don Vasco encouraged the Indians to discuss all
community decisions thoroughly, before taking a significant action. As
a good lawyer, he thought it wise to avoid the Spanish courts and settle
their debates internally.[142] Of course, religious instruction and practice,

138. Quiroga, *La Información en Derecho,* 88.
139. Moran Alvarez, *El pensamiento,* 167, 215, comments on this aspect of Quiroga's thought.
The point is most forcefully presented in José Miranda, "La fraternidad cristiana y labor social de
la primitiva iglesia mexicana," *Cuadernos Americanos* 4 (July–August 1965): 148–58.
140. Marcel Bataillon, "Don Vasco de Quiroga Utopien," *Moreana* 4, no. 15 (1967): 385–94,
esp. 389–90; Moran Alvarez, *El pensamiento,* 97; Moreno, *Fragmentos,* 146; Warren, *Vasco de
Quiroga,* 24.
141. Martínez, "Reorientaciones," 104; Schwaller, *Church and Clergy,* 193.
142. Quiroga, *Reglas y ordenanzas,* 260–64.

supervised by either Vasco de Quiroga or a member of the missionary orders, was woven into the fabric of daily life. Outside of this area, however, community members enjoyed substantial autonomy, and were protected from external labor drafts and other abuses of Spanish colonialism.

The functioning of these communities may have been furthered by Don Vasco's emphasis on practical concerns. His *Reglas* contains a considerable amount of pragmatic advice. For example, he observes that investing in the maintenance of public buildings was cheaper than repairing them once they had collapsed. He also gives specific information concerning the most useful types of crops and animals to be raised, some indigenous to the region, and others imported from Europe and other parts of New Spain.[143] Legend has it that Don Vasco introduced the banana into the local diet. Moreno claims that Vasco de Quiroga brought three types of banana to the region from the island of Santo Domingo, all of which became quite popular. Apparently, one of these species ultimately served as the bread of the Tierra Caliente, or hot Pacific coastal and inland region of Michoacán.[144] In addition to his innovations concerning crop selection, Vasco de Quiroga emphasized the need to plant double the amount needed for any one year, so as to build up a surplus for times of bad harvest.[145] Although the banana legend needs additional verification, it is true that in his writings Don Vasco paid considerable attention to pragmatic details, a useful legacy for those moved by utopian visions in centuries to come.

The social organization of labor was central to his project. In keeping with his sense of status, Don Vasco did not require the "padres de familia" to engage in manual labor. However, he stressed that it would be a great example and inspiration for their subordinates if they would occasionally put "their hands to work."[146] All were educated in the production of food and fiber for clothing, although in gender-specific ways. Since everyone would labor efficiently, no one would have to work more than "two or three workdays from sunrise to sunset each week." They were also responsible for six hours of community work, which included various maintenance duties, labor in the hospitals, and "other pious tasks."[147] In addition, there were limits to

143. Ibid., 254–56.
144. Moreno, *Fragmentos,* 92–93.
145. Quiroga, *Reglas y ordenanzas,* 256.
146. Ibid., 254.
147. Ibid., 245–48, 254–55.

community generosity. Anyone who did something revolting or scandalous, was a bad Christian, got drunk, or was exceedingly lazy and did not want to keep the ordinances, could be expelled from the community. In these cases, the property of expelled members would revert back to the common ownership, since members received only usufruct and not permanent possession of the land.[148]

In the context of the 1530s, Don Vasco's desire to pursue a reformist strategy seriously challenged other powerful sectors of the Spanish colonial establishment. It is plausible to suggest that this challenge created an important space for indigenous peoples in the emerging colonial order, at a time when other possible experiences included physical abuse, death, and the destruction of entire peoples. In this regard, it is interesting to note that the waves of indigenous millenarianism which swept through various Mexican regions in the late sixteenth and seventeenth centuries apparently bypassed Michoacán.[149] These millenarian outbursts generally incorporated deeply felt rejections of colonial attempts to impose Christianity into broadly based social movements. Their absence in Michoacán perhaps testifies to the success of Vasco de Quiroga and his reforms, which may have enhanced the legitimacy of the colonial Church in the eyes of Michoacán's indigenous peoples.[150]

Conclusion

As we have seen, Vasco de Quiroga opposed the cruelty and inhumanity of warfare, though his moral stance was permeated by colonial assumptions. Although Vasco de Quiroga positioned himself as an opponent of war and indigenous enslavement, his appropriation of the Indian—as a site for description, analysis, and the enactment of social reform—reproduced notions of social hierarchy and cultural superiority essential to the colonizing venture. As it turns out, he and his fellow Spaniards shared a similar sixteenth-century

148. Ibid., 266–67.
149. Alicia Barabas, *Utopías indias* (Mexico City, 1987), 104–7. Interesting comparative material for the phenomenon of indigenous millenarianism can be found in Stern, *Peru's Indian Peoples*, 51–71.
150. The testimonies of several indigenous witnesses who are generally critical of the initial generation of Franciscan missionaries, as well as the Spanish settler population, but generous in their praise of Quiroga, are quite important concerning this point. "Residencia," in León, *Documentos ineditos*, 60–66.

imperialist vision, a reality that did not preclude debates over how that vision was to be implemented.

In an extended passage in the *Información,* Vasco de Quiroga argues that the authority of the Roman Catholic Church, which he fervently believed to be the only legitimate expression of religious sentiment, descended directly from God and Jesus Christ, through Peter, the first bishop of the Church, and all subsequent popes.[151] In Vasco de Quiroga's interpretation, the social distribution of power under Spanish colonialism, endorsed by the Catholic God as long as the Spanish met their obligation to evangelize, was ultimately rooted in the divine ordering of the universe.

As part of his defense of the authority of the institutional hierarchy of the Catholic Church, and by implication the Spanish colonial presence in the New World, Don Vasco states: "This is the order of things; this is the correct hierarchy, [the] supreme law of he who speaks with the voice of thunder: that in all parts the inferior is subject to his superior and whoever violates or resists the power upsets he whom God put in place, the supreme order."[152] Although Vasco de Quiroga proposed a reformist effort highly critical of the practice of Spanish colonialism, he intended to substitute a reformed hierarchy, an order that obviously placed indigenes in a subordinate position. This firm belief in hierarchy as the natural basis of order also placed Vasco de Quiroga himself very near the apex of the colonial pyramid. From this position, he could countenance the tightly circumscribed use of violence against the indigenous population, "not in order to destroy them but to humiliate them from their strength and bestiality."[153] This emphasis on hierarchy, moral education of the colonized, and the art of teaching backed, if necessary, by instruments of violence and humiliation, demonstrates the authoritarian tendencies in Vasco de Quiroga's thought.

The writings of Vasco de Quiroga provide the most sustained guide to his actual practice available today. Based on the evidence these sources contain, it is plausible to suggest that his behavior was what one would have expected from a "good *encomendero.*" During the first generation of Spanish colonialism in the Americas, a "good *encomendero*" could certainly build a power base, and even a sense of loyalty among subordinates. However, in the absence of evidence to the contrary, it would be imprudent to define the

151. Quiroga, *La Información en Derecho,* 88–90.
152. Ibid., 90.
153. Ibid., 79.

relationship between Vasco de Quiroga and the indigenes of Michoacán as more than this type of "patron-client" relationship, at least in the era prior to his death.[154] Indeed, even the careful assertion that Vasco de Quiroga's *Información* can be read as "a bridge between the Purhépecha and Spanish Christian worldviews" is arguably more hopeful than justified by fact.[155] Over the centuries, a bridge would be formed and a colonial culture built, but precisely when, and how and to what effect, remains to be determined. The precise nature of indigenous responses to Vasco de Quiroga's evangelization efforts during his lifetime quite possibly will remain a mystery of the past.

154. On the "love" of the Indians for Tata Vasco, see Warren, *Vasco de Quiroga*, 117, and Siller, "La iglesia," 220. More thorough citations and an "archaeology" of this notion can be found in Chapter 5.

155. The quotation concerning the *Información* as a bridge between cultures comes from Verastíque, *Michoacán and Eden*, 110.

Part Two

REFLECTIONS

4

REPRESENTING THE "SPIRITUAL CONQUEST"

The *Crónica de Michoacán* [1788]

There is no doubt that this diversity of opinions among contemporary historians, much embarrasses a historian lover
of the truth, but some rays of light do not cease to manifest
themselves among so much darkness.
—Fr. Pablo Beaumont, *Crónica de Michoacán*

The *Crónica*

The Franciscan historian Pablo de la Purísima Concepción Beaumont wrote of diverse opinions, embarrassment, and the difficult
search for historical truth in the *Crónica de Michoacán*, a massive
late colonial history of the conquest and evangelization of Michoacán.[1] As we shall see, the *Crónica* provides a conservative
creole representation of the "spiritual conquest," one that glorifies the role of the missionary orders in the sixteenth-century
evangelization of New Spain. Throughout the text, Beaumont

---

1. Pablo Beaumont, *Crónica de Michoacán,* 3 vols. (Mexico, 1932). A useful introduction to Beaumont's work is Luis González, "Viaje a las crónicas monásticas
de Michoacán en busca de los purépecha," in Miranda, *La cultura Purhé,* 50–70,
esp. 61–63. Historical background can be found in Rodolfo Pastor and Maria de
los Angeles Romero Frizzi, "Expansión económica e integración cultural" and
"El crecimiento del siglo XVIII," in Florescano, *Historia general de Michoacán,*
2:163–91, 195–211; María Ofelia Mendoza Briones and Marta Terán, "Repurcu-
siones de la política borbonica," in ibid., 2:218–33; and David Brading, *Church
and State in Bourbon Mexico* (Cambridge, England, 1994).

incorporated themes and images pervading Spanish colonial historiography—and a substantial amount of previously published work—into a new, at times unique synthesis.[2] Thus, it is a fascinating site for the analysis of conquest narratives and the politics of historical interpretation.[3]

Beaumont's reproduction of many sixteenth-century documents, archival materials, and secondary accounts, including several that have since been lost, has led many historians to treat his account as a direct witness to the events of the conquest. Indeed, the *Crónica* has been described, accurately, as "the source most frequently cited" by those interested in the initial Franciscan evangelization of Michoacán.[4] The implications of this text, however, are much broader in scope than the regional history of a missionary order, and the truths it presents as self-evident—the unmitigated superiority of European Christian, specifically, Spanish Catholic, culture—are from a modern vantage inevitably and self-evidently subjective.[5]

By the eighteenth century, many of the ambiguities of the early colonial "encounter" appear to have diminished, at least in Beaumont's account. The *Crónica,* produced in a context quite different from that of the *Proceso,* the *Relación,* and the writings of Vasco de Quiroga, reveals continuities and transformations in colonial discourse over time. Beaumont wrote after an early-eighteenth-century resurgence of Franciscan missionary zeal, when Franciscans from Michoacán and elsewhere participated in the evangelization of Texas. His writings indicate some of the enhanced religious fervor of this moment, but unlike his sixteenth-century counterparts they are also

2. On the formation of Spanish colonial historiography, see Rabasa, *Inventing America;* Enrique Pupo-Walker, *La vocación literaria del pensamiento histórico en América* (Madrid, 1982), 156–90; and Mignolo, *The Darker Side of the Renaissance,* esp. 6.

3. On history and interpretation, see Russell Jacoby, "A New Intellectual History?" *American Historical Review* 97, no. 2 (April 1992): 405–24, and Dominick LaCapra, "Intellectual History and Its Ways," ibid., 425–39. Also see Anthony Pagden, "Rethinking the Linguistic Turn: Current Anxieties in Intellectual History," *Journal of the History of Ideas* 49 (1988): 519–29, esp. 525; Lloyd S. Kramer, "Literature, Criticism, and Historical Imagination: The Literary Challenge of Hayden White and Dominick LaCapra," in *The New Cultural History,* ed. Lynn Hunt (Berkeley, Calif., 1989), 97–128; Edward W. Said, "Criticism Between Culture and System," in *The World, the Text, and the Critic,* 178–225; and Gayatri Chakravorty Spivak, "The Politics of Interpretations," in *In Other Worlds* (New York, 1987), 118–33, esp. 118, 121–22, and "Subaltern Studies: Deconstructing Historiography," in *Selected Subaltern Studies,* ed. Ranajit Guha and Gayatri Chakravorty Spivak (Oxford, 1988), 5.

4. Warren, *Conquest of Michoacán,* 329.

5. On the distinction between absolute and relative notions of truth, see Hulme, *Colonial Encounters,* 8.

Figure 2 Vasco de Quiroga and Fray Jerónimo de Alcalá discuss the move of the bishopry from the City of Tzintzuntzan to the City of Pátzcuaro. In Beaumont, *Crónica de Michoacán,* copy of 1792 (translated by the author).

marked by a defensive tone. Beaumont responded directly to Bourbon attacks on the privileges of the missionary orders. In Michoacán, these occurred in the 1750s, when his Franciscans lost access to a network of parishes they had controlled since the sixteenth century.[6] Ironically, he celebrates the activities of the first generation of missionaries after the influence of the religious orders had been sharply curtailed, and at a time when the colonial system they helped to found was showing signs of decline. This may account for the impassioned nature of his defense, presented as a factual reconstruction of what has come to be known as the "spiritual conquest."[7]

Although Beaumont drew on established traditions, he also defined them in new ways. This creative process was not necessarily benign. A harsh tone,

6. Brading, *Church and State in Bourbon Mexico,* 32–38.
7. The concept of the "spiritual conquest" received its most systematic elaboration in Robert Ricard's classic *The Spiritual Conquest of Mexico.*

at times quite jarring to readers from a different era, permeates the *Crónica*. At many points in the text, Beaumont's defense of the Spanish conquest and the colonial order it inaugurated becomes a frank celebration of violence, a celebration that is grounded in an emphatic belief that the end of Christian evangelization justified such means. This distinguishes him from the missionaries and settlers of the sixteenth century. The desire of Beaumont's predecessors for converts and their need for labor led to debates over the legitimacy of violent colonization, factional power struggles, and varied colonization strategies. In addition, historical/technological constraints in practice resulted in substantial indigenous autonomy, despite ethnocidal intentions.[8] As we shall see, in his descriptions of the indigenous "other," Beaumont embraced violence with a certainty—and even a passion—absent in much of the initial missionary-Indian "encounter," although not entirely without precedent.[9]

The Author of the Text

Today, at a distance of more than two hundred years, the *Crónica* remains to be consulted. Its author has long since passed into historical memory. Much like the missionary author of the *Relación*, and Vasco de Quiroga prior to his time in New Spain, there are significant gaps in our knowledge of Pablo Beaumont. Nevertheless, our understanding of the *Crónica* is enhanced when we consider the biographical information that remains. We know that Beaumont arrived at his "creole" interpretation of the Spanish Conquest through a process of cultural appropriation, despite his frequent references to "our Spaniards" in the text.[10] He was born, most probably in the 1720s, as the son of Blas Beaumont, a French doctor in the service of Philip V.[11]

---

8. Sweet, "Ibero-American Frontier Mission," 43; J. Jorge Klor de Alva, "The Postcolonization of the (Latin American) Experience: A Reconsideration of "Colonialism," in *After Colonialism,* ed. Gyan Prakash (Princeton, 1995), 241–75. I agree with much of what Klor de Alva writes about cultural hybridity, *mestizaje,* and the specificity of Latin American history, while considering his claim that the term "colonialism" is inappropriate in this context to be an overstatement.

9. Rivera, *Violent Evangelism;* Rabasa, *Inventing America,* 151–64.

10. Beaumont's references to Spaniards as "ours," usually as a way of distinguishing them from the Indian population, are pervasive, even constant, throughout the text. A few examples among many are Fr. Pablo Beaumont, *Crónica de Michoacán* (1788; Mexico City, 1932), 1:372, 532, 2:104, 3:31.

11. González, "Viaje," 61. See also Rafael López's (1932) introduction to the *Crónica de Michoacán,* xi.

His French nationality distinguished him from the American-born Spanish creole elite, and of course he always remained quite distant from New Spain's Indian, African, and multiracial plebeian masses. Beaumont comments directly on this cultural distance only once in the text, by expressing concern about his facility with Spanish, or "Castilian." "Of the style I can only advise, the Castilian language being something strange to me, by circumstances of my education, I will not be able to be as polished as I would want."[12] However, at no point did Beaumont express deep concern about his status as a foreign national. It is likely that his years of service in New Spain, similar class position, and shared Catholicism served to bridge any cultural distance from the creole elite in social terms. His habit of "borrowing" heavily from existing Spanish colonial historiography—to be discussed promptly—played a similar intellectual role.

Thus, although one would think that Beaumont's French descent might have inclined him to be a particularly ardent supporter of the Bourbon monarchy, his ideological posture is closer to that of the conservative Spanish-American creole elite. Beaumont does maintain a fervent pro-monarchy position throughout his *Crónica,* as did many creoles up through Independence. Indeed, he even "praised" elements of the Bourbon reforms, although faintly. For example, Beaumont noted that Charles III "with inexpressible liberality, ceding of his just rights" considerably reduced the amount of mercury available for the refining of silver, by establishing the Real Junta de Minería (Regional Mining Council); however, "in these years of 1778 and 1779" an extremely successful remedy had been devised, and mining had recovered tremendously.[13] This muted praise cloaking a rather harsh criticism stressed the possibility of remedying the negative effects of imperial reform. It is plausible to assume that Beaumont would have enjoyed a similar remedy to the negative effects that he perceived in the late colonial treatment of the religious orders.

Beyond the central fact of his nationality, specific details about Beaumont's life prior to writing his *Crónica* are elusive. At one point in the text, Beaumont referred to his experience of a Mexican earthquake in 1749, making it plausible to suggest that he had arrived there as a relatively young man.[14] Apparently, like his father—no mention is made of his mother, or her

12. Beaumont, *Crónica de Michoacán,* 1:14.
13. Ibid., 3:181.
14. Ibid., 183.

family—Beaumont had received medical training. At least, he had authored a book on surgery prior to writing his *Crónica*.[15] Beaumont defined himself as an intellectual, which he undoubtedly was. In his introductory remarks, he speaks of "the continual reading of various histories and memoirs of almost all the nations of the world, and of their kingdoms, in distinct languages, that has been the genial occupation of my entire life."[16] By the time he began writing the *Crónica* he had been forced to retire from an active missionary life because of an unspecified chronic illness, which he blamed in part for the ungraceful, even awkward quality of his Spanish prose.[17] Other than these small glimpses, however, most of the details of Beaumont's life remain unknown.

Beaumont died prior to finishing his *Crónica*, in which he had intended to detail—year by year—missionary activity from the discovery of the Americas through at least 1639, in order to fill a gap he perceived in the work of Alonso de la Rea, a Franciscan chronicler of the seventeenth century.[18] Because of his illness, he only made it to 1565, the year of the death of the bishop Vasco de Quiroga. Indeed, when the *Crónica* is read in its entirety, one gets the sense that Beaumont was racing against the clock of his own physical frailty. The *Aparato*, which examines the Spanish Conquest from Columbus through Cortés, is much more polished than the *Crónica* proper. This latter, unfinished portion of Beaumont's work—massive in its own right—borrowed more heavily from prior scholarship, and reproduced more documentation, than did the *Aparato*. At times, particularly during the final chapters of the *Crónica*, Beaumont appears to be simply compiling evidence to support arguments he had sketched out earlier, lending the latter parts of his work the quality of a rough draft. The hurried and unprocessed nature of much of the *Crónica* can be traced in large part to Beaumont's deteriorating physical condition.

In this regard, Beaumont spoke frankly in an extended passage that commented on his fragile health, revealed Enlightenment influence, and acknowledged his habit of "borrowing"—which today we would refer to as plagiarism—while also situating it in the proper context. "With total sincerity," as he put it, Beaumont stated:

15. González, "Viaje," 61.
16. Ibid., 1:3–4.
17. Beaumont, *Crónica de Michoacán*, 1:3.
18. Ibid., 4–5; González, "Viaje," 57.

If death cuts the thread of my life before the conclusion of my *Crónica,* advise to the public that the disposition of the *Aparato* that precedes it is mine, but that the manuscript of the cited priest Espinosa has served me as a guide for the composition of the body of this *Crónica,* and that it is almost one and the same, less the historical combination and collation of some botanical and geographic species, and of diverse erudition, useful to the State and to religion, corresponding to the description of the kingdom of Michoacán and to all that which touches on the continuous parallel of both conquests, spiritual and temporal of that kingdom, as also I have part in some corrections and to the style more fit to mine, in the relation of the lives of our primitive fathers, from which I have pared some events credible in a small degree and certain extraordinary passages ultimately apocryphal, ultimately founded in vulgar traditions.[19]

Indeed, Beaumont's *Crónica* "borrows" not only from Isidro Félix de Espinosa—a Franciscan intellectual of the late seventeenth and early eighteenth century—but also from Muñoz, La Rea, Vetancour, Torquemada, Gonzaga, Mendieta, López de Gomara, Garcilaso de la Vega, Diez de la Calle, Las Casas, Columbus/Colón, Fernando Colón, Herrera, Solís, Acosta, Herrera, Basalenque, Moreno, and Tello, among others.[20] Beaumont's use of these authors ranged from simple citations and critical commentary, to the lifting of entire passages. However, as the quotation above indicates, even when this borrowing was most direct—as in the case of Espinosa—it involved some editorial influence.

My purpose in this essay is not to trace the intellectual lineage of Beaumont's work, or to provide a comprehensive biography of the author. Rather, I seek to evaluate how a distinct historical context and various subjective factors influenced a specific text, one that rewrote the narrative of the conquest of Michoacán. Given Beaumont's influence, we must consider the *Crónica* a product of the late colonial period. However, because of its manner of composition, we may also consider it to be a repository of motifs that informed Spanish colonialist discourse for more than two centuries, reconfigured in a late colonial context.

19. Beaumont, *Crónica de Michoacán,* 1:9.
20. González, "Viaje," 61–63; Warren, *Conquest of Michoacán,* 329.

Truths, Contexts, and Colonialisms

How does one evaluate a work as enormous as Beaumont's *Crónica,* the modern edition of which consists of nearly sixteen hundred pages divided into three volumes? Obviously, any critique will be partial. Nevertheless, even a fragmentary analysis can prove to be extraordinarily revealing. As Luis González has indicated, Beaumont's search for "truth," and his professed desire for "knowledge for knowledge's sake," indicates the influence of Enlightenment thought.[21] These Enlightenment influences served to distinguish his *Crónica* from the hagiographies produced by previous generations of missionary intellectuals.[22] Beaumont believed he could reconcile conflicting interpretations by sifting through their distortions, ultimately arriving at the truth, or as he put it, "There is no doubt that this diversity of opinions among contemporary historians much embarrasses a historian lover of the truth, but some rays of light do not cease to manifest themselves among so much darkness."[23]

The "diversity of opinions" that Beaumont refers to are the contrasting interpretations of the meaning of the Spanish Conquest. The dispute centered on the writings of European intellectuals about the initial Spanish military occupation of the "Isla Española," or the "Spanish Isle," which today consists of Haiti and the Dominican Republic.[24] For Beaumont, this dispute boiled down to a debate between those who condemned the alleged depravity of the indigenous peoples at the time of their "discovery" and those who focused on the atrocities committed by the Spanish conquistadores.[25] Initially, Beaumont assumed an apparently neutral posture and questions the motivations of the various authors he considered to be embroiled in controversy. He argued that it is possible:

21. González, "Viaje," 61, reproduces some of the passages "borrowed" by Beaumont and traces them to their original authors.

22. González, "Viaje," 61. See also Brading, *Church and State in Bourbon Mexico,* 20–39.

23. Beaumont, *Crónica de Michoacán,* 1:230.

24. Ibid., 228–29.

25. One aspect of this "depravity" is, of course, the allegation that these indigenes practiced cannibalism. For a discussion of the debate over the definition and existence of cannibalism during the initial Spanish encounter with the natives in the Americas, see Peter Hulme, *Colonial Encounters: Europe and the Native Caribbean, 1492–1797* (London, 1986); López Austin, *The Human Body and Ideology,* vol. 1, esp. 375–84; and Clendinnen, *Aztecs,* esp. 87–110, 236–63.

to see in some [. . .] love of nation has guided their pens, so as to diminish to the extent possible the investigation of the public and of posterity against their fathers and countrymen, and in others excessive zeal for religion, motives that animated them to attribute with exaggeration these and other excesses, to make hateful or exculpate the authors of the cruelties that were executed against these Indians, who desired to finish [them off] rather than attract them to the cult of the true God.[26]

At this point in the text Beaumont is setting the stage for his own interpretation by discounting the passions—nationalistic fervor and religious zeal—that clouded the judgments of others.

Beaumont explicitly defines himself as a "lover of the truth" when he discusses conflicting depictions of conquistadors and Indians. The historians causing embarrassment by their diverse opinions remain unspecified, except for fleeting references to Oviedo and Herrera, authors Beaumont sought to defend against an anonymous assault. For those obscuring the absolute Truth Beaumont believed could be found in this past there was "no pretext better than to represent these peoples on the one hand, as that they had no more than the form of men, and that they were given to the greatest abominations; and on the other, painting them to the contrary as men without vices nor passions."[27] Beaumont argued that one could avoid falsehood by looking to "the middle of these two extremes." For Beaumont, this middle ground could be constructed by acknowledging the "cruelties" of the first generation of Spanish conquistadores. However, he insisted—rather passionately—that any such acknowledgment must recognize how "the Spanish nation" censured these cruelties, which he believed were widely condemned in their own time.[28] Beaumont's flexibility in recognizing the atrocities of individual Spaniards—presenting them as punished, and peripheral to the consolidation and maintenance of the colonial order—is not reproduced in his discussion of disputes over the image of the Indian.

In fact, Beaumont's search for the rational center between what he proposed as two extremes collapses in his discussion of indigenes. Beaumont

26. Beaumont, *Crónica de Michoacán*, 1:230.
27. Ibid., 230–31.
28. Ibid., 231.

considered his strategic acknowledgment of Spanish atrocities to be matched by a recognition that "Oviedo, Herrera and other historians" correctly reported "that these Indians were abundant in the nefarious sin, except the women, who abhorred it, not due to shame or scruples, being very lascivious, but because this infamous commerce took no account of them." Of course, Beaumont's term "nefarious sin" refers to unspecified sexual activity among men. Beaumont continued by charging that "the women were continent with the natives, and dishonest with the Castilians, and communicated to them the venereal virus."[29] This latter statement transformed realities of rape, cross-ethnic male commerce in women, and other types of sexual unions, into a plot by indigenous women to transmit venereal disease.[30] Undoubtedly, Beaumont considered all of this to be evidence of the alleged "barbarity" of Indians. These statements drew on a deeply rooted tradition in Spanish colonial historiography, which sought to justify colonial rule by demonstrating what Spaniards believed to be the "perverse otherness" of indigenous peoples, conceived of in sexual and other terms.[31]

Beaumont's strategic acknowledgment of Spanish atrocities, in the context of reproducing a most ethnocentric justification for Spanish colonial rule, demolishes his pretense of rational objectivity. Indeed, the collapse of Beaumont's rather shaky binary opposition reveals his history for what he intended it to be, a defense of Spanish colonialism as it had developed from the first years of the Spanish Conquest until the late colonial Bourbon reforms. Most important, he sought to justify privileges granted missionaries during the "heroic" phase of early colonial evangelization. Since the Bourbon reforms had largely succeeded in curbing the power of the religious orders by the time Beaumont wrote, and nonetheless ultimately failed to preserve Spanish colonialism, it is fair to characterize Beaumont's attempt as a failure.

29. Ibid.
30. Gayatri Chakravorty Spivak, "Can the Subaltern Speak?" in *Marxism and the Interpretation of Culture,* ed. Cary Nelson and Lawrence Grossberg (Urbana, Ill., 1988), 287. See also Montrose, "The Work of Gender." On syphilis and the New World "encounter," see Alfred W. Crosby, *The Columbian Exchange* (Westport, Conn., 1972), 122–64. Beaumont does mention colonial rape, and the tendency of the Spaniards to take indigenous women as mistresses. See *Crónica de Michoacán,* 1:188 and 247.
31. Goldberg, "Sodomy in the New World," 46–56.

Nevertheless, lest we rush to hasty judgments that obscure our understanding of complex historical processes, we should recall that the initial achievement of Mexican independence hearkened more toward the colonial past than to the national future. Beaumont's reactionary defense of pre-Bourbon colonialism presaged what John Lynch appropriately titled "the conservative revolution," the ascension to power of Agustín de Iturbide in 1821.[32] Iturbide was a former royalist who responded to liberal reforms in Spain by leading Mexico into independence, and declaring himself emperor. He continued using the power of the state to destroy the popular movements and social reformism surrounding the leaders Hidalgo and Morelos, figures who would become heroic icons associated with the demise of Spanish colonialism in Mexico. This use of the state by postinsurgency elites to subdue popular mobilizations, followed by a process of incorporating vanquished popular leaders into a revolutionary pantheon of heroes, is a pattern that has been repeated throughout Mexican history.[33] Eighteenth-century conservative creole ideology had a nineteenth- and twentieth-century future, as did a glorified version of the sixteenth-century missionary past.

Beaumont and History

"One must observe that from the beginning of the conquest of the kingdoms of Michoacán and Jalisco until these years, of which events we are treating, the entire administration was in the custody of the regulars of the two religions of our father Saint Francis and of our great father Saint Augustine." Throughout his *Crónica,* Beaumont strives to demonstrate that the religious orders made an important contribution in "civilizing" New Spain. In writing this particular passage, Beaumont wanted that "the reader see with distinction and clarity" how "the houses of both religions, . . . fraternized in order to obtain the instruction and conversion of so many pagan and barbarian Indians."[34] Perhaps his characterization of the Franciscan and

32. See John Lynch, *The Spanish American Revolutions, 1808–1826* (1973; New York, 1986), 319–23.
33. For twentieth-century examples of similar processes, see Ilene V. O'Malley, *The Myth of the Revolution* (Westport, Conn., 1986).
34. Beaumont, *Crónica de Michoacán,* 3:430.

Augustinian orders as distinct "religions" testified to the strength of institutional rivalries within the colonial Church, a reality echoed in Beaumont's desire to find and portray a golden era of mutual cooperation. His discussion of the colonial Church focused on the religious orders, especially his own Franciscans. His tone in "recovering" this history was simultaneously celebratory and defensive.

For example, in his discussion of Church activities during the conquest of Hispaniola, Beaumont distinguishes the efforts of the Franciscans from those of other priests and bishops. He argues that "the Franciscan missionaries . . . with their doctrine and good example" along with "many miracles that Our Lord showed for confirmation of the truth, bore the greatest fruit in the hearts of those people." Later in the text, he asserts that "the first ministers of this Indian Church were not ignorant, as some falsely and maliciously wanted to say."[35] He is highly critical of the efforts of Vasco de Quiroga, the legendary first bishop of Michoacán, despite his recognition of Don Vasco's role in helping to found the regional Church. Toward the end of the *Crónica*, Beaumont harshly condemns what he believed to have been Quiroga's attempts to wrest control of the area from the Franciscans who had preceded him. Beaumont bitterly complains about these actions, and claims that the "persecution" of the religious orders by the bishops has continued until "present times." The end result, according to Beaumont, was that the original missionaries had been "almost totally despoiled" of the fruits of their original Indian ministry.[36]

To consider these statements as isolated comments would be to misconstrue their meaning. Their defensive tone suggests that they existed as part of an unfolding "dialogue," however strained it may have been. In making these remarks, Beaumont was responding to perceived attacks on the religious orders from the Bourbon monarchy and the "secular" Church. In so doing, he was also defending Catholicism, and Spain, from European proponents of what has come to be termed the "Black Legend." Beaumont prefaced his *Crónica* with a lengthy *Aparato*, which discusses the Spanish Conquest from Columbus through Cortés. This might seem a curious choice for an author concerned with the missionary history of western

35. Ibid., 1:243, 2:124.
36. Ibid., 3:407.

Mexico, but for Beaumont it was necessary to consider the Spanish Conquest in its entirety. Beaumont completed the *Aparato,* which was the section of the entire work that he considered most uniquely his own, on February 20, 1788. Most probably, he drafted the remainder of the text after writing the *Aparato.*[37]

By 1788, the Spanish colonial system had begun to show signs of decline, a reality evident in the regions most familiar to Beaumont.[38] Indeed, Beaumont comments on many of the signs of imperial decay. For example, he rues the loss of Florida to the British, a "disgrace" occurring in 1763, and he condemns the corruption of his day.[39] In addition, Beaumont complains about the burgeoning mixed racial population that had emerged in colonial Mexico. He does so in a remarkable passage that testifies to elite perceptions of racial and cultural difference, as well as to the increased social tension of the late colonial period. In a discussion of the sixteenth-century slave trade, Beaumont states that

> with this introduction of negroes, although few at first, have come forth damned castes, as of *castizos, mestizos, lobos, coyotes, salta-atrás, tente-en-el-aire, joveros, mulatos,* who in an infinite procession proceed from the mixing of whites, Indians, Chinese, and among one and another they form with so much variety of physiognomies and colors a people so extravagant and much more in customs, that they have come to be very prejudicial to all of these reigns of the Indies, as experience demonstrates it daily.[40]

37. Beaumont, *Crónica de Michoacán,* 1:8 (*Aparato* as most uniquely his own), 566 (date of completion). A useful introduction to Beaumont and the corpus of missionary writings on western Mexico can be found in González, "Viaje," 50–70, esp. 61–63.

38. Oscar Mazín, *Entre dos Majestades* (Zamora, Mexico, 1987), esp. 127–72. See also William Taylor, "Banditry and Insurrection: Rural Unrest in Central Jalisco, 1790–1816," in *Riot, Rebellion and Revolution: Rural Social Conflict in Mexico,* ed. Friedrich Katz (Princeton, 1988), 205–46, esp. 232–34. On the social and economic transformation of western Mexico in the eighteenth century and its link to violence, see Claude Morin, *Michoacán en la Nueva España del siglo XVIII* (Mexico City, 1979), and Eric Van Young, *Hacienda and Market in Eighteenth-Century Mexico* (Berkeley, Calif., 1981), esp. 273–342.

39. Beaumont, *Crónica de Michoacán,* 1:284, 557.

40. Ibid., 316. J. I. Israel, *Race, Class, and Politics in Colonial Mexico, 1610–1670* (London, 1975), 67. On the African slave trade in Mexico, see Palmer, *Slaves of the White God.* On colonial racial classification, see Aguirre Beltrán, *La población negra de México,* 163–79. An innovative recent study is R. Douglas Cope, *The Limits of Racial Domination* (Madison, Wis., 1994).

Beaumont considered this extensive mixed racial population to be danger-ous, noting—ominously, from the perspective of a colonial elite—that these plebeian peoples were capable of "whatever uprising."[41]

Nevertheless, despite his fears of popular turmoil, and comments about imperialist rivalry, the strongest challenge to the privileged lifestyle that Beaumont enjoyed came not from below, or from without, but rather from above, through metropolitan efforts to reform a declining colonial system. At one point in the *Crónica*—after reviewing the political infighting that broke out among Columbus and his subordinates in 1496—he remarks that "when a person is found invested with authority (as happens to a foreigner or to a man of new nobility), this one must educate himself a lot on rendering acceptable, diminishing the effect of his power and softening its severity."[42] Beaumont's editorial comment might have been addressed as much to the colonial authorities of his day, as to the historical reconstruction of the expe-rience of Columbus. To understand the "challenge from above" that influ-enced Beaumont's definition of the meaning of the Spanish Conquest, we must briefly examine the impact of the late colonial Bourbon reforms on the Church in western Mexico.

The Bourbon administrations, beginning with Philip V (1700–1746), and especially under Charles III (1759–88), pursued an aggressive policy of ad-ministrative and economic reforms that attempted to bring colonial regions more firmly under the control of the Crown. Although partially successful, the Bourbon reforms failed to prevent the ultimate collapse of Spanish colo-nialism, which occurred in Mexico between 1810 and 1821.[43] The institutional Church, being one of the pillars of the colonial system, could not avoid the process of change initiated by these top-down reforms. Beginning around 1749, the Bourbon administrations confronted the religious orders in west-ern Mexico, including Beaumont's own Franciscan order, with a campaign of secularization. In this context, "secularization" meant shifting primary con-trol of areas formerly dominated by the religious orders to the "secular" Church, i.e., to parish priests directly responsible to bishops, and through

41. Beaumont, *Crónica de Michoacán*, 1:316–17.
42. Ibid., 131.
43. Useful introductions to and analyses of the Bourbon reforms can be found in George Reid Andrews, "Spanish American Independence: A Structural Analysis," *Latin American Per-spectives* 44 (Winter 1985): 105–32, esp. 109–10; Lynch, *Spanish American Revolutions*, 7–24, and on Mexico, 295–333; and Gibson, *Spain in America*, 160–81.

the bishops to the pope. In theory, at least, this would enable the Bourbons to control particular regions more effectively.[44]

In many ways, these campaigns paralleled—and carried to completion in "peripheral" regions, such as Michoacán and rural Jalisco—Crown efforts of the second half of the sixteenth century, when royal authorities used "secularization" as a way to bring the remnants of the first missionary generation into line. Generally, the Spanish state had a more decisive influence over the appointment of bishops—who in turn appointed parish priests, and oversaw the administration of parishes—than over the members of the religious orders. These latter individuals belonged to something of a parallel hierarchy within the Roman Catholic Church, being accountable only to superiors within their own orders, and through them to the pope.[45] Thus, the status, power, and privileges that members of the religious orders had enjoyed in many regions—in some cases, as with the Franciscan experience in western Mexico, since the initial moments of Spanish colonialism—faced a substantial challenge at the close of the colonial period.[46] This challenge influenced Beaumont's understanding of his world, and of the past.

"In effect, for all those who look at things with Christianity, and for every Catholic breast, the discovery of the New World has always been of highest regard," explained Beaumont.[47] What better forum to pursue a defense of the issues dearest to Beaumont's heart than a historical study of the Spanish Conquest? We must recognize that the political struggles of Beaumont's day influenced his representation of the Spanish Conquest, although this understanding does not exhaust the complexity of his text. In its glorification of the founders of Spanish colonialism—including Queen Isabella, Columbus, Cortés, and other "secular" figures, as well as various missionaries and other "religious" individuals—Beaumont's *Crónica* typified a conservative creole ideology in the process of being redefined. Ironically, creole nationalism reached its full fruition in Mexico with the severing of political ties to the imperial center—in response to reformist movements in Spain—several years

44. On institutional Church politics in eighteenth-century Michoacán, see Mazín, *Entre dos Majestades*, esp. 37–44, 153–61, and Taylor, "Banditry and Insurrection," 232–34, which examines "secularization" and the social impact of Church reforms.

45. For a somewhat dated, although still useful discussion of the colonial Church, see Gibson, *Spain in America*, 68–89, esp. 77–78.

46. In this instance, the most substantial challenge was faced by the Jesuit order, expelled from the colonies in 1767. Gibson, *Spain in America*, 80–85, esp. 82.

47. Beaumont, *Crónica de Michoacán*, 1:2.

after Beaumont's death.[48] In the end, it is the organization of the *Crónica* itself that provides the strongest evidence of contextual influences.

Throughout the entire work—beginning with Columbus and the conquest of the Caribbean, including Cortés and the conquest of Mexico's central valley, and finishing with the conquest of Michoacán, Jalisco, and regions to the north—Beaumont focuses on the achievements of the religious orders, with a primary emphasis given to his own Franciscans. Even in those areas where he discusses other individuals—for example, in his treatment of the "good" conquerors Columbus and Cortés in the *Aparato,* or "bad" conquerors like Nuño de Guzmán, or his presentation of the "good, but in some ways quite bad" bishop Vasco de Quiroga—he utilizes them strategically, as a way of enhancing the reader's appreciation of the religious orders. In the end, Beaumont's selection of the topic of inquiry—namely, the chronicling of the contributions of the missionaries to the "civilization" of New Spain— defined his entire representation.

Defined, but did not exhaust. Of course, the complexities of individual motivation cannot be reduced simply to social determinations. Also, recognizing that social context and political orientation influence textual production does not grant the reader license to ignore, or gloss over, the ambiguities evident in every text. Indeed, these contradictory and imprecise areas often indicate the most productive moments of creative tension. The scattered comments cited as the most visible demonstrations of the political nature of Beaumont's *Crónica* forms only a paragraph or two in a multivolume work. An argument that they indicate more than would be the case on strictly quantitative grounds is defensible, since they reveal concerns that shaped the *Crónica* at the level of selecting the topic of inquiry, and the content of the entire work. Nevertheless, any serious reading of Beaumont's *Crónica* must recognize that the richness of the text is not exhausted, or even adequately addressed, by a discussion focused exclusively on its political implications. This is especially the case when we define "politics" narrowly, as disputes among elites over colonial administrative reforms.

48. David Brading, *The First America* (Cambridge, England, 1991); Andrews, "Spanish American Independence," 111–13, 126–29; Lynch, *Spanish American Revolutions,* 319–26; Benedict Anderson, *Imagined Communities* (London, 1983). For an insightful critique of Anderson and an innovative recognition of the complexities of national identity, see Julie Skursi, "The Ambiguities of Authenticity in Latin America: Doña Barbara and the Construction of National Identity," *Poetics Today* 15, no. 4 (Winter 1994): 605–42.

The Baroque, the Enlightenment, and the *Crónica*

In his *Crónica,* completed by about 1788, Beaumont incorporated elements of "baroque" and "Enlightenment" thought into a distinctively Latin American historiographical effort.[49] As such, his work does not fit easily within rigid intellectual categories established in a European context.[50] Scholars generally consider the ornate, massive, and at times redundant intellectual production evident in Beaumont's *Crónica* as a hallmark feature of the baroque. However, precisely what constitutes a baroque work, or even the exact dates of the baroque era, appear to be somewhat fluid. Irving Leonard claims that the baroque period stretched from around 1550 to 1750. He argues that baroque texts display "a tendency to shift from content to form, from ideas to details, to give new sanction to dogmas, to avoid issues, and to substitute subtlety of language for subtlety of thought; [the baroque] served to express rather than liberate the human spirit, and to divert by spectacle, by overstatement, and by excessive ornamentation." While there may be some substance to Leonard's characterizations, at times his condemnations of the baroque era seem excessively dismissive. He continued by noting that during the baroque period "through medieval religiosity chaotic feelings vented themselves in a fierce fanaticism which spawned an arid dogmatism, an uncompromising intolerance, an implacable persecution and a degrading superstition."[51] Although Leonard's fierce intolerance forced him into an uncompromising interpretation of the baroque, Anthony Pagden's characterization of a specific baroque text as "ponderous and heavily freighted with a superfluous encyclopedic learning" seems a fair designation for many of the epoch.[52]

A more sympathetic characterization of the baroque has been made by Luis González. González dated the baroque era from the "last years of the great adventures of discovery, conquest and evangelization until the first restlessness in favor of national independence." Among its many characteristics, González cites reduced populations—presumably caused by

---

49. For a discussion of similar works, see Pupo-Walker, *La vocación literaria,* esp. 90–92, 156–90.

50. Chartier, "Intellectual History or Sociocultural History?" esp. 16.

51. Irving Leonard, *Baroque Times in Old Mexico* (Ann Arbor, Mich., 1959), 28–29.

52. Anthony Pagden, *Spanish Imperialism and the Political Imagination* (New Haven, Conn., 1990), 93.

relatively frequent, devastating epidemics—and "apostolic poverty and much liturgical sumptuosity, contorted art and prophetic sermons."[53] Beaumont's work contained traces of the baroque as discussed by all of these authors, although it includes much more, and thus defies easy categorization.

González distinguished Beaumont's work from that produced by earlier generations of missionary intellectuals by noting that he sought "knowledge for knowledge's sake." He contrasted Beaumont with seventeenth-century authors such as Diego de Basalenque and Alonso de la Rea (also Larrea and Larra), and those from the early eighteenth century, such as Matías de Escobar and Isidro Félix de Espinoza, who sought to write heroic accounts of their order's founding fathers for the purpose of influencing the "norms of conduct" of contemporary friars. While this is arguably overstated, since Beaumont relied heavily on these other sources and certainly provides a heroic narrative of sixteenth-century evangelization, it is true that at times his *Crónica* displays a critical spirit commonly associated with the Enlightenment. This is most evident in Beaumont's critique of other scholars, whose judgment he describes as impaired by "love of nation" and "excessive zeal for religion." It is also evident in Beaumont's respect for, and analysis of, historical evidence—documents, archival materials, and the works of established scholars—which Beaumont considered to be the foundation upon which he built his *Crónica*. Indeed, Beaumont even felt confident enough in his own rational capabilities to speak of "an ancient map, that escaped from the incendiary hands of the ignorants."[54] This was a remarkable comment, since Beaumont must have been aware that his sixteenth-century Franciscan brethren were among those who zealously destroyed priceless legacies of indigenous cultures. Despite this Enlightenment influence, however, it is not entirely accurate to claim that with Beaumont "we arrive at the eve of scientific history."[55]

The fusion of elements of the baroque with elements of the Enlightenment distinguished Beaumont's *Crónica* as a distinctively creole work of historiography and literature. As such, it should be considered more as an

53. González, "Viaje," 63. See also Brading, *Church and State in Bourbon Mexico*, 18–19. On the Spanish baroque, see José Antonio Maravall, *Culture of the Baroque*, trans. by Terry Cochran (Minneapolis, 1986). On recent interpretations of the baroque in Latin America, see Mabel Moraña, ed., *Relecturas del barroco del Indias* (Hanover, N.H., 1994).

54. Beaumont, *Crónica de Michoacán*, 1:230, 514.

55. J. Benedict Warren, "Comentario," in Miranda, *La cultura Purhé*, 71–72.

American synthesis—albeit a rough and incomplete one—than as a transitional text lying between two rigidly defined intellectual eras. The apparently contradictory relationship between baroque and Enlightenment tendencies in Beaumont's *Crónica* can be seen most vividly by contrasting his commitment to a narrowly defined rationalism, with his treatment of the "fantastic." Here, Beaumont's Enlightenment skepticism clashes with his profoundly held conviction that the Spanish Conquest of the Americas had been divinely ordained. As he put it, in a discussion of the comets that allegedly appeared to indigenous peoples prior to the Spanish Conquest:

> I am not ignorant that the philosophers hold these signs on account of natural effects, and many physicists, principally among the moderns, consider the comets as a strip of small stars and they ridicule among themselves the preoccupation of the populace, that fixes on their minds a terror panic when they appear; but I must, in such circumstances as were those that preceded the conversion of this American paganism, call these portentous signs, with Saint Augustine, heavenly speech; they are notices from God, that He deigns to make known to us from time to time, according to His most elevated ends.[56]

Thus, a text that on the one hand exalts Beaumont's rationality and freedom from excessive zeal for religion, also repeatedly refers to instances of divine intervention and miraculous occurrences during the founding of Spanish colonialism.

A few examples can be drawn from among the many to be found in this work. Some of the Spaniards involved in intrigues against Columbus were killed in a shipwreck during a terrible storm. As Beaumont put it, they were "paying for their sins," as "proven" by the fact that weaker, less-prepared ships managed to survive. Prior to the Spanish arrival in what would become New Spain, a pyramid-shaped flame shot up to the sky. Loud voices were heard, proclaiming the end of the "Indian monarchy," and armed men appeared in the sky, fighting until they had annihilated one another.[57] According to Beaumont, these supernatural manifestations continued throughout

56. Beaumont, *Crónica de Michoacán*, 2:66.
57. Ibid., 187–88, 65–66.

the Spanish Conquest. In a battle for what would become Querétaro—which Beaumont dates at 1530, in an account "borrowed" from his fellow Franciscan Espinosa—he recorded that "there is a tradition, that in this conflict appeared the image of the Holy Cross and the Apostle Saint James [Santiago]; that the sun stopped itself, and in the end, that all heaven declared itself in favor of the Catholic arms."[58] During a pivotal battle in the Mixton War—which erupted around Zacatecas, in the northernmost reaches of New Spain, throughout the 1540s—Beaumont recorded that a knight on a white horse appeared to urge the Spaniards on to victory, inspiring them to triumph over the "enemies of God."[59]

The point is not to hold fragments of Beaumont's text up to ridicule by evaluating them according to present-day standards. Rather, it is to demonstrate that in Beaumont's *Crónica*, the repeated portrayal of divine intervention and miraculous happenings at crucial moments coexisted in a sometimes tense, but for the most part quite happy relationship with the highly esteemed rationality, and almost "modern" historiographical techniques, of an Enlightenment scholar. Many Enlightenment scholars and scientists also believed in the hand and inspiration of Providence, and did not construe reason as necessarily excluding divine plan or intervention. The *difference* is the tendency to explain events and nature through a discourse of natural order and causation, rather than a discourse of "miracles" and "superstition." Beaumont's *Crónica* clearly falls within the latter realm, particularly as regards his justifications for Spanish colonial rule.

Missionaries and Conquests

"The infantry gave no quarter at all to the Indians on foot and in this battle without doubt heaven fought on our behalf, because the plazas and streets of the city were full of corpses and streams of blood flowed, consistent with the multitude of Indians that died thus in the attack." This passage from the *Crónica* describes the Spanish reconquest, in 1541, of the fortress-city of

58. Ibid., 3:110. On the history of Santiago and the Conquest, see William Taylor, "Santiago's Horse: Christianity and Colonial Indian Resistance in the Heartland of New Spain," in *Violence, Resistance and Survival in the Americas,* ed. William Taylor and Franklin Pease G. Y. (Washington, D.C., 1994), 153–89.
59. Beaumont, *Crónica de Michoacán,* 3:32. On the Mixton War, see Philip Wayne Powell, *Soldiers, Indians and Silver* (Berkeley, Calif., 1952).

Guadalajara. The battle—and subsequent slaughter—resulted in the Spanish recovery of a strategic frontier outpost, which had been temporarily overrun by insurgent indigenes. As Beaumont portrayed it, the Indians' temporary military advantage due to their enormous numbers allowed them to occupy Guadalajara. According to the *Crónica,* "they entered dancing and singing to walk through the streets of the city and the first [thing] that they did was to sack the Church and profane it; afterwards they burned it and set fire to the houses of the city."[60] Of course, for Beaumont this lack of respect for the Christian God—and by definition, those divinely ordained to subdue a "barbarian" population—could not triumph, or go unpunished. Hence, the "miraculous" recovery of the Spaniards, their subsequent victory, and the massacre of Indians, all presented as a manifestation of God's will.

Obviously, this was a contorted interpretation. Inflating the enemy death toll, and minimizing friendly casualties, has been a standard public relations ploy, possibly as old as war itself. Beaumont, in a manner as zealous as it was absurd, claimed that "more than fifteen thousand Indians" died in this battle, and only one Spaniard.[61] While his account obviously does not conform to "what really happened," it is quite revealing in terms of how Beaumont—and by implication, most other colonial intellectuals, overwhelmingly affiliated with the Church in this era—conceived of the Spanish Conquest. Most obviously, this passage illustrates the belief that the Conquest had been divinely ordained, as indicated by God's willingness to intervene on the Spanish side. This belief pervades Beaumont's *Crónica*—and Spanish colonial historiography.[62] To my knowledge, Las Casas, late in his life, was the only possible exception.[63]

For Beaumont, the spread of Christianity—which he defined exclusively in terms of Roman Catholicism—served as the final, indeed only, reason for the Spanish Conquest, and hence granted legitimacy to the entire colonial order built upon this event.[64] In his mind, the spiritual and military aspects of the Spanish Conquest were inextricably linked, and the one

60. Beaumont, *Crónica de Michoacán,* 2:429, 428.

61. Ibid., 429.

62. In this specific instance, Beaumont based his account on the writing of Fray Agustín Tello, a seventeenth-century Franciscan historian of western Mexico. Ibid., 428.

63. Gutiérrez, *Las Casas,* Rivera, *Violent Evangelism,* 63–86.

64. A particularly straightforward statement of Beaumont's views can be found in Beaumont, *Crónica de Michoacán,* 1:11. See also 17, 63–64, 398; 2:32, 228; 3:105, 110. These are only a few of the most pertinent citations, selected from many possibilities.

justified the other. Indeed, he composed the *Aparato*—that part of the text which he considered to be most uniquely his own—so that readers would "see better the beautiful link that both conquests, spiritual and temporal, observe between themselves, this last arranging itself to the first." Beaumont continued, by stating precisely how Christian evangelization served as the ultimate justification for the Spanish Conquest. "Then only did the discovery of the New World gain merit and importance, with regard to opening the way for the conquest of innumerable souls to the faith of Our Lord Jesus Christ."[65] Many of Beaumont's ideas exist in contradictory tension. However, while he criticizes particular aspects of the behavior of Spanish settlers, soldiers, and even missionaries, his belief in the Conquest as divinely ordained never wavers.

Beaumont writes frequently, in a straightforward, even calculating manner, about this issue. He notes that the congregation of Indians into concentrated settlements, which facilitated evangelization, occurred "consistent with the progress of our victorious arms." He refers constantly to "both conquests, spiritual and temporal."[66] In his *Crónica,* divine sanction justifies battles producing "streams of blood" from a "multitude of Indians," and he writes proudly of massacres where "our Spaniards tired from killing Indians."[67] Indeed, in his description of the reconquest of Guadalajara, Beaumont claims that the Spaniards tortured the surviving Indian prisoners: "To some, they cut their noses and to others their ears and hands and a foot and later they cured the wounds with boiling oil." Beaumont notes, approvingly, that this punishment, combined with the earlier massacre, was sufficiently severe to prevent any further sieges of the city since that time.[68]

Whether or not these events occurred—and they did with enough frequency to be recorded by Beaumont—is not precisely the point. Beaumont considered his descriptions to be accurate, even factual, supported by the evidence and sanctioned by God. His description of the sacking and reconquest of Guadalajara employs a powerful explanatory device, one with a long and enduring life in rationalizing military conflict. For several centuries, European and colonial intellectuals utilized the notion of divinely

65. Ibid., 1:11, 8.
66. Ibid., 9, 10, 14, 503.
67. Ibid., 2:429, 3:31.
68. Ibid., 2:430.

sanctioned Christian evangelization to justify, among themselves, the violence necessary to establish and maintain a colonial order. In his *Crónica,* Beaumont considered the "truth" of the Spanish Conquest, as a manifestation of God's will, to be self-evident. This explanatory mechanism can be discerned in his discussion of "divine intervention" during the reconquest of Guadalajara. However, perhaps ironically, the ideological depth of this deeply rooted belief in violence justified by divine sanction can be measured most effectively in areas of the text where he does not explicitly defend the Spanish Conquest.

For example, in an extended passage Beaumont condemns the atrocities committed in Michoacán and Jalisco by the conquistador Nuño de Guzmán. As the reader may recall from our analysis of the *Proceso* in Chapter 1, Guzmán's infamous campaign through western Mexico began with the execution of the Cazonci, or indigenous ruler of Michoacán. Beaumont describes Guzmán as someone who had killed "more than twelve thousand friendly Tarascan and Mexican Indians," and he blames Guzmán for the Cazonci's "atrocious death." However, during the course of his description, Beaumont tempers his condemnation by acknowledging that

> one cannot negate, that by his good hand and industry he himself obtained the acquisition, conservation and advancement of the most vast lands, of those that today are known as New Galicia and Vizcaya, affording the entrance to Sonora and New Mexico, that was made with a variety of outcomes, in the years following, and now more than ever, is the particular object of our ministry, so as to secure the conversion of infinite barbarians to our holy faith, that live brutally dispersed in so vast and mountainous regions of the north of this New Spain.[69]

This quotation demonstrates that Beaumont considered the "spiritual conquest" an open-ended event, one that continued in his own day. It also affirmed his recognition of the efficacy of the violence of the Conquest from a missionary perspective. A passage even more removed from the issue of directly defending the Spanish Conquest—yet one that vividly illustrates the

69. Ibid., 2:333, 334.

depth of disregard for indigenous life in colonial discourse—discusses the Indians of "Hispaniola." In a passage laced with scientific pretensions, in which he discusses the physical characteristics of the island's original inhabitants, Beaumont coldly reproduces an early colonial insight. Indian skulls, he wrote, were unusually hard. To illustrate the point, he noted that "the Spaniards broke their swords to bits more than one time."[70]

As Beaumont reported, the Indians—"possessed of the furor that the love of liberty engenders"—burned the church in Guadalajara, in 1541.[71] In the text, this is presented merely as a temporary setback in the "spiritual conquest," one rectified by Spanish military might and celestial assistance. However, Beaumont's depiction of this incident reveals an important issue related to the very nature of the Spanish Conquest itself. For Beaumont, the Spanish Conquest did not exist as a single epoch—say, from the discovery by Columbus of a "new world" to the fall of Tenochtitlán—but rather represented a process constantly challenged and continually recreated over time.[72] Indeed, Beaumont portrays the Conquest as rooted in the Iberian past, and played out through the centuries until his American present. While for Beaumont this represented an ever-unfolding struggle that would result, ultimately, in the triumph of God's will, we can read his account against the grain. When we do so, we see traces of an indigenous struggle for dignity against an oppressive ideology, or, at least, against an ideology applied oppressively.

There is no doubt that a profound, even vicious, religious intolerance underlay Beaumont's understanding of the Conquest as divinely inspired. He began the *Aparato* with the following proclamation: "At last the light of the Gospel dawned in this hemisphere, God permitting in light of his impenetrable decrees, that they began to discover the Indies that we call Western, or the New World, when Luther and other heretics would pervert so many of the faithful with their damned sects in Germany." He continued by noting that at the same time the *reyes catolicos,* or Catholic kings—of what was in the process of becoming Spain—had finished conquering Granada, driving Islamic peoples from their last Iberian stronghold. For Beaumont, these

70. Ibid., 1:228.
71. Ibid., 2:430.
72. On definitions of terminology to describe the indigenous peoples of central Mexico, see Clendinnen, *Aztecs,* xiii, also 1–11.

"victories" provided proof of the unfolding of God's will, since they provided Spain's Catholic rulers with the "most vast territories," in which "to propagate his most holy religion." Indeed, the discovery of the "New World" brought "true light to such a multitude of souls that had such necessity of it, inasmuch as they lived, or, better said, perished in the utter darkness of the most barbarous and bestial idolatry, as in the discourse of this *Crónica* we shall see."[73] In fact, "discovery" preceded extended processes of conquest, followed by the consolidation of colonial rule. This entire series is repeated several times, in different regions and eras, throughout Beaumont's *Crónica*. Although Beaumont viewed discovery, conquest, and the consolidation of Spanish colonialism as the inevitable unfolding of God's will, his representation of these events also includes the recurring theme of indigenous resistance. Indeed, a careful reading of Beaumont calls into question one of his own central tenets, namely the belief that sixteenth-century missionaries successfully pursued a "spiritual conquest" of the peoples they called Indians.

The conquest of Hispaniola, the first American island "discovered" by Columbus, served as a paradigm for Beaumont, one reproduced throughout the text. On this island, missionaries enjoyed what they perceived to be initial success. Indeed, as Beaumont puts it, the Indians of Hispaniola followed their leaders with "blind obedience," and the missionary strategy of targeting Indian rulers paid off with the conversion of the cacique Guarionex and his followers. However, this apparent "victory" did not last. Inspired by the "common enemy"—for Beaumont, Satan—some high-ranking subjects convinced Guarionex that the Christians "were perverted ones and they had taken from him his land by force."[74] As Beaumont portrayed it, the missionaries—identified as Fray Román Pane and Fray Juan Borgoñon—realized that Guarionex had "insensibly erased from his heart" Christian teaching, and left in search of another cacique to convert. After they left, Indians under the influence of Guarionex entered the house where the missionaries had lived, and desecrated a sanctuary left by the friars. They trampled images the priests had left for some of the converts, and cried out mockingly: "Now

---

73. Beaumont, *Crónica de Michoacán*, 1:17–18.
74. Ibid., 129, 128. On the Devil in colonial Mexico, see Fernando Cervantes, *The Devil in the New World* (New Haven, Conn., 1994).

your fruits will be good and great!" The mother of Guarionex, whom Beaumont labeled a "perverse woman," even pulled a chili plant up and claimed its roots formed a cross. Apparently, she believed this was a great miracle, a sign from God.[75]

At this point in the narrative, Spanish colonial authorities intervened to restore order, forestalling what Beaumont believed could have developed into a serious uprising. The mother of Guarionex took her miraculous root-cross to a "captain Ojeda," a member of the Spanish force encamped on the island. Somehow, according to Beaumont and the Spanish colonial sources he utilized, she overcame the language barrier and explained her discovery. As she allegedly put it "God made this miracle, and He knows why." Immediately thereafter, in a sequence of events not entirely clear, the Spaniards found the desecrated images buried underground. They responded swiftly to what they perceived to be a transgression of priestly, hence civil, authority. As Beaumont recorded, without regret, "to make an example with these impious ones . . . they were burned alive."[76]

Beaumont considered the possibility of indigenous rejection, even treachery, to be omnipresent. He describes a variety of ways that these tendencies manifested themselves in the various Spanish conquests he examined. Thus, in Cuba, the legendary cacique Hatuey taunted his captors by stating that if Spaniards were in heaven, he preferred hell. The Spaniards, hoping to oblige, promptly burned him alive. During the long march on Tenochtitlán, the priest Bartolomé de Olmedo and Juan Díaz—identified as a "licenciado," or holder of a university degree—pleaded with Cortés not to leave crosses in the villages of their newly "conquered" allies. They argued that "it would be imprudent to trust the holy cross to some poorly instructed barbarians, that could do some indecency with it, and pay homage to it with superstitious venerations."[77]

Following the military triumph at Tenochtitlán, the Mixton war challenged Spanish efforts at Christian colonization in northwestern Mexico. As Beaumont portrays it, this uprising struck at the core of what he defined as Christian conversion, namely Spanish colonial attempts to regulate

75. As an aside, at this point in the text Beaumont states that in "various scientific academies" in Europe, different configurations had been noted in the roots of plants, including those resembling Christ and the Most Holy Virgin. Beaumont, *Crónica de Michoacán,* 1:128–29.

76. Ibid., 128–29.

77. Ibid., 272, 394.

indigenous sexuality: "In a short time they converted them and subjected them to the laws of a legitimate matrimony, this is, to the true monogamy, and converted, ultimately the demon made of them his, so as to return them to their abominations, and thus (the year of 1541) they rose in rebellion against the Spanish nation."[78] Once again, the issue is not the extent to which Beaumont's description conforms to "reality." My purpose is not to highlight, ironically, the inadequacy of Beaumont's explanation for social turmoil. Rather, it is to note that although Beaumont's *Crónica* glorifies the missionary evangelization of the sixteenth century, an unintended subtext of missionary failure—linked to a conscious recognition of the "need" for continual reconquest—permeates his text.

Thus, in 1541 the Indians burned the church in Guadalajara.[79] Despite this and other setbacks, missionaries continued to evangelize. Beaumont records missionary efforts around Lake Chapala, and in "the most remote missions of California, Monterrey, Sonora, Upper and Lower Pimerias, Tarahumara, Texas and others of this continent." He also discusses the roles of missionaries in Coronado's exploration of New Mexico and regions further to the north, and describes the famous wanderings of Cabeza de Vaca, from his shipwreck in Florida through what became the southeastern and southwestern United States. During all this activity, Beaumont records failure more than success, in terms of the goal of Christian conversion. He claims that the "Chichimecas," or seminomadic peoples of northern Mexico, "in order to revenge themselves of the injury that was done to their God and their sacrilegious rites, did whatever possible to destroy the temples dedicated to the true God." He lists several churches that Indians had burned, and referred to instances of executed priests.[80] All of these events demonstrate a point far from the author's intention, that is, the failures of the "spiritual conquest." Beaumont repeatedly produces evidence of these failures, in the sixteenth century and up until his day. As we shall see, he does so not only for "peripheral regions," but also for the "core" of Spain's colonial empire, in areas that had endured the most sustained missionary efforts for several centuries.

Beaumont blames the failures of the missionaries on the innate characteristics of indigenes. In his view, these colonial subjects frequently proved unable to rise above—or quickly returned to—their primitive state, linked

78. Ibid., 2:413.
79. Ibid., 428–29.
80. Ibid., 3:188, 1:503, 2:323, 3:15–17, 3:383, 419, 420.

to an essential identity deeply rooted in the indigenous past. Indeed, for a variety of reasons, Beaumont makes a considerable effort to discuss the origins of Indians. He describes the ancestors of New Spain's original inhabitants in the following terms: "These ancient inhabitants of New Spain were wild and maintained themselves with fruits and roots from the country; they did not live in society; they resided in the foothills and mountains, walked naked, slept on the ground, and had no type of public order." Despite what Beaumont viewed as the successes of Spanish colonialism—such as the fact that Spaniards "have aggregated innumerable Indians of the center of New Spain, Michoacán and Jalisco" and had achieved the "subjection of the inhabitants of New Galicia, New Mexico, Texas and other provinces"—he considered indigenous identity as essentially unchanged, from what he believed to be a prior primitive state. Beaumont rued missionary failures, claiming that the Indians "with ease have returned to their ancient barbarism."[81]

Most important, Beaumont believed this to be especially the case in Michoacán, among the Purhépecha, the region and people with whom he was most familiar. In a passage seeking to justify the sixteenth-century destruction of Purhépecha "paintings and other monuments," Beaumont comments on the Franciscan missionaries' need "to erase from the spirits of their natives this innate propensity, that they have still . . . for idolatry and superstition." Toward the end of his *Crónica*, he writes of the Church "still having much need of instruction, and of ministers, of whom there is still great lack in the clergy so as to finish to perfection this conversion of pagans, and of Tarascan [Purhépecha] Indians in the faith still very addicted to superstition and to idolatry."[82] Despite his glorification of sixteenth-century missionaries, Beaumont repeatedly indicates that the "spiritual conquest" was at best partial and incomplete, and at worst a failure.

A modern scholar might—and, indeed, should—view this acknowledgment of failure within Beaumont's discourse as a reflection of a profound indigenous struggle to maintain some type of spiritual autonomy, within an oppressive context.[83] Beaumont, however, had a decidedly different view of the nature of indigenous resistance, which he linked to what he considered to be the essentially barbaric identity of Indian peoples. For Beaumont,

81. Ibid., 1:511, 503.
82. Ibid., 3:384, 385, 407.
83. Sweet, "Ibero-American Frontier Mission."

Indian peoples most clearly expressed their "real" identity prior to European contact, and they lived in constant danger of a return to their previous condition, which he defined as barbaric.[84]

Beaumont's perception of the colonial Indian and his understanding of the Spanish Conquest as divinely ordained, continually challenged, and constantly re-created, led him to an extremely authoritarian appreciation of sixteenth-century missionary activities. In short, just as Beaumont—in the main—condoned the violence of the military conquest, so too did he condone the violence of the spiritual conquest. In the abstract, Beaumont could condemn "the incendiary hands of the ignorants" who had destroyed unspecified relics of indigenous cultures. However, he heartily approved of all the specific instances of missionary violence that he reviewed. The most vivid example of this tendency can be found in Beaumont's depiction of the founding of the Church in Michoacán, the core event of his entire narrative. Beaumont's account centers on the activities of Fray Martín de la Coruña who forcibly introduced Christianity to Tzintzuntzan, the primary urban center of the Purhépecha kingdom. Although Beaumont claimed this occurred in 1526, recent scholarship indicates that 1525 was a more likely year.[85]

Through an interpreter, Friar Martín had explained to the Indians "the abominable errors in which they had lived," the horrors of "the sacrifices that they made of men," and "the falseness of their idols and gods, that were no other thing but demonic instruments, images, and portraits." Fortunately, Friar Martín continued, "this great God and absolute Lord from his infinite compassion and mercy" had sent ministers, to free the Indians from "the slavery of the devil." At this point, claimed Beaumont, Friar Martín had won over the Purhépecha king, and many high-ranking Indians. In an extended passage, he describes what happened next: "He attained his fervent zeal to see the entire dominion of the demon demolished; . . . in presence of the populous city of Tzintzuntzan, and in the most numerous assembly of their worshipers, they themselves pounded and broke to bits all the idols that they made the object of their false religion."[86] While Beaumont portrays this as a step the Purhépecha took willingly, his text also indicates a more complex reality. Apparently, the Indians grieved to see their idols, still yet to

84. Beaumont, *Crónica de Michoacán*, 3:503.
85. Ibid., 1:514, 2:110; Warren, *Conquest of Michoacán*, 83.
86. Beaumont, *Crónica de Michoacán*, 2:111–12.

be ejected from their "obstinate heart," treated in such an injurious manner. Despite this grief, the destruction of the idols continued.

As Beaumont describes it, this missionary violence had the full support and participation of the Purhépecha. This was despite their acknowledged "grief," as well as their prior support for indigenous gods that, from Friar Martín's perspective, required the destruction in the first place. Beaumont's account continued:

> They were delivering to him all the idols of gold, silver, and precious stones, and breaking them with great contempt, making of them a great mountain, he hurled them in sight of everyone into the deepest of that lake, which is the same as that of Pátzcuaro; others of wood and of odd stones he compelled them to heap in the middle of the plaza, and on a great pyre he made the fire reduce them to ashes, so that these carried off by the wind struck them in the eyes, and removed them from their blindness in which they had kept themselves for such long years. The idols destroyed, he obtained that the same ones who before had built them with such elaborate effort, demolished them, cast those down, and in order that neither of them still remain a memorial, he made the flame consume, all the wood of the doorways, and roofs, and the stones that before served for sacrifices, then he could go freely introducing in their hearts the catechism, and by means of Holy Baptism, to join and to light that fire that Christ came to light on Earth.[87]

Thus, the missionaries burned the indigenous shrine at Tzintzuntzan. This was not the only—and in terms of human casualties certainly not the worst—incident of imperialist violence recorded by Beaumont. Nevertheless, it strikes at the very heart of his representation of the "spiritual conquest." Beaumont viewed the destruction at Tzintzuntzan as justified, even divinely ordained, since to establish Christianity—in its Spanish colonial Roman Catholic variant—it was necessary to destroy, utterly, all vestiges of Purhépecha religion. Then, and only then, could Friar Martín "light that fire that Christ came to light on Earth."

87. Ibid., 112.

Conquests of fire, and conquests of blood. For Beaumont, there were many conquests, rooted in the Iberian past and extending into his American present. They occurred in different regions—Granada, different Caribbean islands, central Mexico, and throughout the western and northern provinces—at different times, from the end of the fifteenth century to the time of the writing of his *Crónica*. However, one feature remained the same. Spanish colonialism triumphed, or would inevitably triumph, because Beaumont believed a particular set of human, social, and historical relationships had been divinely ordained.[88] Yet, within this fervent evangelical discourse, one can note a persistent, unintended subtext of rejection, resistance, and struggle. According to Beaumont, the Purhépecha had persisted in their "superstition and idolatry" until his era.[89] Indeed, Friar Martín's fiery introduction did not even prevent the Purhépecha from rejecting him, despite their apparent earlier acceptance. As Beaumont recorded, the Purhépecha forced the missionaries to abandon their initial evangelization effort, and leave the region.

For once, Beaumont did not place the blame for this rejection on the Indians. Rather, he blamed the abuses of the conquistador Nuño de Guzmán.[90] While celebrating the role of missionaries and evangelization as ideological justification for imperialism, Beaumont condemned the failures of individual conquistadors, and the incapacities of indigenes. This brings us to different, though related, aspects of his work.

Conquerors and Conquered

"The first concern of Cortés was to give thanks to God, purifying the city with great fires, so as to take away the pestilence of the corpses that they had interred in the most enormous piles in their houses."[91] The spiritual and military conquests must be considered as part of the same social process, the founding of the Spanish colonial order. Beaumont recognized this basic fact,

88. Though contested, this belief would continue to exist through the late twentieth century. For an account of a more recent celebration of the Spanish Conquest, and the twentieth-century controversy surrounding it, see Howard W. French, "Dissent Shadows Pope on His Visit," *New York Times*, October 14, 1992, A15.

89. Beaumont, *Crónica de Michoacán*, 3:407.

90. Ibid., 2:174.

91. Ibid., 1:470.

as did Cortés and the other Spanish conquistadores. A belief in divine sanction profoundly influenced colonial discourse throughout the centuries of European imperialism. Beaumont adhered to this vision, and it influenced all aspects of his *Crónica*. Nevertheless, Beaumont's actual practice in elaborating this belief—the motifs he developed through engagement with the historical record—displayed a certain ambiguity, rooted in the paradoxes of colonial rule itself.

Although Beaumont mentioned abuses by some missionaries, his remarks in this regard can be characterized, easily, as peripheral and isolated. This was not the case for his treatment of Spanish conquistadores, and for the Indian populations they conquered. In these areas, Beaumont exalted and condemned, indicating a contradictory tension in his own thought that can be observed throughout Spanish colonial historiography. Beaumont's tendency to exalt, and condemn, both conquerors and the conquered indicates complicated social realities that in practice mediated relationships of power in Spanish colonial society. At these points in the *Crónica*, we can discern divisions among the ruling elite—and even the distant reflection of the struggles of the dispossessed—that influenced the daily practice of social life under Spanish colonialism. Indeed, these types of tensions can be noted in most colonial texts, even those, like Beaumont's *Crónica*, marked by extreme ethnocentrism.

González has noted, accurately, that for the most part Beaumont's *Crónica* excludes the history and perspectives of indigenous peoples.[92] Beaumont himself admitted difficulty in obtaining information about the Indian population. As he describes it, "these poor ones" viewed inquiries about the past suspiciously, believing that "the end is to despoil them of their lands."[93] It would be mistaken to think that these perspectives can be recovered through a reading of Beaumont's *Crónica*. Nevertheless, much can be gained by examining Beaumont's representation of those he portrays as conquered, as well as conquerors, because it allows us to examine contradictions within colonial discourse.[94]

Beaumont explained examples of colonial brutality as aberrations, a problem of subordinates pursuing their own goals at the expense of the well-

92. González, "Viaje," 66.
93. Beaumont, *Crónica de Michoacán*, 1:6.
94. Spivak, "Can the Subaltern Speak?" 308; Pierre Bourdieu, *The Logic of Practice*, trans. Richard Nice (Stanford, Calif., 1990), 20.

intentioned Spanish Crown. He tended to divide conquistadores simply into "good" and "bad" groups. For Beaumont, a "good" conquistador implemented the Crown's just decrees, while loyally gaining new lands and peoples for the "spiritual conquest." A "bad" conquistador abused his power—entrusted in him by the king, and ultimately by God—for personal gain. His most prominent examples of the former were Christopher Columbus and Hernán Cortés, while Nuño de Guzmán fell into the latter category. Beaumont's focus upon these three individuals demonstrates, once again, his fundamental preoccupation with Franciscan concerns. Columbus and Cortés, whom he exalts, enjoyed particularly close relationships with the Franciscan missionaries engaged in the initial evangelization of New Spain.[95] Nuño de Guzmán, whom he condemns, engaged in legendary conflicts with Cortés, Mexico's first bishop the Franciscan Juan de Zumárraga, and with most of the Franciscan order in Mexico.[96] While Beaumont discusses other conquistadores, his descriptions fall within the boundaries established in his presentation of these three major figures.

Beaumont's portrayal of the conquistadores—and his construction of "good" and "bad" conquerors—is an attempt to reconcile his belief in the Spanish Conquest as an expression of God's will, with the realities of indigenous resistance, and the centrality of violence in establishing colonial rule. Thus, Beaumont presents Columbus as "enlightened without doubt from heaven," "the most skillful sailor of Europe," an "extraordinary man."[97] After noting that Columbus died in poverty, enjoying neither the fame nor the wealth Beaumont believed he deserved, he comments that "Don Christopher Columbus certainly merits the greatest eulogies, for having undertaken the discovery of the New World, from which resulted the conversion of innumerable souls to the faith of Jesus Christ, and the so great increase of the Catholic kingdoms."[98] Beaumont explicitly defines his discussion of Columbus—which occupies a substantial portion of the *Aparato*—as a defense, from critics of Columbus in the conquest era, and from the spreaders in late colonial times of what has come to be known as the "Black Legend."[99] To defend Columbus, Beaumont employs a process of rejection

95. Phelan, *Millennial Kingdom*, 19, 31–34.
96. Liss, *Mexico Under Spain*, 51, 77–79.
97. Beaumont, *Crónica de Michoacán*, 1:36, 20, 21.
98. Ibid., 221.
99. Ibid., 21, 118.

through partial incorporation. That is, he concedes that atrocities occurred during the initial conquest of the Caribbean, but he portrays these atrocities as aberrations, sharply contradicted by the behavior of Columbus, who for Beaumont manifested the "true" nature of Spanish colonialism.

My purpose here is not to expose how Beaumont's portrayals of Columbus, Cortés, Guzmán, and other conquistadores varied from what "really happened," although they are demonstrably false, and this distinction matters. Rather, I seek to demonstrate an explanatory strategy utilized by a late colonial elite to render the massive violence of the Conquest acceptable, primarily to an audience of his peers. Thus, Beaumont recognized that Spanish conquistadores raped indigenous women, and abused their power in other ways. In his discussion of why the cacique Guarionex rejected Spanish missionaries, after initially appearing to welcome them, Beaumont spoke of "the brutal action of one of our own, who abused by force his beloved wife, after having her violently removed from him, and the tyrannical proceeding of some Castilians with his Indian vassals." Beaumont's description of the rape of Guarionex's wife contrasts sharply with his description of the behavior of Columbus. According to Beaumont, upon arriving at Hispaniola, Spanish soldiers captured an Indian woman, whom they delivered to Columbus. At this point, Columbus "presented her many bells and strings of glass beads; he ordered her to put on an undergarment and other women's trinkets and after having hugged her, giving her many little things and without doing her any harm, he sent her directly to her dwelling."[100] This pattern of distinguishing the "good" conquistador Columbus, exemplar of royal and divine intention, from other "bad" conquistadores, continued throughout Beaumont's discussion of the Spanish Conquest in the Caribbean.

Beaumont explicitly links Columbus to what he perceived as Spain's benign civilizing mission, defined as royal ambition and divine will. He describes the situation on the eve of the second voyage of Columbus in the following terms: "Everything being arranged, and the admiral instructed of the particular rule that his superiors intimated to him, that the Indians should be well treated and with gifts and good works attracted to our holy faith and that if the Castilians treat them poorly, they ought be severely punished." Of course, the almost total extinction of Caribbean Indian populations during

100. Ibid., 188, 45.

the first generations of colonial rule left a historical legacy difficult for any partisan of Spanish colonialism to deny. Beaumont comments on this population decline in a manner harshly critical of some conquistadores. He states: "In the *Aparato* to this history I have touched on the so barbarous conduct of the first conquistadores, that without distinction, and without reparation, finished off the Indians of the Indies."[101] Although he acknowledges that epidemics played a part in this decline, he attributes the spread of disease to the disruption of indigenous communities through warfare. He notes that many Spaniards became infuriated at the resistance they found in their "new vassals," whom they ruthlessly repressed.[102] Beaumont recognizes that "abandoning themselves to all types of licentious military acts," Spanish soldiers committed "the most excessive violent acts" with the islanders.[103] Indeed, Beaumont concludes his discussion of the initial Spanish invasion of the Caribbean by reproducing part of the famous sermon of Antonio de Montesinos, given in 1511 in Santo Domingo.

In this sermon, Montesinos confronted an audience of conquistadores and colonial officials. He claimed that "a conduct so foreign and so contrary to the spirit of Christianity had been the cause that already a million men had perished."[104] Montesinos went on to argue that the Spaniards, through greed, had betrayed any rightful claim they might have had to the "New World." Beaumont presented Montesinos's condemnation as just, an accurate comment on Spanish failures. However, he did not believe that the issue of Spanish atrocities—even when defined as aberrations, instead of as fundamental to the establishment of colonial authority—merited sustained attention, and did not probe them in any depth. As he put it: "I will not relate here their cruelties, detested by their own nation." These cruelties were "detested by their own nation" at home, and in the field by Columbus, whom Beaumont portrays as the embodiment of Spanish colonial benevolence. Beaumont claims that "the virtuous Columbus cried out uselessly against those horrors."[105] Thus, for Beaumont Columbus maintained the integrity of Spain's divinely sanctioned mission, despite the havoc wrought by his fellow explorers and conquistadors.

101. Ibid., 1:89, 2:342.
102. Ibid., 1:113–14.
103. Ibid., 105.
104. Ibid., 264.
105. Ibid., 113, 114.

Hernán Cortés plays a similar role in Beaumont's discussion of the first generation of Spanish colonialism in Mexico. Beaumont's most revealing characterizations of Cortés come late in the text—long after his discussion of the Conquest itself—when he notes the occasion of Cortés's death. As Beaumont portrays it:

> This hero finished the glorious course of his life, at sixty-two years of age, having gained the notable surname Captain, and of the most famous that the centuries relate. Examining the singular events of the Conquest of Mexico, that he led with dexterity as far as to leave almost all of New Spain discovered, and subject to his sovereign, one will recognize, his military skill, his magnanimity, his valor, and loyalty, and, in the end, his great piety so that his virtuous actions come to be his most truthful eulogy.

The entire occasion of the death of Cortés—as represented by Beaumont—stands as a remarkable affirmation of creole identity, the fusion of the spiritual and military conquests, and the bond between ecclesiastical and civil authority under Spanish colonialism. As Beaumont portrays it:

> His body was carried to internment with great pomp, and universal grief from all of Spain, accompanied by many nobleman of the first distinction, by the venerable clergy, and religious, to the chapel of Medina-Sydonia, and some time [having] passed, his bones were brought to New Spain, and placed, first, in a noble tomb of the monastery of Our Father Saint Francis of Texcoco, and in the year of 1619, were deposited in the main altar of the great convent of Saint Francis, of Mexico, accompanied, and with much authority of the Knighthood, and of the entire nobility of that great city, as also of her lord Archbishop, and religious orders, with the pomp and ostentation that corresponds to a captain general, and notable conquistador, of these vast dominions of New Spain.[106]

Beaumont prefaces his discussion of Cortés, and the Spanish Conquest of Mexico, by noting that "perhaps of no other conquistador of the New World

106. Ibid., 3:184.

has such good and such bad been said."[107] However, his actual portrayal of the Conquest is curiously silent on issues that might have led to such contradictory interpretations. Instead, Beaumont focuses on the military narrative of battles, defeats, and victory that has served as the story of the Spanish Conquest, from Bernal Díaz del Castillo through Prescott into modern historiography.

Beaumont did recognize, indirectly, the inherent violence of this entire process. For example, he speaks of "our Spaniards" committing "great slaughters," at times recognizing some priestly Spanish dissent, while also viewing the large numbers of Indians killed—in contrast to few Spanish casualties—as further evidence of God's will.[108] However, he persists in describing the Conquest as "the most just and holy undertaking." He warns that "these passionate and poorly founded judgments of some authors ought to be heard with contempt, who behold with [a] frown the ease with which the great work of the Conquest of the Indies was finished, and of New Spain in particular, being evident that in this especially is the finger of God acknowledged, with evidence." "In the end," Beaumont argues, "they cannot deny that with these instruments was obtained the conversion of that paganism," a statement which could be turned, ironically, on Beaumont himself.[109] In Beaumont's *Crónica*, the condemnation of atrocities—generally viewed as aberrations, although with an occasional recognition of their functional nature—occurs only with his portrayal of other conquistadores. Foremost among these was Nuño Beltrán de Guzmán, the infamous conqueror of western Mexico, whom Beaumont characterizes as "of a cruel heart."[110]

Beaumont frames his condemnation of Guzmán in terms of his legendary conflict with the Franciscans. Beaumont writes of Guzmán's "transit through this region of Michoacán, where he did so many excesses of cruelty, that he was the principal cause of the aversion of the natives to the soft yoke of the Gospel." Beaumont claims that Guzmán "unjustly" executed the Cazonci, ruler of the Purhépecha, giving him an "atrocious death," despite Franciscan attempts to intervene.[111] He condemns "the furor of Guzmán,"

107. Ibid., 1:337.
108. Ibid., 372, 374, 397, 398, 402, 405.
109. Ibid., 406.
110. Ibid., 2:334.
111. Ibid., 177, 188, 333.

and the atrocities committed during the conquest of Jalisco. According to Beaumont, and the sources he utilized, these included summary executions, torture, the sacking and burning of villages to the ground, and the branding of thousands of Indians as slaves.[112] However, even for Guzmán, whom he characterizes as viciously abusive of power, Beaumont felt compelled to point out that "it cannot be denied, that by his good craftiness and industry was obtained the acquisition, conservation, and advancement of the most vast territories."[113] Given the weight of divine sanction within colonial discourse, Beaumont had a relatively easy task rendering acceptable even acts he initially defined as most heinous crimes.

In his discussion of Cortés, Beaumont argues that the supposed ease of the Conquest of Mexico stands as the strongest proof of this event's divine support. He tends to reproduce—quite mechanically—those portions of the historical record which reinforce this belief. Of course, the historical record itself was a product of colonial social relationships, permeated by the conscious biases and implicit assumptions of those holding power. In the study of Spanish colonialism, the most enduring assumption built into the historical record is the designation of the colonial order—indeed, America itself—as an exclusively European creation. One need not believe, as Beaumont did, that a European-dominated colonial order expressed God's will, to reproduce this assumption.[114] Nevertheless the *Crónica* is permeated by an unintended subtext of indigenous rejection, which led Beaumont to portray the Conquest as essentially unfinished business. This, then, is the great contradiction in Beaumont's depiction of indigenous peoples, which entirely destabilizes his representation of the Spanish Conquest.

Evangelizations and Failures

Beaumont's understanding of "Indians," as well as of racially mixed peoples, is marked by a profound suspicion indicative of a betrayed paternalism, and perhaps bordering on hatred. His late-colonial views contrast with the reformist hopes of the first generation of Spanish missionaries. Thus Beaumont

112. Ibid., 198–206.
113. Ibid., 334.
114. The classic statement of this position is Edmundo O'Gorman, *The Invention of America* (Bloomington, Ind., 1961).

reproduced a letter from Fray Martín de Valencia from June of 1531, in which Fray Martín spoke of the "honesty" and "womanly shame" naturally possessed by Indian women.[115] Nevertheless, in those portions of the text that he claimed as most authentically his, he preferred to portray indigenous women as conspiring to infect Spaniards with syphilis. His depiction of the "poor Indians" of the Caribbean living "in their simplicity" showed a faint glimmer of the paternalism associated with European conceptions of the "Noble Savage." However, his characterization of the same Indians as capable of refusing to plant crops in the hope of starving out occupying Spaniards betrayed the hard-edged vision of a late colonial elite.[116] Indeed, while Beaumont shared with other creole and baroque authors a tendency to glorify the indigenous past—thus heightening the colonial achievement—he also made a considerable effort to demonstrate what he believed to be the original, barbaric roots of Indian peoples. In a passage once again marked by scientific pretensions, he claimed that they were descendants of the "Tartars."[117] It is at the nexus between Beaumont's belief in the Conquest as divinely ordained, and his perception of indigenous peoples as prone to relapses into an essentially "barbaric" identity that his representation of the "spiritual conquest" falls apart. For relapse into barbarism was how Beaumont explained missionary failures to himself.

Conclusion

Fr. Pablo Beaumont's *Crónica* is an enormous, and enormously rich, source of information about religion, politics, and history in colonial Mexico. For the most part, scholars have utilized the *Crónica* as a primary source detailing the sixteenth-century history of missionaries in western Mexico. Here I have taken a different approach, interpreting the *Crónica* historically, as a text produced by a late colonial elite. Viewed in this light, Beaumont's

115. Beaumont, *Crónica de Michoacán*, 2:150.
116. Ibid., 112–13, 153.
117. Ibid., 40–44, 412–13, 480–97. On the exaltation of the past in creole authors, and the baroque, see Pagden, *Spanish Imperialism*, 95–103; Anthony Pagden and Nicholas Canny, *Colonial Identity in the Atlantic World, 1500–1800* (Princeton, 1987), 67; and Brading, *The First America*. On European searches for indigenous "origins," see Michael T. Ryan, "Assimilating New Worlds in the Sixteenth and Seventeenth Centuries," *Comparative Studies in Society and History* 23, no. 4 (October 1981): 519–38.

Crónica is an example of conservative creole ideology, one with deep roots in the colonial experience and undergoing substantial redefinition at the end of the eighteenth century. In its fusion of baroque and Enlightenment tendencies, this work can also be considered to be an example of Spanish colonial historiography as incipient American literature, albeit in a rough and incomplete form. It is also an elaborate exercise rendering the violence necessary to establish and maintain a colonial order acceptable for colonial elites, by presumably proving—"with evidence," as Beaumont puts it during his discussion of the ease of the Conquest of Mexico—that the entire process had been divinely ordained.

Beaumont did not consciously intend to reproduce evidence of the centrality of violence to the colonial project. His intent was to defend colonial missionary history as an expression of God's will, and in so doing to defend the privileges granted to the missionary orders during the sixteenth century. Given that this history was inextricably linked to Spanish colonialism, his work inevitably stood as a defense of the Spanish Conquest, and the social order that followed it. He exalted indigenous civilizations, to render more epic the missionary efforts at evangelization. He conceded indigenous resistance to justify Spanish repression. Nevertheless, a persistent, unintended subtext of indigenous rejection—which calls into question his entire representation of the Spanish Conquest itself—permeates his *Crónica*.

A growing body of historical and anthropological literature has called into question the very notion of a "spiritual conquest" in the sixteenth century.[118] This scholarship emphasizes that the indigenous reception and redefinition of Christian ideology always involved substantial cultural autonomy, creativity, and resilience. This was an active process that took place over centuries, rather than one generation. It involved significant resistance as well as

118. The classic treatment of the sixteenth-century "spiritual conquest" was Robert Ricard's *The Spiritual Conquest of Mexico*. The death knell for Ricard's interpretation was sounded in another classic, Charles Gibson's *The Aztecs Under Spanish Rule* (Stanford, Calif., 1964). In recent years, the full implications of Gibson's work have been realized and transcended by a number of other scholars. See James Lockhart, *The Nahuas After the Conquest* (Stanford, Calif., 1992), 203–60, and *Nahuas and Spaniards* (Stanford, Calif., 1991), 159–200; Jorge Klor de Alva, "Spiritual Conflict and Accommodation in New Spain: Toward a Typology of Aztec Responses to Christianity," in *The Inca and Aztec States, 1400–1800:* Anthropology and History, ed. George A. Collier, Renato I. Rosaldo, and John D. Wirth (New York, 1982), 345–66, and "Spiritual Warfare in Mexico: Christianity and the Aztecs" (Ph.D. diss., University of California, Santa Cruz, 1980); Clendinnen, *Ambivalent Conquests;* and MacCormack, *Religion in the Andes.* A useful comparative work is Rafael's *Contracting Colonialism* (Ithaca, N.Y., 1988).

accommodation and historical change for all those involved in the colonial equation. More than two centuries after its composition, Beaumont's *Crónica* now appears to be a remarkably ethnocentric text, one that considers the fact that the Spanish Conquest was divinely ordained to be a truth beyond dispute. Ironically, Beaumont's recognition of the continuing need for missionary activities—not only on the frontier, but also in regions where missionaries had been present for centuries—undermines this "truth," which for him was self-evident.

5

REMEMBERING TATA VASCO

It is satisfactory for the archdiocese of Don Vasco, at the completion of four hundred and fifty years of life, to rely upon more than a dozen native priests from the Pur[h]épecha indigenous communities, several of them working among their people, thus following the example of our first bishop, whose sowing continues giving its fruits.

—Pastoral message of the archbishop of Morelia, in *Vasco de Quiroga y Obispado de Michoacán*

It has been said, with reason, that Don Vasco was not a communist, but with the same reason it could be affirmed that if Don Vasco existed now, he would be accused of being one.

—Alfonso Caso, 1965

The voluminous secondary literature tells one less about Quiroga than about the mentality of commentators.

—Ross Dealy, 1976

Of all those involved in the first generation of Spanish colonialism in Michoacán, Vasco de Quiroga is the most widely revered in contemporary Mexico.[1] He is remembered, across many social and ideological divides, for the founding of communal villages among the "Indians" in a world he believed to be new. In this chapter I trace the emergence and transformation of the legendary Vasco de Quiroga, from the "good *encomendero*" of the sixteenth century into the humanist icon of today. Here I contend that the traditional image of Vasco de Quiroga as a saintly

1. On the contemporary salience of the mythic figure, see Francisco de Miranda, "Vasco de Quiroga, artifice humanista de Michoacán," in Herrejón, *Humanismo y ciencia,* 131–49.

father figure, who understood and was beloved by his Indian charges, is an after-the-fact reconstruction, rooted more in colonial discourse, creole perceptions, and the formation of modern Mexican nationalism than the sixteenth-century past.[2]

This investigation extends my analysis of Michoacán's conquest historiography into the nineteenth and twentieth centuries. In these eras Vasco de Quiroga received more favorable and extensive treatment than he did in Beaumont's *Crónica*. As we shall see, Vasco de Quiroga has been celebrated as a pragmatic social reformer across a remarkably wide ideological spectrum in Mexico, throughout Latin America, and beyond. For example, the Mexican historians Silvio Zavala and Carlos Pereyra, and the Chilean woman of letters Gabriela Mistral, wrote favorably about his intellectual debts to Thomas More's *Utopia* and his supposed reorganization of regional craft production.[3] Fintan B. (J. Benedict) Warren, a historian from the United States, set out to recover the history of the village-hospitals attributed to Quiroga's evangelical efforts. In 1963 Warren claimed that "the traditional image of Quiroga is that of a very fatherly and saintly man, a man with a far-reaching love for the poor and oppressed, the miserable and defenseless. This image can be verified from his written works (e.g. the 'Información en Derecho,' the 'Reglas y ordenanzas para los hospitales de Santa Fe,' the 'Testamento') as well as from the actual works of charity for which his name is remembered."[4] In 1984, Warren qualified this portrayal somewhat by noting Quiroga's role in censuring the Franciscan linguist Maturino Gilberti, although he

2. A crucial moment in the elaboration of the legend was the 1766 appearance of Juan José Moreno's *Fragmentos*. Brading, *Church and State in Bourbon Mexico*, 38; Francisco Miranda, "Vasco de Quiroga," 148.

3. The classic work of Silvio Zavala is brought together in *Recuerdo de Vasco de Quiroga*. On Mistral and Pereyra, see José Zavala Paz, *D. Vasco de Quiroga* (Morelia, Mexico, 1964), 76–77. The precise influence of Vasco de Quiroga and other Spanish colonials on preexisting craft production remains disputed, although multiple influences are evident. See García Canclini, *Hybrid Cultures*, 144, 152–70, and *Las culturas populares en el capitalismo* (Havana, 1982), 63, 82; Becker, *Setting the Virgin on Fire*, 112–13; R. A. M. Van Zantwijk, *Servants of the Saints* (Assen, Netherlands, 1967), 64–66; George M. Foster, *Empire's Children*, asst. by Gabriel Ospina (Washington, D.C., 1948), 17–18, and *Tzintzuntzan* (Boston, 1967), 24; Pedro Carrasco, *Tarascan Folk Religion* (New Orleans, 1952), 26–29; and Robert C. West, *Cultural Geography of the Modern Tarascan Area* (Washington, D.C., 1948), 57.

4. Warren, *Vasco de Quiroga*, 24.

stopped short of a sustained investigation of the authoritarian aspects of Quiroga's thought and practice.[5]

Heroic definitions of Don Vasco's activities continue to surface in current scholarship. Writing in the mid-1980s, Eduardo Galeano looked back on Don Vasco as a "dreamer who riveted his eyes on a hallucination to see beyond the time of infamy."[6] In 1990, Carlos Fuentes stressed his importance as an example for an increasingly troubled Mexico, noting that he "did not come to denounce, but to transform utopia in history."[7] In Spain, also in the early 1990s, Francisco Martín Hernández claimed that "Don Vasco was not only the great protector of the Indians, but their untiring apostle from the very moment that he arrived on American soil." Paz Serrano Gassent commented that he currently is "well regarded as founder of the State, as protector and preserver of indigenous life."[8] More than four centuries after his death, Vasco de Quiroga has proven to be remarkably enduring as an attractive symbol of humanitarian reformism and utopian hope.

There is nothing innately objectionable—and, indeed, much to be admired—in the values that many have attributed to Vasco de Quiroga. Nevertheless, as we have seen, our knowledge of his activities rests on a slender documentary base capable of sustaining multiple readings, some of which challenge our basic assumptions about him. The mythic Vasco de Quiroga owes as much to the needs of various "historical presents" as he does to the real history of the sixteenth century. As Chapter 5 seeks to demonstrate, one can make this claim in a spirit of open-ended dialogue, without fixing past or present meanings in an essentialist way.

Of Buildings and Bones

Today, Vasco de Quiroga's bones can be found in La Basílica de Pátzcuaro, in a new mausoleum constructed in 1990. They have been placed in an urn

5. See J. Benedict Warren, "Los estudios linguisticos en Michoacán en el siglo XVI: Una expresión del humanismo cristiano," in Herrejón, *Humanismo y ciencia*, 113–24, esp. 119. A recent study that does so is Verastíque's *Michoacán and Eden*, esp. 94, 107–9, 139.

6. Eduardo Galeano, *Memory of Fire*, vol. 1, *Genesis*, trans. Cedric Belfrage (New York, 1985), 132.

7. Carlos Fuentes, *Valiente mundo nuevo* (Madrid, 1990), 64. Fuentes misidentifies Quiroga as a Dominican. It should also be noted that he was not a Franciscan, as claimed in Burkholder and Johnson, *Colonial Latin America*, 86, and Pagden, *Uncertainties of Empire*, xii.

8. Martín Hernández, *Don Vasco de Quiroga*, 19; Quiroga, *La utopía en América*, 44.

REFLECTIONS

located in the hollow of a Tuscan pedestal that serves as a foundation for his tomb. On the four sides of the pedestal, imprinted on plates of copper, are four coats of arms: those of Don Vasco and the cities of Tzintzuntzan, Pátzcuaro, and Valladolid-Morelia.[9] The juxtaposition of these coats of arms indicates the honorable status of Vasco de Quiroga, and his contribution to the forging of a new culture in Michoacán: the bringing together of Tzintzuntzan, the urban center of the Purhépecha kingdom; Pátzcuaro, the site where he chose to implement his vision of a reformed church under firm sixteenth-century Castilian Catholic tutelage; and Vallodolid-Morelia, from 1580 on the center of church and state administration and the regional Spanish presence.[10] Don Vasco's remains are now situated between an exalted indigenous past and the birth of a mestizo nation, to be viewed as a uniquely Mexican example of early modern Christian humanism.

Vasco de Quiroga's bones have been moved before, and the various locales of their public display reveal much about the construction of his mythic image.[11] The reinterring of Vasco de Quiroga's remains in 1990 was preceded by a long campaign to find a burial site "worthy of the virtues and memory of so illustrious [a] man" under way by 1940.[12] In that same year, the international Indigenist Congress met in Pátzcuaro, shortly after the 1938 founding of the Regional Museum of Popular Arts and Industries in the same city. These were critical moments in the elaboration of a modern, postrevolutionary Mexican national identity, a process consolidated during the era of President Lázaro Cárdenas (1934–40), one of the leading sons of the state of Michoacán.[13] Interest in Vasco de Quiroga after the revolution was remarkable at least in part because recognition of his historical significance was shared by the largely anticlerical intelligentsia of the newly stabilized ruling party, as well as by practicing

9. A detailed description is provided in Martín Hernández, *Don Vasco de Quiroga,* 261.
10. On the historical and specifically Castilian nature of early colonial Catholicism in Mexico, see Poole, *Our Lady of Guadalupe,* 19.
11. For a discussion of the enduring importance of material culture, and specifically architecture, in recalling the Latin American past, see Eric Van Young, "Material Life," in *The Countryside in Colonial Latin America,* ed. Louisa Schell Hoberman and Susan Midgen Socolow (Albuquerque, 1996) 49–74, esp. 69–71.
12. Toussaint, *Pátzcuaro,* xii, 126.
13. William Rowe and Vivian Schelling, *Memory and Modernity* (London, 1991), 65; García Canclini, *Las culturas,* 76; Becker, *Setting the Virgin on Fire,* 159.

Catholics, many of whom were opponents of the regime.[14] Indeed, one could argue that Don Vasco's posthumous ability to straddle the ideological divides that frame understandings of the Mexican past has been his most significant legacy.

From the early 1940s on, Vasco de Quiroga's bones were kept in a safe in the baptistery of the basilica of Pátzcuaro.[15] This building's initial construction is attributed to Don Vasco's desire for a cathedral that would demonstrate the magnificence of his reformed Church. The architect Toribio de Alcaraz drew up the original design between 1545 and 1547. It called for a central nave, with five adjoining structures. The colonial art historian Mina Ramírez Montes suggests that these may have been intended for each of the four barrios of indigenes in Pátzcuaro, along with a separate but adjoining wing for Spaniards.[16] In viewing colonial religious architecture, and reflecting upon sixteenth-century labor conditions, this observer at least is reminded of Walter Benjamin's famous aphorism: "There is no document of civilization which is not at the same time a document of barbarism."[17] As planned, Don Vasco's cathedral would have rivaled the largest edifices known to sixteenth-century Mexico. Many of his contemporaries considered the project a grandiose monument to his ambition, one that wasted resources and abused workers. These complaints should not be dismissed simply as a reflection of the Spanish factional politics of the time, although that was certainly a factor. The Indians of Tzintzuntzan formally protested the labor drafts and tribute required for the project, and in 1555 Viceroy Luis de Velasco relieved them of this duty.[18]

In the end, Vasco de Quiroga died before the building was completed, although the single nave constructed would be designated as the cathedral from 1573—with the arrival of the Jesuits in Pátzcuaro—until 1580. At this time, the center of colonial administration in Michoacán—including

14. For an example of Vasco de Quiroga's appeal drawn from popular culture, and a nuanced discussion of Cárdenismo in Michoacán, see Becker, *Setting the Virgin on Fire*, 141. Toussaint, *Pátzcuaro*, an artifact of this era, also provides evidence for this position; see xi–xii, 126. On the Cárdenas era in Mexico, see Nora Hamilton, *The Limits of State Autonomy* (Princeton, 1982).

15. Toussaint, *Pátzcuaro*, 126.

16. Ibid., 107–9, 126; Ramírez Montes, *La catedral*, 63–100, esp. 67.

17. Walter Benjamin, *Illuminations*, ed. Hannah Arendt and trans. Harry Zohn (New York, 1968), 256.

18. Ramírez Montes, *La catedral*, 80–85; Toussaint, *Pátzcuaro*, 108.

Church-sponsored institutions such as the cathedral and the Colegio de San Nicolas—was moved to the "Spanish" town of Valladolid, renamed Morelia in 1826 after José María Morelos, leader of the popular insurgency during the wars for Mexican Independence.[19] The building continued to function as a parish church, and eventually served as a sanctuary and collegiate chapel. The structure itself was added to and substantially transformed over time, with major modifications—walls built and then improved, additional towers added, and the interior redesigned—beginning in the mid-eighteenth century. In the nineteenth century, a series of earthquakes—on March 25, 1806, November 23, 1837, and April 7 and 10, 1845—effectively destroyed it; in 1867, during the French Intervention, crowds under the command of General Régules burned what was left. By the twentieth century, the only part remaining that could plausibly date from the sixteenth century was a winding staircase in the interior. The 1924 designation of the building as a basilica concluded a rehabilitation effort that began in 1893 under the Most Illustrious Archbishop of Michoacán, Don José Ignacio Arciga. In 1899, the edifice received its modern decoration, and on December 8 of that year the Imagen de Nuestra Señora de la Salud, patroness of Don Vasco's utopian communities, was transferred to this site.[20] In the early 1940s, Don Vasco's bones were also placed in the basilica, and there they stayed until their reinterring in 1990.[21]

Prior to this time, his "precious remains" had been stored in a building known as the Colegio de la Compañia de Jesus, or Jesuit College, in reference to its colonial function.[22] According to local tradition, Vasco de Quiroga had built this building originally by around 1540, on one of the

19. Francisco Miranda, *Don Vasco de Quiroga*, 223–27; Peter Gerhard, *A Guide to the Historical Geography of New Spain* (Norman, Okla., 1993), 350; Lynch, *Spanish American Revolutions*, 306–19.

20. Toussaint, *Pátzcuaro*, 107–12. On the importance of Marian devotion in regional popular culture, see Becker, *Setting the Virgin on Fire*, 10–38. Brading, *Church and State in Bourbon Mexico*, 97, notes a "flood-tide" of women's vocations in the late nineteenth century. For wider contextual setting, see Silvia Marina Arrom, *The Women of Mexico City, 1790–1857* (Stanford, Calif., 1985), 259–68.

21. Toussaint, *Pátzcuaro*, 123–26. Benjamin Jarnes's account, also published in 1942, makes no mention of the transfer to the Basilica, locating the remains instead in the Colegio de la Compañia. This leads me to conclude that they were moved sometime in 1942. See Benjamin Jarnes, *Don Vasco de Quiroga, obispo de utopia* (Mexico City, 1942), 311.

22. Nicolás León, *El ylmo. señor Don Vasco de Quiroga primer obispo de Michoacán* (Morelia, Mexico, 1903), 138, 142.

most important sites of prehispanic worship. It served as his church while he awaited completion of his cathedral. After Don Vasco's death in 1565, his corpse was placed in a niche to the right of the presbytery, where it remained until 1897, undisturbed for three hundred and thirty-two years.[23] When the Jesuits arrived in Michoacán, the *cabildo* or municipal authority of Pátzcuaro ceded them the building. Despite the transfer of ecclesiastical institutions to Valladolid in 1580, they managed the property as a local college until 1767, when the Bourbon monarchy expelled them from the Spanish colonies. From 1767 until 1854, the "iglesia de la Compañía" was used for primary education, and in 1854 it passed from clerical control.[24]

Nicolás León, resident of Michoacán and a famous Porfirian intellectual, and "one of Mexico's greatest anthropologists and bibliographers,"[25] notes, in his 1903 biography of Vasco de Quiroga, that by 1897 the tomb was in a state of "abandon and uncleanliness." León provides a detailed description of the public ceremonial surrounding the 1897 refurbishment of this site, another project sponsored by Archbishop Arciga. He repeatedly stressed that this effort brought together "individuals of all the classes" with the region's indigenous peoples, perhaps reflecting late-nineteenth and early-twentieth-century Catholic concern for social cohesion as well as Don Vasco's symbolic utility for that era's definitions of Mexican national identity.[26] The culmination of the event was the placement of the bones in a new crypt in the same building, and the installation of an inscribed marble slab testifying to the "greatness of our first bishop and the disinterested piety of an illustrious successor."[27] There they remained throughout the first four decades of the twentieth century, amidst the turmoil unleashed by the revolution and the consolidation of the postrevolutionary state.

León's biography relies heavily on Juan José Moreno's earlier work (1766), and like Moreno he complains about a lack of documentation detail-

23. Jarnes, *Don Vasco*, 311; León, *El ylmo. señor*, 138.

24. Toussaint, *Pátzcuaro*, 123–26.

25. "Porfirian" refers to the era of the authoritarian ruler Porfirio Díaz (1876–1910). See Michael C. Meyer and William Sherman, *The Course of Mexican History* (Oxford, 1991), 466–79, and Donald D. Brand, *Quiroga: A Mexican Municipio*, asst. José Corona Nuñez (Washington, D.C., 1951), 6.

26. León, *El ylmo. señor*, 127, 138–46; Grayson, *The Church in Contemporary México*, 9–11; Reich, *Mexico's Hidden Revolution*, 8–11. Interesting comparisons can be found in Barbara A. Tenenbaum, "Streetwise History: The Paseo de la Reforma and the Porfirian State, 1876–1910," in Beezley, Martin, and French, *Rituals of Rule, Rituals of Resistance*, 127–50.

27. León, *El ylmo. señor*, 146.

ing Quiroga's achievements.[28] As he states: "In the archive of the church cathedral of Michoacán neither any document of the Most Illustrious Sr. Quiroga nor any of the things of his epoch remain because of their having been destroyed, with many others, in a fire that occurred in the seventeenth century."[29] In February 1903, perhaps in order to fill this void, León sought to apply scientific techniques to generate new data. With a positivist flourish characteristic of intellectuals of the late-nineteenth and early-twentieth century, he carried out a precisely detailed anthropometric study of Don Vasco's cranium. León's research in the name of what subsequent generations would dismiss as pseudoscience was conducted with the full permission of ecclesiastical authorities, and was uncontroversial in his time.[30]

León's investigation was the last of a series of measurements and inventories of Vasco de Quiroga's remains that stretched back almost a century. In 1884, León had verified the results of an earlier study by the doctor Don Francisco Javier Orozco. This earliest examination had been carried out on August 16, 1831, in the presence of six witnesses and a notary, who recorded the entire proceeding. In his biography, León reproduced the results of all of these studies, despite their overlaps, and an additional one he viewed as truly definitive. On April 1, 1897, as part of the ceremonies surrounding the placement of Don Vasco's bones into the newly constructed crypt, the doctors Don Nicolás Luna and Don José Laris—in the presence of Archbishop Arciga and the bishops of Querétaro and Sonora, eight other witnesses, and a notary—demonstrated that the material remains of Don Vasco de Quiroga consisted of "the complete cranium and the lower maxillar; two femurs, two tibiae, two fibulae, a humerus, a complete ulna, two radii, a complete clavicle and two fragments of another; two iliac bones, two fragments of a jawbone; the sacrum, seven complete vertebrae and two fragments; two fragments of the omoplate; a fragment of the sternum, two complete calcaneum; an astragalus, also complete, fourteen

28. Moreno, *Fragmentos,* 9–15; Brading, *Church and State in Bourbon Mexico,* 38.
29. León, *El ylmo. señor,* 151.
30. Ibid., 148–49. In a neocolonial context, scientific fetishism combined with the anthropologist's power to define subjects for analysis could have explosive implications. León's colleague Carl Lumholtz, who admired Quiroga's reformism and alleged reorganization of craft production, provoked a near riot by attempting to purchase the corpse of a recently deceased Purhépecha male for scientific experimentation. In 1902, Lumholtz recounted this experience with indignation at what he believed to be indigenous savagery. Carl Lumholtz, *Unknown Mexico* (New York, 1902), 2:392–97, 415.

fragments of ribs and four bones without possible classification."[31] In order to avoid damaging the relics, whose value was believed to be inestimable, all of these operations were conducted on location, in the Colegio de la Compañía de Jesus.

According to Manuel Toussaint, in 1940 this building—although formally reserved for use as a federal school—was in a "lamentable state of deterioration." Moreover, despite the weight of local tradition, not much of the existing architecture linked it to the sixteenth century. On the basis of his own investigation and the work of his students, Toussaint concluded: "It is indisputable that of the original buildings little remains, therefore that which we see in the present appears to date entirely from the eighteenth century."[32] The shifting locales for public display of Vasco de Quiroga's remains demonstrate increasing interest in his historical significance. Though his bones remained undisturbed until 1897, three hundred and thirty-two years after his death, there is substantial evidence that the revival of interest in Quiroga that culminated in the increasingly prominent display of his remains received a substantial boost in the late eighteenth century.

Myths and Origins

Don Vasco loved the Indians. What is more, the Indians loved him. Indeed, they loved him so much that in their own language they refer to him as "Tata Vasco," and insist that Tata Vasco lives on "in the heart of the Pur[h]épecha people."[33] This assertion is central to the legend of Vasco de Quiroga, and it resurfaces almost universally in writings about him.[34] *Tata* is an indigenous term that literally means "father," but its usage here refers to legitimate male authority.[35] In Michoacán, there is not only Tata Vasco, but also Tata Lázaro, in reference to Lázaro Cárdenas, and at the village level *tata diosa* refers to a male saint, or perhaps more appropriately to the image of a male

31. León, *El ylmo. señor,* 143–48, esp. 144–45.

32. Toussaint, *Pátzcuaro,* 126.

33. Alfonso Caso, "Presencia de Don Vasco," *Cuadernos Americanos* 141, no. 4 (July–August): 139–47, esp. 147.

34. For example, ibid., 150; León, *El ylmo. señor,* 121, 127, 141; Jarnes, *Don Vasco,* 306–8; Warren, *Vasco de Quiroga,* 117; Zavala Paz, *D. Vasco,* 23, 61; Siller, "La iglesia," 220; and Martín Hernández, *Don Vasco de Quiroga,* 19, 24, 153

35. Maturino Gilberti, *Arte de la lengua de Michoacán,* ed. J. Benedict Warren (1558; Morelia, Mexico, 1987), and *Diccionario de la lengua tarasca* (1559; Morelia, Mexico, 1983), 107.

saint.[36] While this usage reveals much about masculinity and definitions of legitimacy within local political culture, it is less useful as a demonstration of love, especially a love projected back through almost five centuries.[37] As with so much else, the notion of Don Vasco's love for the Indians, and their love for him, is prominently displayed in Juan José Moreno's 1766 biography, and can ultimately be traced to Vasco de Quiroga's writings themselves.[38]

Even in the present, love is a complicated thing, and in this instance there simply is no evidence permitting an assessment of the emotional attachments of sixteenth-century indigenes. In fact, we know very little about the inner workings of Vasco de Quiroga's village-hospitals during his lifetime. Despite the presence of village-hospitals throughout west central Mexico, it has been proven definitively only that Don Vasco founded two communities, Santa Fe de México and Santa Fe de Michoacán.[39] The village-hospital, based on the congregation of dispersed indigenous populations into more easily monitored population centers, was the west central Mexican variant of a widespread colonial trend. In this area, one major congregation of the population took place in the 1530s, and another after the epidemic of 1545–48.[40] These resettlements facilitated and were made easier by a substantial regional decline in indigenous population levels, from an estimated 60,750–105,000 at contact to 40,000–75,000 by 1550, and a severe drop to under 10,000 by 1650.[41]

The task of resettling the newly conquered populations fell primarily to the Church as an arm of the colonial state. In Michoacán this institution was divided between regulars, or members of the religious orders—in this case especially the Franciscans and, later, the Augustinians and Jesuits—and secu-

36. Grayson, *The Church in Contemporary Mexico,* 19; Carrasco, *Tarascan Folk Religion,* 23.

37. For pioneering research on the connections between masculinity and legitimate political authority in the colonial period, see Stern, *Secret History of Gender.* See also Ana María Alonso, *Thread of Blood* (Tucson, Ariz., 1995). On "Tata Lázaro," see Becker, *Setting the Virgin on Fire,* 155–62.

38. Moreno, *Fragmentos,* 150.

39. Warren, *Vasco de Quiroga,* 3–7; Herrejón, "Dos obras señaladas," 66; Warren, *Vasco de Quiroga,* 48–50, 84; Muriel, *Hospitales de La Nueva España,* 1:85–86. There is no doubt that this pattern was extensive, although the claim by José Bravo Ugarte, based on Muriel, that 92 of the 111 hospitals founded in sixteenth-century New Spain were located in the bishopric of Michoacán seems excessive. See José Bravo Ugarte, *Historia sucinta de Michoacán* (Mexico City, 1962), 2:77–81.

40. Gerhard, *Guide,* 349–50.

41. Pollard, *Tariacuri's Legacy,* 79.

lars, or those priests that were not. The most famous secular of this early colonial period was Vasco de Quiroga.[42] These groups were locked in struggles for institutional power from the first moments of their arrival in a world they believed to be new. In Michoacán, the definitive triumph of the "seculars" came about only with the Bourbon reforms of the eighteenth century, and especially with the rule of Charles III (1759–88).[43] An inconclusive and at times bitterly partisan polemic has been waged over the centuries by intellectuals affiliated with these groups, who have sought unsuccessfully to prove that it was they, or rather their predecessors, who had founded the regional Church.[44] Although the pattern of establishing village-hospitals was extensive, in fact the precise origins and founder of most of them cannot be established.

We also lack substantial information about daily life in these communities during Vasco de Quiroga's lifetime and for several centuries after his death.[45] Given what Gruzinski terms "the poverty and rarity of the memories of Michoacán," it is unlikely that this absence will be filled or reconfigured by the discovery of new sources of information, especially for the era prior to 1565.[46] In addition, there are sound reasons for questioning the quality of Vasco de Quiroga's communication with the peoples he intended to save. As late as 1563, two years prior to his death—as the legend has it, at the probably fictitious age of ninety-five—Vasco de Quiroga still required the use of a translator in order to preach to the indigenous peoples.[47] In addition, although he served as bishop of Michoacán from 1538 to 1565, his time there was interrupted by an extended absence in Spain from 1547 to 1554.[48] All of these factors justify questioning assumptions about his reception by the local population.[49] After the 1580 transfer of colonial administration, including

42. Muriel, *Hospitales de la Nueva España*, 1:55–110; Martínez, "Reorientaciones," 150, 149–60.

43. Brading, *Church and State in Bourbon Mexico*, 20–39, and *The First America*, 492–513; Mazín, *Entre dos Majestades*; Lynch, *Spanish American Revolutions*, 7.

44. Muriel, *Hospitales de La Nueva España*, 1:77; Fidel de Lejarza, O.F.M., "Don Vasco de Quiroga en las crónicas franciscanas," *Missionalia Hispanica*, 23, no. 68 (1966): 129–256.

45. For example, note the absences in Felipe Tena Ramírez, *Vasco de Quiroga y sus pueblos de Santa Fe en los siglos XVIII–XIX* (Mexico City, 1977).

46. Gruzinski, *Conquest of Mexico*, 75.

47. Warren, "Writing the Language of Michoacán," 311.

48. Ibid., 322; Martínez, "Reorientaciones," 98.

49. On the ambiguities of communication during colonial evangelization attempts, see Rafael, *Contracting Colonialism;* MacCormack, "The Heart Has Its Reasons"; and Clendinnen,

ecclesiastical offices, from Pátzcuaro and the indigenous highlands to the Spanish town of Valladolid, the institutional hierarchy of the Church became more distant from the daily operation of the village-hospitals. Although the enhanced autonomy probably facilitated local control, and might explain regional loyalty to this form of social organization throughout the colonial period, the reality is that this situation has also created a void in the historical record. Attempts to discern the reality of Vasco de Quiroga's relationship to the indigenes in the sixteenth century are largely speculative.

Once it is acknowledged that it is not possible to recover initial popular reception of these efforts at all—and that nonelite perceptions of Vasco de Quiroga have not been investigated with anything approaching rigor until the mid-twentieth century—one can suggest plausibly that local articulations of the myth existed, and also that they reverberated back and influenced intellectuals. Thus, it is not necessary to deny Moreno's claims that "the offices of the hospital have not ceased until today," or even that "the veneration of this memory, and burning desire to conserve it, is a very manifest and constant motive for the people of Michoacán."[50] Increasing awareness of Vasco de Quiroga's significance at an elite level is demonstrated by a portrait painted at Santa Fe de México in 1737, and another one of his entire body painted and hung above his remains in 1755, at the Colegio de la Compañía de Jesus in Pátzcuaro.[51] These are the earliest known images of Quiroga; none exist that date from his lifetime.[52] Moreno also indicated that the Jesuits had an interest in his study because they possessed Vasco de Quiroga's remains, demonstrating recognition as well as an absence of knowledge.[53] Among intellectuals, then, increasing awareness of Don Vasco is evident by the eighteenth century, and Moreno's 1766 biography provides the most crucial moment in the elaboration of the myth.

The emergence of more popular forms of veneration cannot be precisely dated, and they have come to the attention of historians only through the power-laden filter of writing and the construction of a historical archive. Rather than an objective and disinterested retrieval of transparent events, the

Ambivalent Conquests, and especially "Disciplining the Indians: Franciscan Ideology and Missionary Violence in Sixteenth-Century Yucatán," *Past and Present* 94 (February 1982): 27–48.

50. Moreno, *Fragmentos,* 71, 184.

51. Martín Hernández, *Don Vasco de Quiroga,* 260; León, *El ylmo. señor,* 122.

52. Personal communication, Armando Maurico Escobar Olmedo.

53. Moreno, *Fragmentos,* 9.

notion of mutual love between Don Vasco and the indigenous population of Michoacán during the sixteenth century is the product of a colonialist historiography defining the "Indian" as subject.[54] During the construction of this myth, the subaltern did not speak; or, at least, at times conflicting subaltern voices did not control their own representation in the world of writing.[55] This reality is ignored in heroic representations of Vasco de Quiroga, and the deeply imbedded nature of this denial is evident in the celebratory accounts that continue to be produced. For example, in a 1993 hagiography Francisco Martín Hernández claims that "the natives of those lands still remember him with love."[56] A more appropriate claim would be that some indigenes "now remember him with love"—if they indeed do. The problem with this type of depiction is that it perpetuates colonialist assumptions that simultaneously deny the complexities of the present and conceal the contradictions and ambiguities of the past.[57]

Making this claim is not to ignore the late-twentieth-century insights of Catholic intellectuals like Francisco Miranda and Ramón López Lara. These scholars' finely grained knowledge of contemporary life in Purhépecha villages testifies to the current vitality of Don Vasco's image, although the recent spread of evangelical Protestantism and the persistence/re-creation of indigenous traditions should temper assumptions about the homogeneity of local culture.[58] Rather, given the absence of evidence concerning the nature of sixteenth-century responses to Vasco de Quiroga's activities, it is appropriate to ask where the mythic figure of the saintly father came from, and when; and how it was circulated and redefined over time.[59] Asking these kinds of questions does not deny that indigenes have influenced,

54. Florescano, *Memory, Myth and Time in Mexico*, 81; González, "Viaje."
55. See Spivak, "Can the Subaltern Speak?" Two intelligent responses to Spivak are Frederick Cooper's "Conflict and Contention: Rethinking Colonial African History," *American Historical Review* 99, no. 5 (December 1994): 1516–45, and Stuart B. Schwartz's "Introduction," in *Implicit Understanding*, 1–19.
56. Martín Hernández, *Don Vasco de Quiroga*, 24.
57. Sider, "When Parrots Learn to Talk."
58. Miranda, "Vasco de Quiroga, artifice"; Ramón López Lara, "Los Hospitales de la Concepción," in Miranda and Briseño, *Vasco de Quiroga*, 112–28, esp. 127. See Ma. del Socorro Sánchez López et al., *Ixiti juchiti irieta: Asi es mi pueblo* (Morelia, Mexico, 1987), 105. This is not a systematic study, but contains several Purhépecha testimonies about local life. For comparison and context, see Sheldon Annis, *God and Production in a Guatemalan Town* (Austin, Tex., 1987); Phillip Berryman, *Stubborn Hope* (New York, 1994); David Stoll, *Is Latin America Turning Protestant?* (Berkeley, Calif., 1990); and John Burdick, *Looking For God in Brazil* (Berkeley, Calif., 1993).

appropriated, and at times even internalized the myth. Nor is it to negate the significance of sixteenth-century events, to the extent that they can be recovered. Instead, it is to suggest that the construction of the legendary Vasco de Quiroga can be traced to the Spanish and creole populations, and that the most significant moments in this process came centuries after his death.

It is widely recognized that Juan José Moreno's 1766 biography played a crucial role in the compilation of historical knowledge pertaining to Vasco de Quiroga. As Miranda notes, "The Licentiate Moreno has the responsibility, in great measure, of rescuing from oblivion" the figure of Don Vasco.[60] It is also recognized that Moreno's portrayal is properly read as an intervention in eighteenth-century political struggles pitting the secular clergy against the regular. According to David Brading, "Written at a time when the bishop and chapter were enforcing with considerable enthusiasm the Crown's directive to secularize the parishes still administered by the mendicants, the life of Quiroga was designed to provide an historical justification for the assertion of episcopal authority and to demonstrate the role of a secular bishop in the foundation of a Mexican Church."[61] Moreno, a secular priest, was rector of the Colegio de San Nicolás in Valladolid. This institution traced its lineage to the college founded by Vasco de Quiroga in Pátzcuaro in 1540, and as Moreno stated, "from here the bishopric has been provided ministers for more than two hundred years."[62] At this point, Don Vasco became the heroic founder of the regional Church, a status that conformed well with the needs of local "seculars" and the Bourbon regime. As the crisis of late Spanish colonialism deepened, other definitions emerged.

In 1792, Miguel Hidalgo y Costilla was appointed rector of the Colegio de San Nicolás, following in the footsteps of Moreno and Quiroga. Hidalgo would later achieve fame and martyrdom as the leader of the first wave of armed insurgency during the Mexican wars for independence (1810–11), and he is now remembered as a founder of the modern Mexican nation. José María Morelos, leader of the most popular phase of the insurgency (1811–15),

59. For interesting comparisons with Vasco de Quiroga, see Beezley, Martin, and French, "Introduction: Constructing Consent, Inciting Conflict," in *Rituals of Rule, Rituals of Resistance,* xii–xxxii, and William Taylor, "The Virgin of Guadalupe in New Spain: An Inquiry into the Social History of Marian Devotion," *American Ethnologist* 14 (1987): 9–33.

60. Miranda, "Vasco de Quiroga, artifice," 148.

61. Brading, *Church and State in Bourbon Mexico,* 38.

62. Moreno, *Fragmentos,* 61.

would also be associated with the college and was active throughout Michoacán.[63] The creole nationalism of this region made the Colegio de San Nicolás a focal point of independence sentiment, and enhanced the status of its founder as an opponent of the abuses of Spanish colonialism.[64] In 1847, control over the institution passed from Church to state.[65] Ultimately, the Colegio de San Nicolás was renamed the Universidad Michoacana de San Nicolás de Hidalgo, Valladolid was renamed Morelia, and the rest, as they say, is history. The influence of this institution in Michoacán over four hundred and fifty years was recognized during the 1990 reinterment of Vasco de Quiroga's bones.

It is plausible to suggest that historical memory of Don Vasco was maintained primarily in the Colegio de San Nicolás during the sixteenth and seventeenth centuries, and was spread throughout the region by priests trained there. Local peoples of all ethnic categories may have responded to and internalized versions of the myth; but if they did so, precisely when, how, and why is a mystery of the past. Don Vasco was "rediscovered" by Moreno in 1766. Moreno himself argued convincingly that during the two centuries after Vasco de Quiroga's death he had been remembered poorly if at all among intellectuals, and only in ways difficult if not impossible to recover at the popular level. The tentativeness evident in his introduction, and in his selection of the title "Fragmentos de la vida . . . ," drops out of the body of his text, and also disappears in many subsequent accounts.[66] Moreno's biography established Vasco de Quiroga as an important symbol in an emerging regional discourse that was to blend creole nationalism with nineteenth-century liberalism, and in the twentieth century with the social-reform strand of the Mexican Revolution. Perhaps surprisingly—given the polarized and at times intensely violent clerical and anticlerical dynamic that would mark regional political culture in the late nineteenth and early twentieth centuries—in its initial manifestations this late colonial phenomenon blended Enlightenment rationalism with religious sentiment. After Independence, in a manner that is perhaps unique, the myth of Vasco de Quiroga continued to

63. Martín Hernández, *Don Vasco de Quiroga,* 268–69.
64. Lynch, *Spanish American Revolutions,* 306–19; Miranda, *Don Vasco de Quiroga,* 233–40. Pastor and Frizzi, "El crecimiento del siglo XVIII," in Florescano, *Historia general de Michoacán,* 2:195–218, esp. 218.
65. Martín Hernández, *Don Vasco de Quiroga,* 269; Miranda, *Don Vasco de Quiroga,* 233–41.
66. Moreno, *Fragmentos,* 9–16.

be elaborated by intellectuals drawn from the ranks of the Church and the liberal, revolutionary, and postrevolutionary intelligentsia.

Independence officially came to Mexico in 1821, and it ushered in decades of struggles between liberals and conservatives for control of the emerging republic. During this time, regional alliances and the reciprocal though authoritarian ties of *caudillismo* were always interwoven in ideological disputes.[67] In Michoacán, liberals came to believe that their challenges to the colonial order, and especially the privileged position of the Catholic Church, resonated with Vasco de Quiroga's reformism. Conservatives also claimed aspects of the legend, although they drew different conclusions. Both groups claimed the symbol of Don Vasco, and would continue to do so throughout the nineteenth century. The first inventory of Quiroga's remains was carried out in 1831, by a select group of local gentlemen who enjoyed the full support of the Church.[68] In 1852, Nicolás León's hometown of Cocupao was renamed Quiroga, by order of Melchor Ocampo, the liberal governor of Michoacán in the 1840s and 1850s. This decree—signed by a famous anticlerical intellectual renowned for his familiarity with the works of Voltaire, Rousseau, and Balzac, as well as his translations of Pierre Proudhon—paid homage to the memory of Don Vasco while recognizing Cocupao's contributions as a liberal stronghold during post-Independence conflicts.[69]

Not all nineteenth-century observations of Don Vasco's significance can be reduced to liberal and conservative political struggles, or to the increasing influence of Enlightenment rationalism. Other understandings, indigenous and female, can be noted, although in this instance only as they are reflected in elite, male, and Spanish texts.[70] For example, in a footnote to his massive five-volume history of Mexico, Vicente Rivas Palacio told of certain facts that he believed demonstrated the love of the "Tarascans" for Vasco de Quiroga. He noted that there was a point in the sierra of Nahuachín called *Obispo Tirecua*, which means the place where the bishop ate, because as legend had it this was a place where Vasco de Quiroga had once stopped for food. He also recalled that in 1866, when moving through the sierra of Paracho with a

67. For a detailed and nuanced discussion of the multiple elaborations of Mexican conservatism, liberalism, and revolutionary ideology in the nineteenth and twentieth centuries, see Florencia Mallon, *Peasant and Nation* (Berkeley, Calif., 1995).

68. León, *El ylmo. señor,* 147.

69. Brand, *Quiroga,* 100; León, *El ylmo. señor,* 129; Meyer and Sherman, *Course of Mexican History,* 373–74.

70. See Jean Franco, *Plotting Women* (New York, 1989), xi–xxiv, 79–101.

division of infantry during the war against the French, many of his troops broke ranks to approach an "altar or rustic monument" placed over an indentation in the ground. They were followed by the women traveling with the troops, who carried any children that they might have to the site. Upon arriving, each person placed his or her right foot into the hole. When Rivas Palacio inquired about what was happening, he was told that at that spot a footprint of Vasco de Quiroga had been preserved, and that for more than three centuries the Indians had paid homage to it in this way.[71]

In 1873, Doña Manuela de Betancourt, a resident of the village of Tangamandapio, wrote:

> I have seen from afar an arc of light that came out from the sepulchre of Don Vasco de Quiroga, to the camarin of the Most Holy Virgin, and a procession, presided over by the same most illustrious Señor who surrounded by many people, went forth from the Iglesia de la Compañía and arrived at the camarin of the Most Holy Virgin. On another occasion I saw him go out from the same camarin, with greater pomp and ceremony, he went to the Iglesía de la Compañía and there came forth other bishops to receive him. I am resolved to sell as much as I have, to collect all of my interests and go to Rome to promote the cause of the beatification of this Most Illustrious Señor.[72]

This fascinating letter displays the mysticism of a woman of means during an age increasingly dominated by positivism and science. Attributions of the miraculous can be noted as far back as Moreno's biography, which details Vasco de Quiroga's alleged divination of water in Pátzcuaro.[73] They continued to be persistent though less acknowledged parts of the legend in the nineteenth and twentieth centuries, a factor emphasized by those seeking beatification and, later, canonization for Vasco de Quiroga. These efforts date from 1873, and received significant boosts in 1903, 1942, and 1965.[74] As a symbol, Vasco de Quiroga also proved capable of attracting attention in more desacralized contexts.

---

71. Vicente Rivas Palacio, *México á través de los siglos,* vol. 2 (Barcelona, 1888–89), 226.
72. Zavala Paz, *D. Vasco de Quiroga,* 152.
73. Moreno, *Fragmentos,* 172–73.
74. See León, *El ylmo. señor,* 140; Jarnes, *Don Vasco;* Zavala Paz, *D. Vasco de Quiroga.*

In 1880, Macario Torres, professor of Latin and Literature at the Colegio de San Nicolás—and an 1867 graduate of this institution, born in the village of Quiroga in 1854—gave a public reading of his ode "To the Memory of Don Vasco de Quiroga." In it, he saluted the "great father of the people of Michoacán," a man who "first planted on our soil the tree of science," which he claimed worked to the benefit of the Indian, as well as the foreigner. Torres introduced his ode by noting that its subject had spent three centuries "in the dark night," only to be raised up as "a majestic figure triumphant from the death of oblivion." As he proclaimed

> Don Vasco de Quiroga: This is your name
> Apostle of progress: This is your glory.[75]

Vicente Rivas Palacio, minister of development from 1876 to 1880 during the early rule of Porfirio Díaz, has been described recently as "the champion of a new group, the 'nationalist mythologizers.'" He and other intellectuals of his generation sought to create a public sense for what they believed to be a shared national history. Their efforts transformed the public spaces of Mexico City, and had a lasting influence on twentieth-century Mexican culture.[76] Although he cited examples of indigenous veneration in a footnote, Rivas Palacio saluted Don Vasco's reorganization of industrial production in the body of his magnum opus, published in 1888–89. He also spoke in glowing terms of Vasco de Quiroga's desire to unify the diverse peoples of Michoacán so as to "avoid ruinous competition," and of his organization of craft production in ways appropriate for "people who are in the infancy of civilization and of culture."[77] In this last quotation, deeply rooted notions of the childlike incapacity of indigenes, a notable feature of colonial discourse, merges with the social Darwinism of the late-nineteenth-century Mexican elite.

Other nineteenth-century remembrances of Vasco de Quiroga include León's 1884 inventory, and the extensive public ceremonial surrounding the 1897 refurbishment of his tomb. In 1903, the results of León's anthropometric investigation and his biography were published with funding provided by the archbishop of Michoacán and the bishops of Querétaro, Tulancingo, Cuer-

---

75. Jarnes, *Don Vasco,* 324–25.
76. Tenenbaum, "Streetwise History," 136.
77. Rivas Palacio, *México,* 225–26.

navaca, and Chiapas.[78] In 1904, a Catholic Social Conference was held in Morelia, one in a series—Puebla (1903), Guadalajara (1906), Oaxaca (1909)— that discussed Pope Leo XIII's 1891 encyclical *Rerum Novarum* in light of Mexican realities.[79] Although not explicitly mentioning Vasco de Quiroga, this increased attention to social problems indicates why Vasco de Quiroga became increasingly useful in symbolic terms within Mexican Catholicism, as well as for a state formally committed to liberal anticlerical principles. In 1903, according to Nicolás León, the reigning archbishop of Morelia Atenógenes Silva wanted to demonstrate his admiration for Vasco de Quiroga. Thus, he gave Don Vasco's name to "a college for Indians that he founded and sustains, at his expense, in the pueblo of Erongarícuaro."[80] In Pátzcuaro, on October 1, 1906, by order of the government of Michoacán, an engraved stone plate commemorating Vasco de Quiroga's founding of the Colegio de San Nicolás was placed at the original site of the college. By this point in time, the nineteenth-century distinctions between liberals and conservatives had blurred with the consolidation of a neocolonial ruling class under the strong-arm rule of Porfirio Díaz (1876–1910). The image of Vasco de Quiroga as a pragmatic social reformer, opposed to the abuses of Spanish colonialism and with a vision of a mestizo nation, would be recognizable to all.

The irony of the "rediscovery" of Vasco de Quiroga in the late eighteenth and nineteenth centuries is that the public exaltation of this figure paralleled the destruction of the land base sustaining the village-hospitals that in legend are attributed to his sixteenth-century efforts. This is especially the case with his appropriation by nineteenth-century Mexican liberals. The village-hospitals existed until the legislation of the liberal governments privatizing communal landholdings—combined with population pressures and absorption by expanding agricultural estates—led to their ultimate demise. This process, accompanied by considerable resistance on the part of the Indian communities, occurred primarily between 1872 and 1877.[81] Despite—and perhaps because of—the decline in communal landholdings, the image of

78. León, *El ylmo. señor,* iii, 138–49.

79. Grayson, *The Church in Contemporary Mexico,* 11. For documents on modern Catholic social teaching, see David J. O'Brien and Thomas A. Shannon, *Renewing the Earth* (New York, 1977).

80. León, *El ylmo. señor,* 130.

81. Tena Ramírez, *Vasco de Quiroga,* 165–68. One study of Franciscan hospitals recovers some of this past and looks at the political implications of their eighteenth-century demise in the neighboring state of Jalisco. Taylor, "Banditry and Insurrection," 205, 232, 234–37.

Vasco de Quiroga retained and even increased its vitality as the twentieth century unfolded.

Vasco de Quiroga in the Twentieth Century

In 1903, Nicolas León remarked that Vasco de Quiroga sought to achieve "the ideal of the original Church or of some modern socialists; that none had a right to the superfluous, but none would lack the necessary."[82] The question of the relationship between Vasco de Quiroga's early modern Christian humanism and the various types of socialism and social reform that developed in the twentieth century became an important issue especially because of the Mexican Revolution. Throughout the social turmoil and political conflict of this event and its aftermath, the legendary figure of Vasco de Quiroga proved to be a remarkably flexible Mexican national symbol.

The revolution itself has been defined in multiple ways: as a series of military confrontations running from 1910 to 1920 that cost Mexico, a country of fifteen million inhabitants, nearly a million citizens through death and emigration; as a process of modern state formation beginning in the 1780s, consolidated by 1940, and contested in the present; as a peasant revolution; as the first great social revolution of the twentieth century; and as no revolution at all, but rather the coming to power amidst substantial violence of a northern bourgeoisie bent on capitalist modernization and carrying to completion the project initiated by Porfirio Díaz.[83] Although its precise meaning remains disputed, it is clear that the revolution substantially redefined the terms of political debate in Mexico and led to substantial innovation in the cultural realm. One important aspect of this innovation was the search for authentically Mexican culture, including historical figures that could be seen as precursors of the egalitarian and social reform dimensions of the revolution. In this milieu, the heroic image of Vasco de Quiroga gained increasing appeal.

In the 1920s—and especially from 1920 to 1924, when José Vasconcelos served as minister of education during the presidency of General Obregón—

82. León, *El ylmo. señor*, 16.
83. Héctor Aguilar Camín and Lorenzo Meyer, *In the Shadow of the Mexican Revolution*, trans. Luis Alberto Fierro (Austin, Tex., 1993), 1–36; Meyer and Sherman, *Course of Mexican History*, 481–566; Mallon, *Peasant and Nation*, esp. 310–30; Paul J. Vanderwood, "Explaining the Mexican Revolution," in *The Revolutionary Process in Mexico*, ed. Jaime E. Rodríguez O. (Los Angeles, 1990), 97–114.

the Mexican State "discovered" the peasantry. This was especially the case for the indigenous peasantry, whose cultural traditions and glorified past became defined as essential components of national identity.[84] The cultural changes promoted by the revolution were stimulated by and deepened the conflict between the state and the Catholic Church. Between 1926 and 1929, open warfare between clerical and anticlerical forces—the so-called Cristero Rebellion—erupted throughout the nation. In Michoacán, which had more Cristeros than any other region, sporadic guerrilla violence continued into the 1930s. In the end, this renewed conflict between primarily peasant insurgent forces and the state resulted in an additional eighty thousand casualties.[85] All of these factors enhanced the utility of Vasco de Quiroga as a symbol whose ambiguous legacy could be claimed across the ideological spectrum.

One artifact from this era is the following statement by Vicente Lombardo Toledano, one of Mexico's most important twentieth-century Marxist intellectuals.[86] In a newspaper article written in 1929, Lombardo Toledano celebrated Vasco de Quiroga's *Reglas y ordenanzas*. These were the rules for daily life in the village-hospitals, known only from their partial—"incomplete from beginning to end"—reproduction in Moreno's biography.[87] Lombardo Toledano claimed that the *Reglas y ordenanzas* were, "without any doubt, the most valuable documents that have marked the history of popular education in our country until today."[88] Despite his own anticlerical views, and the fact that he made this statement in a heightened atmosphere of politico-religious turmoil, Lombardo Toledano still celebrated Vasco de Quiroga's utopian project as an authentically Mexican attempt at social reorganization. The claiming of Vasco de Quiroga by the Mexican Left was also demonstrated by the statement of Miguel O. de Mendizábel, who in 1931 pointed out that the *Reglas y ordenanzas* required only a six-hour day. This proved that Vasco de Quiroga's sense of justice was "so generous for the proletariat that he wished for more in his kindness than the socialists of Chicago in the

84. Rowe and Schelling, *Memory and Modernity*, 64; Franco, *Plotting Women*, 102.

85. Purnell, *Popular Movements*, esp. 48–196; Becker, *Setting the Virgin on Fire*, 6, 40, 125; Meyer, *La cristiada*.

86. On Lombardo Toledano, see Barry Carr, *Marxism and Communism in Twentieth-Century Mexico* (Lincoln, Nebr., 1992), 7, 195–201.

87. Zavala, "Vasco de Quiroga ante las comunidades de indios," 27–35, 34.

88. Vicente Lombardo Toledano, "Don Vasco de Quiroga fundador de la escuela de la acción," *Excelsior* (Mexico City), September 7, 1929, 5, 9.

nineteenth century."[89] Lombardo Toledano's celebration of Don Vasco, and his simultaneous attack on the "enemies of change: the semiliterate masses and the elite of the cults," appears arrogant in the twenty-first century.[90] It is probable that this arrogance offended Catholics more than his understanding of Vasco de Quiroga's significance.

In 1937, Silvio Zavala's classic article demonstrated the influence of Thomas More—whom Don Vasco had described as the "author of that very good state of republic"—on the thought of Vasco de Quiroga.[91] Few historians in twentieth-century Mexico enjoyed the success and esteem accorded to Zavala, and he appropriately remains a widely respected figure.[92] Genaro Estrada, in his introduction to the article, made an explicit reference to the relevance of Vasco de Quiroga's experience for the social reforms of the revolution, which were implemented most fully during the Cárdenas years (1934–40).[93] Not surprisingly, given the Mexican political climate, these interpretations and the more radical proposals of the Mexican Left provoked considerable debate. Justino Fernandez and Edmundo O'Gorman provided an impassioned response. In 1937, these two authors published *Santo Tomás Moro y "La Utopia de Tomás Moro en la Nueva España,"* aimed primarily at Zavala and Estrada.[94] Their work is essentially an attack on those who would posit any relationship between the type of "monastic" communism espoused by Quiroga, and also More, and twentieth-century variants of socialism and/or social reform. Although absent from the works of Zavala and Estrada, the specter of Marx figures prominently in these countercritiques.[95]

89. Miguel O. de Mendizábel, "Don Vasco de Quiroga," *Crisol* (June 1931): 427. As cited in Francisco Rojas Gonzales, "Los tarascos en la época colonial," in *Los tarascos,* Lucio Mendieta y Nuñéz et al. (Mexico City, 1940), 53–102, 65.

90. Lombado Toledano, "Don Vasco de Quiroga," 5. For a fuller elaboration of Lombardo Toledano's views, see his *El problema del indio* (Mexico City, 1973), esp. 191–94. See also Lacas, "Social Welfare Organizer," 76–77. Lacas strongly criticizes Lombardo Toledano's anticlerical tendencies, citing Lombardo Toledano's *El problema de la educación en México* (Mexico City, 1924), 19.

91. Silvio Zavala, "La utopia de Tomás Moro en la Nueva España," in *Recuerdo,* 9–40; Quiroga, *La Información en Derecho,* 216.

92. "Discurso de bienvenida y retrato del doctor Zavala," in Herrejón, *Humanismo y ciencia,* 17–23.

93. Genaro Estrada, "Introducción a la 'Utopia' de Tomas Moro en la Nueva España (1937)," in *Recuerdo,* 164–65.

94. Justino Fernandez and Edmundo O'Gorman, *Santo Tomás More y "La Utopia de Tomás Moro en la Nueva España"* (Mexico City, 1937).

95. Ibid., esp. 20–22, 25, 27–29, 32.

After these studies, the twentieth-century die was cast. Most works on Vasco de Quiroga over the next fifty years forced their discussions onto the grid of communism/anticommunism.

During this period, contrasting views of Vasco de Quiroga and Thomas More were presented by scholars who put forward constructions of these figures as precursors to twentieth-century variants of socialism or social reform, and those claiming a position of Catholic orthodoxy. These polarized positions, until recently most notable for the spectacular unwillingness of either camp to engage the thought of the other, have been fueled by the reality that neither of these thinkers elaborated a full-blown discussion of property rights. The attitude of both is described best as pragmatic, although More presented a stronger condemnation of private property than did Quiroga. Recall his statement: "This wise sage, to be sure, early foresaw that the one and only road to the general welfare lies in the maintenance of equality in all respects. I have my doubts that the latter could ever be preserved where the individual's possessions are his private property."[96] In contrast to More, Don Vasco actually tried to implement his utopian vision. Perhaps for this reason, his approach to the question of property was more flexible.[97] To found communities, he purchased most of the territory needed to sustain them. However, he also petitioned the Crown for "unused lands," took the liberty of occupying and using lands he considered idle while the courts deliberated his petitions, and even threatened armed conflict to those who challenged his claims.[98] When it suited his purposes, Vasco de Quiroga

96. St. Thomas More, *Utopia*, 53. On the debate over More's position on property, see Kenyon, *Utopian Communism and Political Thought in Early Modern England*, esp. 33, 72. For an article which situates Vasco de Quiroga in some of the broader trends sweeping the Europe of his era, see Natalie Zemon Davis, "Poor Relief, Humanism and Heresy," in *Society and Culture in Early Modern France* (Stanford, Calif., 1975), esp. 36.

97. One comparable effort was the failed attempt of Bartolomé de Las Casas to found a colony of Spanish and indigenous settlers in Venezuela in 1517. See Lewis Hanke, *The Spanish Struggle for Justice in the Conquest of America* (Philadelphia, 1949), 54–56. Hanke is a bit harsh to characterize Vasco de Quiroga's effort as merely a copy of Thomas More, after all Vasco de Quiroga's utopian project was more successful than many. For arguments concerning the uniqueness of Vasco de Quiroga and his project, see Jose M. Gallegos Rocafull, *El pensamiento mexicano en los siglos XVI y XVII* (Mexico City, 1951), 191–202, esp. 198; Silvio Zavala, "La utopia de America en el siglo XVI," *Cuadernos Americanos* 141, no. 4 (July-August 1965): 130–38; Miranda, "La fraternidad cristiana," 148–58; and Muriel, *Hospitales de La Nueva España*, 1:87.

98. Carlos Herrejón, "Cinco documentos sobre Vasco de Quiroga," in *Don Vasco de Quiroga y Arzobispado de Morelia*, 163–64, 165–66; León, *Documentos ineditos*, 1–5; Warren, *Vasco de Quiroga*, 43–44, 89, 90–97.

defended indigenous rights to property held prior to the Spanish Conquest.[99] Nevertheless, the history of his village-hospitals indicates that he also believed these rights could be nullified if they conflicted with the more important goal of forced urbanization for the purpose of evangelization. Once the village-hospitals had been established, however, Don Vasco insisted that members be granted only the use of the land, not ownership.[100] Despite this ambiguity, debates over the meaning of the early modern utopianism of Vasco de Quiroga and Thomas More reached an intensity difficult to understand in a post–Cold War world.

Thus, to cite only a few examples, in a 1940 doctoral dissertation at Loyola University, Paul Leitz argued that Vasco de Quiroga was of the Renaissance "but not of that part which might be held accountable for the growth of modern Socialism."[101] In 1950, the Jesuit Constantino Bayle prefaced his brief remarks about Vasco de Quiroga by making disparaging remarks about "Russia." Bayle also noted that Quiroga's communism differed from modern variants, since it was spiritual, and aimed only to bring the Indians to paradise.[102] In 1959, another Jesuit, Paul L. Callens, wrote about "the shame that has fallen upon the foundation of Don Vasco," referring to the Universidad Michoacano de San Nicolás de Hidalgo. He fumed that "times have changed indeed. The teaching of Catechism and of the Gospels has been replaced by the teaching of a new philosophy. Religion is banned from the school since the new masters consider it 'the opium of the people.'"[103] Callens also claimed that in May 1940, a crowd of villagers in Pátzcuaro forcibly prevented the removal of Vasco de Quiroga's bones, allegedly for their transfer to a state dinner in his honor, sponsored by the governor of Michoacán.[104] In 1963, Warren warned against communists, who tried to "uproot Utopia" and replant it in "materialist soil," and argued that one could never confuse monastic and Marxist communism.[105] Finally, in 1977, Tena

99. Warren, *Vasco de Quiroga,* 62–63.

100. Quiroga, *Reglas y ordenanzas,* 266–67.

101. Paul S. Leitz, "Don Vasco de Quiroga and the Second Audiencia of New Spain" (Ph.D. diss., Loyola University, 1940), 138–39.

102. Constantino Bayle, S.J., *El clero secular y la evangelización de America* (Madrid, 1950), 306.

103. Paul L. Callens, S.J., *Tata Vasco* (Mexico City, 1959), 92.

104. Ibid., 128–32.

105. Warren, *Vasco de Quiroga,* 120.

Ramírez took issue with the fact that the name of Thomas More "was included by the Soviets in the civic calendar of the Red Army."[106]

Of course, these Cold War arguments were correct, in the sense that most monks are not Marxists, and the sixteenth-century visions of Quiroga and More were quite distinct from twentieth-century versions of communism, socialism, and social reform. On the other hand, none of the scholars interested in Don Vasco, including those calling themselves "Marxists," would have disputed these points. Aside from occasional bursts of anticlericalism—hardly uncommon, especially among male Mexican intellectuals from the early nineteenth century onward—there seems to be little that is objectionable from a Catholic viewpoint in the existing scholarship on Vasco de Quiroga.

More important, the entire debate no longer seems as significant, because it was based upon the notion of the intellectual precursor. Instead of emphasizing rigid notions of intellectual lineage, conceived of as a direct and uniform relationship between past and future thinkers, we need to come to grips with the complexity and contextuality of thought, noting common patterns as well as unique, historically situated contributions. This is a difficult task, perhaps capable of producing flashes of insight, but far removed from the totalizing pretensions of the past.

There are several indications that the legend of Vasco de Quiroga enjoyed widespread appeal by the 1940s, although precisely what this means is difficult to determine. Once again, shifting historical and political circumstances resulted in new claims on Quiroga's legacy. In 1939, federal troops were sent out to many towns throughout Michoacán.[107] In the 1940s, Michoacán remained an area of substantial political turmoil and occasional outbursts of violence. Struggles between *agraristas*—or those who received lands as a result of the Cárdenas-era land reform—and other peasants continued in indigenous and mestizo communities. Although the strength of the Cristeros waned, *sinarquismo*—an idiosyncratic corporatist movement with possible fascist overtones, although one that rejected formal political involvement and identified strongly with the Church—flourished. During the early 1940s, *sinarquistas* enjoyed a substantial presence in Michoacán, precisely among

106. Tena Ramírez, *Vasco de Quiroga*, 54.
107. Carrasco, *Tarascan Folk Religion*, 21.

peasant and Indian communities in whose name the revolution had supposedly been fought.[108] Elites needed to construct a political culture responding to and at least partially incorporating local demands. Vasco de Quiroga could now be seen as a useful bridge, making the hierarchical, state-dominated reformism of the postrevolutionary government more palatable to a largely Catholic rural population.

In 1940, President Lázaro Cárdenas personally intervened to insure that representatives from indigenous communities would be included at the international Indigenist Conference held in Pátzcuaro, apparently overruling advisers who preferred only academically qualified participants.[109] In that same year, Lucio Mendieta y Nuñéz introduced a collection of articles on Tarascan culture by noting that "the Indian . . . finds himself congenitally incapacitated for accommodating himself to the laws of progress." For Mendieta y Nuñéz, the solution was obvious: "If one desires that the Tarascan Indian be assimilated by modern culture, it would be indispensable to destroy their primitive language, substituting for it the official language of Mexico, which is Castilian."[110] The ethnocidal developmentalist thrust is notable throughout all of the articles. Although Vasco de Quiroga is not responsible for the uses of his image more than three centuries after his death, the authors repeatedly cited his social reforms as precursors for their proposed activities, which they believed would gain strong support in the indigenous communities. As Francisco Rojas Gonzales hopefully noted, the reward for Don Vasco's life "we find in the heart of the Purhépecha people."[111]

In 1941, the artist, architect, and long-time communist Juan O'Gorman painted his mural *La Historia de Michoacán,* in the Biblioteca Pública "Gertrudis Bocanegra" in Pátzcuaro. In this meticulously detailed and intriguing, though narrowly didactic work, images from the colonial past mingle with nineteenth- and twentieth-century figures. Vasco de Quiroga over-

108. Paul Friedrich, *The Princes of Naranja* (Austin, Tex., 1986), esp. 25, 68, 189. The pages cited deal with popular religion, and the emergence of anticlerical politics at the village level, a trend that waxes and wanes in the area, even within individuals. Also see Purnell, *Popular Movements,* 111–68, and Becker, *Setting the Virgin on Fire,* esp. 143–45. For other areas within Michoacán, see Luis González, *San José de Gracia* (Austin, Tex., 1972), 146–214; Jesus Tapia Santamaría, *Campo religioso y evolución política en el bajío zamorano* (Zamora, Mexico, 1986), esp. 179–230; César Moheno, *Las historias y los hombres de San Juan* (Zamora, Mexico, 1985), 133–73; Carrasco, *Tarascan Folk Religion,* 22; and Brand, *Quiroga,* 6.

109. Becker, *Setting the Virgin on Fire,* 159.

110. Mendieta y Nuñéz, *Los tarascos,* lxiv, lxxi.

111. Ibid., 63, 65–66, 133, 162, 235, 278.

sees male and female Indians at work spinning thread to the left of a banner proclaiming "Utopia." To the right, past a partially constructed wall, stand Morelos and Zapata, and to their right are contemporary Purhépecha, armed with tools. On the other side of the mural stands the artist, with a sign that reads "from the latent force of the undefeated Indian race there will arise an extraordinary art and culture."[112] In the same year, the opera *Tata Vasco*, composed by Miguel Bernal Jiménez, premiered in Morelia. At the time, Bernal Jiménez was the director of the Escuela Superior Oficial de Música Sagrada in Morelia, a position he obtained in 1936, after studying from 1928 to 1933 at the Pontifical Institute of Sacred Music in Rome. Although a success in Morelia, fears that "the opera might stir religious conflict" prevented its showing at the Palacio de Belles Artes in Mexico City. In 1948, *Tata Vasco* and its composer received an enthusiastic reception in Franco's Spain.[113]

Scholars in the United States also acknowledged Don Vasco's significance. In 1942, in the robustly titled *Men of Mexico*, James Magner devoted a chapter to Vasco de Quiroga amidst a series of biographies running from Moctezuma II through Lázaro Cárdenas. According to Magner, "the fruitful future of Mexico depends upon the union of the material and the spiritual redemption of the Indian, as Don Vasco envisioned to such practical effect four hundred years ago." He also argued that Mexican "social problems are still in the temperamental order, arising from the natural instability of a mixed, evolving race."[114] More serious and sensitive efforts were soon to be forthcoming in the U.S. academy, as well as in Mexico. Not surprisingly, as a result of regional turmoil the peasant communities, religious traditions, and political culture of Michoacán began to receive substantial attention, especially from anthropologists.

For example, in his study of Tzintzuntzan, published in 1948 and based on fieldwork from 1945, George Foster wrote that "the name of Don Vasco is known to even the most illiterate Indian, and he is universally venerated. In a folkloric sense he has come to be the culture hero of the lake and sierra

112. As quoted in Emily Edwards and Manuel Álvarez Bravo, *Painted Walls of Mexico* (Austin, Tex., 1966), 241, which presents a clear though black and white reproduction of the mural. On the mural and on O'Gorman, see Antonio Luna Arroyo, *Juan O'Gorman* (Mexico City, 1973), esp. 410–14; Ida Rodríguez Prampolini, *Juan O'Gorman arquitecto y pintor* (Mexico City, 1982); and Terukazu Akiyama et al., *The Dictionary of Art* (New York, 1996), 23:369–70.
113. Robert Stevenson, *Music in Mexico* (New York, 1952), 262–64.
114. James A. Magner, *Men of Mexico* (1942; Freeport, N.Y., 1968), v, 141.

region, and is credited with establishing the modern order of things."[115] Another anthropologist, R. A. M. Van Zantwijk, made similar comments in a
1967 study, and in 1974 María Teresa Sepúlveda y H noted that "Tata Vasco"
was especially venerated in the Tarascan communities.[116] Although by the
time of these monographs a general pattern of venerating Quiroga clearly existed, precise meanings remained elusive. For example, Rosendo Ortega, a
Purhépecha, wrote to President Lázaro Cárdenas that despite recent troubles
between Church and state, the citizens of Pátzcuaro wanted their church re-
opened. According to Ortega, they desired this not necessarily to worship,
but because they shared the president's interest in historical preservation.
The church, he claimed, had been built in 1546 by Vasco de Quiroga. Opening it would be a "memorial to its founder who was a true benefactor of the
Indians who still venerate him."[117] Was this a clever, if somewhat transparent, manipulation of recently created folklore or a restatement of a centuries-
old tradition? Or both?

While it is crucial to move beyond rigidly defined notions of intellectual
precursors, it is also true that certain continuities mark the historiography on
Vasco de Quiroga. Juan José Moreno believed that Vasco de Quiroga was
analogous to Peter the Great for having civilized and taught "the occupations of rational life."[118] Nicolás León praised his "redemption of the Indian."[119] Silvio Zavala argued that the example of Quiroga "elevates the civilizing mission of Spain to a rank and a moral purity of which few examples
exist in the history of the thinking of colonization."[120] For Paul S. Leitz "the
variety and degrees of animalism in which the Indian steeped himself are too
well known to need repetition," thus demonstrating the tremendous nature
of Don Vasco's achievement.[121] Fintan B. Warren concluded his work on
Vasco de Quiroga's hospitals by arguing that "we have seen him among his
Indians, teaching them and leading them away from their savagery like a lov-
ing father. He wished to be father of his brown children also in the life of the

115. Foster, *Empire's Children,* 18.
116. Van Zantwijk, *Servants of the Saints,* 64–65; María Teresa Sepúlveda y H., *Los cargos politicos y religiosos en la región del lago de Pátzcuaro* (Mexico City, 1974).
117. Becker, *Setting the Virgin on Fire,* 141.
118. Moreno, *Fragmentos,* 130.
119. León, *El ylmo. señor,* 155–56.
120. Silvio Zavala, "Ideario de Vasco de Quiroga," in *Recuerdo,* 67.
121. Leitz, "Don Vasco de Quiroga," 41.

spirit."[122] Julio Cesar Moran Alvarez claimed that Quiroga gave indigenous peoples "a system of life very far from the old and of an unquestionable moral and human superiority."[123] All of these quotations, spanning the eighteenth through the twentieth centuries, reveal the enduring quality of colonial and neocolonial assumptions, even as they are redeployed in new circumstances, for different purposes.

Twentieth-century struggles to define the meaning of Vasco de Quiroga's past also reflect an underlying social and historical reality. By 1940, indigenous population levels in Michoacán had reached 55,000.[124] By 1980, they had climbed above 80,000, surpassing pre-Conquest levels for the first time.[125] The recovery of indigenous populations and their increasing organizational capacities and political mobilization has enhanced the utility of Tata Vasco as a symbol of cross-cultural harmony. However, as we saw in Chapter 3, the legacy of Vasco de Quiroga is a contradictory one. To the extent that we can recover his vision, we can state that it combined a rhetoric of liberation and the condemnation of specific abuses of colonial power with an authoritarian paternalism permeated by patriarchal, ethnocentric, and "racialist" assumptions. How best do we remember this complex individual today? We can begin a productive discussion of this question by recognizing that colonial power relationships and assumptions are built into the very foundations of our historical knowledge, the written sources produced in the sixteenth century and beyond that record and narrate this history.

122. Warren, *Vasco de Quiroga*, 117.
123. Moran Alvarez, *El pensamiento*, 234.
124. Carrasco, *Tarascan Folk Religion*, 7.
125. Pollard, *Taríacuri's Legacy*, 79.

CONCLUSION

The present-day, ecclesial-Vatican triumphalism which *celebrates* these events, ought to return to painful history and comprehend the ambiguity of this spiritual conquest.
—Enrique Dussel, *The Invention of the Americas*

In Mexico, the foreign observer quickly notes that present and past mingle together in exceptional ways.[1] This reality is aggressively marketed by the tourist industry. Frequently, however, the result is less than picturesque as unresolved disputes reemerge in new contexts. The resurfacing of conflicts traceable to the experience of conquest and colonization is especially notable in the political demonstrations and ferment that always surround the date of October 12. In Mexico and much of Latin America, this day is referred to as the "Día de la Raza"—literally, the Day of the Race—rather than Columbus Day. Instead of celebrating the arrival of Columbus in the Caribbean, Mexicans officially commemorate the origins of *mestizaje,* or racial and cultural mixing.

Debates over the meaning of Columbus's "discovery of America"—or, as Michel-Rolph Trouillot suggests, "the Castilian invasion of the Bahamas"—exist in part because those seeking to understand the past look back at it from various locations, and from different times.[2] Contrasting interpretations, and the fact

1. On the "layers of time" that constitute the present, see Arnold Bauer, "The Colonial Economy," in Hoberman and Socolow, *The Countryside in Colonial Latin America,* 19–20.
2. Trouillot, *Silencing the Past,* 114.

that some are preferable to others, demonstrate that historical writing is inevitably though not entirely subjective. History always involves a dialogue of present and past, though one is not reducible to the other. Throughout this book, we have engaged in a careful evaluation of the evidence and exclusions found in sixteenth-century sources and in subsequent historiography, from a vantage point located in the present.[3] It is time now to consider the contemporary implications of this study of history.

Epigraphs, like footnotes, are never innocent, and the quotation of Enrique Dussel cited at the beginning of this conclusion refers to a specific debate. As recently as January 22, 1999, in Mexico City, Pope John Paul II emphasized that Iberian expansion in the Americas was an expression of divine will, and spoke favorably of Catholic Church sponsored celebrations of the quincentenary of the arrival of Columbus in the Americas.[4] This papal pronunciation echoed earlier statements issued in 1992 during that year's conference of Latin American bishops. Not coincidentally, the 1992 conference began on October 12 and was held at Santo Domingo, in the Dominican Republic, on the anniversary of the day and at least near the place where Columbus is said to have first established a Christian presence in the Americas. As with many public statements, these seemingly confident assertions obscured a context of fierce debate, as Latin Americans and Europeans struggled to find contemporary meanings for a difficult past.[5]

Ironically, much like the late colonial glorification of the "spiritual conquest" found in Pablo Beaumont's *Crónica,* the forcefulness of the 1992 Catholic Church sponsored celebration of the introduction of Christianity into this hemisphere responded to contemporary challenges and institutional decline. This appropriation of the past told us more about the Catholic Church hierarchy's concern with increasing secularism, the spread of

3. In defense of such an authorial strategy, see Linda Hutcheon, *The Politics of Postmodernism* (London, 1995), 67; Mignolo, *The Darker Side of the Renaissance,* 1–25, esp. 7; and de Certeau, *The Writing of History,* 56–113.

4. John Paul II, *Ecclesia en America,* http://www. vatican. va/holy_father/john_paul_ii/apost_exhortations/documents/hf_jp-ii_exh_22011999_ecclesia-in-america_en.html. On the 1999 papal visit to Mexico, see Diego Ribadeneira and Richard Chacón, "Throngs Welcome Pope to Mexico City: In Nation Where Church Is Losing Ground, Pontiff Speaks of Rebirth," *Boston Globe,* January 23, 1999, A1; and Sam Dillon, "A Rebel Creed, Stifled by the Pope, Flickers Still," *New York Times,* January 21, 1999, A4.

5. Alfred T. Hennelly, S.J., "A Report From the Conference," in Hennelly, *Santo Domingo and Beyond,* 24–36.

evangelical Protestantism, and Catholic liberation theologians in Latin America in 1992 than it did about the events of 1492.[6] For this reason, in my view the most important contribution I can make here is to call into question what Dussel terms "ecclesial-Vatican triumphalism," or the celebration of the so-called "spiritual conquest" of the Americas.[7] This tendency, ultimately derived from the conquest-era notion that the "discovery" of the Americas was an expression of divine will, has proven to be remarkably enduring within Catholicism. It is time for a change.

History as a discipline offers tentative truths, offered as part of ongoing conversations. Of course, these truths are subject to revision. Once established, however, they must be engaged. Theologians, like historians, run the risk of perpetuating dogmatism if they are not open to reality.[8] One truth of the sixteenth and seventeenth centuries has been established decisively by social historians over the last several decades. By 1608, the native population had suffered an enormous decline, reasonably estimated at over 90 percent for the densest areas of indigenous settlement. Demographic history—especially for the medieval and early modern periods—is an imprecise science, and population decline varied widely over time and region. Credible scholars have produced plausible estimates of the native population at the time of contact that vary from 30 to 100 million, and the accuracy of the figures has an obvious influence on the quantitative extent of the demographic catastrophe. Nevertheless, no scholar working today denies that one tragic consequence of the conquest and colonization of the Americas was a profound demographic collapse among the indigenous peoples. According to Alfred Crosby, a respected and moderate environmental historian "the conclusion must be that the major initial effect of the Columbian voyages was the transformation of America into a charnel house."[9]

6. Enrique Dussel, *The Invention of the Americas,* trans. Michael D. Barber (New York, 1995), 54. On conflicts and trends within the Latin American Catholic Church, see Edward L. Cleary, "The Journey to Santo Domingo," in Hennelly, *Santo Domingo and Beyond,* 3–23; Berryman, *Stubborn Hope,* 5–22; and Howard W. French, "Dissent Shadows Pope on His Visit," *New York Times,* October 14, 1992, A15A.

7. Dussel, *The Invention,* 54.

8. Jon Sobrino, "The Winds in Santo Domingo and the Evangelization of Culture," in Hennelly, *Santo Domingo and Beyond,* 167–83, esp. 177.

9. The best concise guide to an enormous literature and debate is Alfred W. Crosby, "The Columbian Voyages and Their Historians," in *Islamic and European Expansion,* ed. Michael Adas (Philadelphia, 1993), 160; see 156–58 for a discussion of the literature.

We know that Europeans had endured an earlier cycle of epidemics and population decline caused in part by pathogens arriving along Eurasian trade routes.[10] However, we also know that the explanation for the sixteenth-century indigenous population decline in the Americas is not strictly biological. Social factors such as warfare, overwork, malnutrition, colonial resettlement strategies, and other abuses of power resulted in deaths and enhanced the spread of disease. Scholars also now recognize that the "Columbian exchange" and Iberian colonial expansion inaugurated the transfer of approximately 10 million Africans across the Atlantic, in a brutal and inhumane system of enslaved labor.[11]

The painful truth is that historically specific forms of Christian ideology served to legitimate colonialism, and thus were complicit in these and other abuses of power. This complicity should be acknowledged and atoned for, and it is impossible to do this while simultaneously celebrating the arrival of Columbus. We have seen how the power dynamics and social hierarchies of the colonial context permeated the thought of even the legendary reformer and dissident Vasco de Quiroga, and then were recreated over time in subsequent historiography. At this time, for reasons both ethical and historical, it is necessary to disrupt and revise this celebratory narrative, which seeks to reinscribe archaic notions of divine will and the ethnocentric assumptions of the early modern era.

Support for a more critical understanding of sixteenth-century evangelization comes from an unlikely source. Robert Ricard's classic, *The Spiritual Conquest of Mexico,* originally published in 1933, set the tone for twentieth-century celebrations of the sixteenth-century missionary evangelization of Mexico. Ricard carried out his research in the 1920s, when Mexico was wracked by an intensely violent civil war.[12] Without question, in his work he sought to defend the Catholic Church, and the text is permeated by a heroic tone. Nevertheless, some aspects of Ricard's classic appear to have been ignored by subsequent generations. In 1940, while teaching at the University of Algiers, Ricard wrote a preface to the 1947 Spanish edition. Here he

10. A classic work is William H. McNeill, *Plagues and Peoples* (New York, 1976). See also Alfred W. Crosby, *Ecological Imperialism* (Cambridge, England, 1986).

11. Crosby, "The Columbian Voyages," 159.

12. Ricard, *Spiritual Conquest of Mexico,* vii–viii. The classic work on political/religious conflict in 1920s Mexico is Meyer, *La cristiada*. See also Becker, *Setting the Virgin on Fire,* and Purnell, *Popular Movements*.

explained that his book "tried to show that certain aspects of the activity of the Spanish missionaries, especially their attitude of 'tutelage' toward the Indians, and their decision to keep them out of the priesthood and the religious Orders, had unfavorable consequences for the history of the Church and perhaps for the Mexican nation itself."[13] He continued by arguing forcefully that "a Mexican Church was not founded [at all], and a Creole Church was barely founded. What was founded, before and above all, was a Spanish Church, organized along Spanish lines, governed by Spaniards, in which the native Christians played the minor part of second-class Christians."[14]

These reflections in the preface to the Spanish edition built upon a connection Ricard had made earlier, in the concluding chapter of the first edition. In a statement with interesting implications—especially given the subsequent war for Algerian independence from French colonialism—Ricard had mused that "however odd it may seem at first glance, the difficulties of Mexico bring to my mind the situation in Algeria."[15] Those recalling the so-called "spiritual conquest" of the sixteenth-century evangelization of the Americas would benefit from considering Ricard's observations. Is this really an event that merits celebration?

History and Theory

Throughout this book, I have stressed the presence of multiple meanings at all levels of historical interpretation. In addition, my findings reinforce a notion of lengthy intellectual pedigree, namely that the ability to speak and be heard, and to be recorded in historical archives and preserved in memory, is circumscribed by social, hence historical, relationships of power.[16] One need not master the at times byzantine world of contemporary theory to appreciate the significance of this reality, in life or for the practice of history. Nevertheless, a brief discussion of the theoretical concerns informing this book will facilitate the necessary task of clarifying my own interpretive stance. Ideally,

13. Ricard, *Spiritual Conquest of Mexico*, 297, 309; the quotation is from page 303.
14. Ibid., 308.
15. Ibid., 292.
16. Stern, "Paradigms of Conquest. " Recent work discussing the influence of social power on the construction of historical sources includes Silverblatt, "Interpreting Women in States," 140–71, esp. 142, 161–63, 165; Trouillot, *Silencing the Past;* Nathan Wachtel, *Gods and Vampires,* trans. Carol Volk (Chicago, 1994), 30–31; Florescano, *Memory, Myth and Time in Mexico,* 64, 65–99, 228–32; and Gruzinski, *Conquest of Mexico,* 1–5.

my comments will also serve to demystify and render accessible complex arguments that I have found to be of vital importance to my project.

The late Michel de Certeau reminded us that historians rooted in present times and places pursue real pasts, knowable only through language and the imagination.[17] Although not a new insight, especially in a Latin American context, this point has been asserted with increased vigor in recent years.[18] This is undoubtedly due to the shifting historical circumstances of the contemporary (postmodern?) world, which—as in the past—have decisively influenced epistemology and historical interpretation.[19] My more limited goal has been to refine our understanding of the history and historiography of early colonial Michoacán. Throughout this book, my emphasis has been on historical representation as a social process linking present and past.[20] I have sought to demonstrate the influence of historical context on the compilation and interpretation of written records, while also recognizing that "historical context" is itself discursively configured. In short, I emphasize "the historicity of texts" and "the textuality of history."[21]

As my research and writing developed, I entered into a productive and open-ended engagement with poststructuralist theory. The single most important influence has been de Certeau, but his writings represent only one element of a larger philosophical and historical project. In my view, the most

17. De Certeau, *The Writing of History,* 9–11, 29–30, 35, 38, 42–44. Also see Hayden White, *Metahistory* (Baltimore, 1973); Gayatri Chakravorty Spivak, "The Rani of Sirmur: An Essay on Reading the Archives," *History and Theory* 24, no. 3 (1985): 247–72, esp. 249–52; Edward Said, "Introduction: Secular Criticism," in *The World, the Text, and the Critic,* 1–30, esp. 4; and Eric Van Young, "The Cuautla Lazarus: Double Subjectives in Reading Texts on Popular Collective Action," *Colonial Latin American Review* 2, no. 1–2 (1993): 3–8.

18. John Beverly and José Oviedo, eds., "The Postmodernism Debate in Latin America," *boundary* 2, 20, no. 3 (Special Issue 1993). To gain a sense for the location and influence of Latin American history within the institutional space provided by the United States's academy over the last thirty years, see Steve J. Stern, "Africa, Latin America, and the Splintering of Historical Knowledge: From Fragmentation to Reverberation," in *Confronting Historical Paradigms,* ed. Frederick Cooper et al. (Madison, Wis., 1993), 3–20.

19. David Harvey, *The Condition of Postmodernity* (Oxford, 1989). Harvey's emphasis on "time-space compression" in the nineteenth and twentieth centuries is complemented nicely by Walter D. Mignolo, "The Movable Center: Geographical Discourses and Territoriality During the Expansion of the Spanish Empire," in Cevallos-Candau et al., *Coded Encounters,* 15–45.

20. Important comments in this regard can be found in Van Young, "The Cuatla Lazarus," 10, and Rolena Adorno, "Reconsidering Colonial Discourse for Sixteenth- and Seventeenth-Century Spanish America," *Latin American Research Review* 28, no. 3 (1993): 138–39.

21. Louis A. Montrose, "Professing the Renaissance: The Poetics and Politics of Culture," in *The New Historicism,* ed. H. Aram Veeser (London, 1989), 20.

important contribution of poststructuralism has been to reaffirm the indeterminacy of language—with a vigor that is arguably unprecedented—while making explicit the implications this has for our descriptions of reality, past and present.[22] Accepting this contribution, as developed by de Certeau, should not be equated with nihilism, radical skepticism, the denial of history, or a belief in its end. Rather, it indicates a recognition of the deeply rooted human desire to understand the past—in a sense, to transcend death—and a willingness to identify and question the factors that allow some accounts of the past to circulate, while excluding others.[23] Asking hard questions of history, and historical methods, should not be equated with a negation of their utility.

The insights and limitations of poststructuralism, and the other apparently proliferating "posts-" of the late twentieth and early twenty-first centuries, will remain contested into the foreseeable future.[24] My concern with poststructuralism in this book is limited to my appreciation of de Certeau's philosophy of history, and poststructuralism's influence on scholars from a variety of disciplines studying colonial Latin America. Current debates over the relevance of poststructuralist theory for the investigation of sixteenth- to eighteenth-century Latin America have clustered around the concept of "colonial discourse," which has been derived from but also challenges poststructuralism.[25] There are multiple intellectual origins for this concept as it is

22. On poststructuralism and the study of Latin America's colonial experience, see Van Young, "The Cuautla Lazarus"; Adorno, "Reconsidering Colonial Discourse," 138; and Franco, "Remapping Culture," esp. 176–77.

23. On the first point, see de Certeau, *The Writing of History,* 99–102. On the second, Mignolo, *The Darker Side of the Renaissance,* vii–25.

24. Those interested in pursuing current theoretical debates should consult the following: Tony Bennett, "Texts in History: The Determinations of Readings and their Texts," in *Post-Structuralism and the Question of History,* ed. Derek Attridge, Geoff Bennington, and Robert Young (Cambridge, England, 1987), 63–81; Montrose, "Professing the Renaissance," 15–36; and Micaela di Leonardo, "Gender, Culture and Political Economy: Feminist Anthropology in Historical Perspective," in di Leonardo, *Gender at the Crossroads of Knowledge,* 1–47. On the conflictual blending of poststructuralist criticism into "postmodernism," see Best and Kellner, *Postmodern Theory,* and E. Ann Kaplan, ed., *Postmodernism and Its Discontents* (London, 1988).

25. A recent, very productive exchange in the *Latin American Research Review* summarizes the issues. Patricia Seed's "Colonial and Postcolonial Discourse" *Latin American Research Review* 26, no. 3 (1991): 181–200, frames the issues and draws a series of interesting responses. See Adorno, "Reconsidering Colonial Discourse," 135–52; Walter Mignolo, "Colonial and Postcolonial Discourse: Cultural Critique or Academic Colonialism?" *Latin American Research Review* 28, no. 3 (1993): 120–34; Hernán Vidal, "The Concept of Colonial and Postcolonial Discourse: A Perspective from Literary Criticism," ibid., 113–19; and Seed, "More Colonial and Postcolonial

currently understood. A crucial moment in its elaboration, however, came with Edward Said's critical engagement with Foucauldian notions of discourse and discourse analysis.[26] Said's investigations into the explanatory strategies of colonial power resulted in pioneering work on the enduring cultural legacies of nineteenth- and twentieth-century British and French imperialism, especially as they pertain to representations of the colonial and neocolonial worlds.

In essence, "colonial discourse" refers to the political and cultural process of Europe's "othering" of the rest of the world during the centuries of colonial rule. It also recognizes the influence this experience has had on the definition, organization, and circulation of knowledge during and after the colonial centuries.[27] In the Latin American context, attention to the rhetoric of empire dates back at least to the work of Edmundo O'Gorman.[28] In recent years, a number of studies have returned to this theme, although in new ways, informed by different concerns and interpretive strategies. As is to be expected, these works—which together may or may not represent a "trend"—have generated substantial debate.[29] In my view, the overall impact of poststructuralism, and the introduction of the concept of "colonial discourse" into Latin American studies, has been positive. The net result has been renewed attention to questions of interpretive power, and the social and political factors that facilitate the construction of historical memory.

Discourses," ibid., 146–52. An overview and critique of recent debates from the perspective of a historian of Latin America's nineteenth and twentieth centuries is Florencia Mallon, "The Promise and Dilemma of Subaltern Studies: Perspectives from Latin American History," *American Historical Review* 99, no. 5 (December 1994): 1491–515.

26. Edward Said, *Orientalism* (New York, 1978). See Foucault, *The Order of Things* (1966; New York, 1970), esp. 34–42, 367–73. For productive critiques of Said, see James Clifford, "On Orientalism," in *The Predicament of Culture*, 255–76, and Aijaz Ahmad, *In Theory* (New York, 1992), 159–219, esp. 173–79.

27. For a succinct definition of "colonial discourse," in terms of Latin American culture, see Franco, "Remapping Culture," 176–77.

28. O'Gorman, *Invention of America*. This work involves a substantial elaboration and reworking of ideas sketched out in *La idea del descubrimiento de America* (Mexico City, 1952).

29. Recent works include Hulme, *Colonial Encounters*; Rabasa, *Inventing America* and "Writing and Evangelization"; Patricia Seed, "Taking Possession and Reading Texts: Establishing the Power of Overseas Empires," in Williams and Lewis, *Early Images of the Americas*, 111–47; and Stephan Greenblatt, ed., "The New World: Essays in Memory of Michel de Certeau," *Representations* 33 (Special Issue, Winter 1991). On O'Gorman, see Mignolo, "Colonial and Postcolonial Discourse," 120–34. For the contours of contemporary theoretical debates, in addition to the issue of the *Latin American Research Review* and the other works cited above, see *The Hispanic American Historical Review* 79, no. 2 (May 1999).

These theoretical issues can provide intriguing insights when pursued in reference to specific historical narratives.

The History of Michoacán

Historians, philosophers, rhetoricians, and others have long recognized that power creates plausible approximations of reality, although less attention has been paid to the specific mechanisms by which power is created, co-opted, subverted, neutralized, and ignored.[30] The recognition of agency—the ability to act, respond, define, and contest—allows us to note that even the most European of colonial sources bear the traces of an indigenous presence, if only in a distant and distorted way.[31] When one opens the sources preserving and transmitting the memory of Michoacán's "spiritual conquest" to this type of re/reading, several dominant colonial images are called into question.

These images include triumphant—though, at times, admittedly rapacious—conquistadors, in Michoacán represented by Nuño de Guzmán. As we saw in Chapter 1, the triumph of Nuño de Guzmán was short-lived. Rather than being "deviant," his actions—especially the execution of the Cazonci—proved to be quite functional for the founding of the colonial order in Michoacán. Ironically, the abuses associated with Nuño de Guzmán benefited not only his allies but also his opponents within the newly forming colonial elite. This latter category included the Franciscan missionaries, Vasco de Quiroga, and even opportunists like Cuinierángari or Don Pedro drawn from the indigenous male elite. Another image that must be revised is that of the Church as the "defender of the Indians." The sixteenth-century "encounter" between missionaries and indigenes involved destruction far

30. On attention to colonial rhetoric in Latin America prior to the emergence of poststructuralism in Europe, see Mignolo, "Colonial and Postcolonial Discourse. " For European philosophical background, see Richard Schacht, *Hegel and After* (Pittsburgh, 1975), and Best and Kellner, *Postmodern Theory*, 1–75. For varied responses to social power, see Scott, *Domination and the Arts of Resistance*. On varied strategies for negotiating gender hierarchies in colonial Mexico, see Stern, *Secret History of Gender*, esp. 148–50.

31. On postmodernism's inability to provide an adequate theory of agency, see Hutcheon, *The Politics of Postmodernism*, 3. On the indigenous presence in colonial sources, see Rolena Adorno, "Arms, Letters and the Native Historian in Early Colonial Mexico," in Jara and Spadaccini, 1492–1992, 201–24, esp. 202–8, and Sherry B. Ortner, "Resistance and the Problem of Ethnographic Refusal," *Comparative Studies in Society and History* 37, no. 1 (January 1995): 173–91, esp. 189. A pioneering work is Hulme's *Colonial Encounters*.

more than defense, and missionaries proved as susceptible to the attractions of power as any colonist. To the extent that moral concerns encouraged dissidents to protest, this was a good thing and should be acknowledged, though not to the extent that it deflects attention from the complicity of the colonial Church with Iberian imperialism. This complicity was demonstrated in detail in Chapters 2 and 3, in the examinations of the *Relación de Michoacán* and the writings of Vasco de Quiroga.

In Chapter 3 I sought to present Vasco de Quiroga in terms of his own sixteenth-century milieu. More than anything, this chapter demonstrates the gaps in our knowledge about this individual during his lifetime. The image that emerges from a handful of sources is of a "good *encomendero*," who succeeded in building a power base among a faction of indigenes through patron-client ties. In the early colonial period, a "good *encomendero*" would have been better than a "bad" one, but the image of Vasco de Quiroga as a successful missionary who understood and was loved by his indigenous charges stands in need of serious revision. Finally, the images of the natives as passive recipients of conquest, or conversely, as actors uniformly engaged in resistance, must also be revised. Tzintzincha Tangaxoan, the Cazonci, clearly maintained his authority in Michoacán until the moment of his execution. In fact, this was why settlers allied with Nuño de Guzmán killed him. To do so, he engaged in varied forms of resistance, including savvy alliance building with the faction of Spaniards led by Hernán Cortés. Years after his death, the newly installed opportunistic indigenous ruler Cuinierángari, or Don Pedro, recalled the Cazonci's execution for his Franciscan ally, who hoped to use this knowledge to influence the policies of the colonial state.

In the second part of this book I evaluated representations of early colonial history created at the distance granted by the passage of time. In these chapters I did not deny the reality of the past; instead, I emphasized that knowledge of the past comes to us through filters traceable to the needs of various "historical presents." In Chapter 4 I demonstrated this reality through a close reading of Pablo Beaumont's history of the "spiritual conquest." As I argued in Chapter 4, the forcefulness of Beaumont's search for heroic origins reveals an unintended subtext of indigenous rejection. His aggressive glorification of the colonial past also ironically indicated the Franciscans late-eighteenth-century position of increasing political and institutional weakness in Michoacán.

In Chapter 5 I continued this investigation of history and historiography by evaluating various definitions of Vasco de Quiroga from the eighteenth through the twentieth centuries. Despite varied interpretations, one can note remarkable continuity in the assumption that "Tata Vasco" understood and was loved by the indigenous peoples of Michoacán during his lifetime. It is precisely this colonial assumption that I seek to undermine by placing Vasco de Quiroga in his own historical context, and then asking where did the legendary figure come from, when, and in whose interest has the myth been elaborated? Vasco de Quiroga provides us with an example of a national symbol that blurs the lines between elite and popular culture. Nevertheless, it is plausible to argue that an emerging creole nationalism in the eighteenth century, liberal and conservative elites in the nineteenth century, and the Mexican Revolution in the twentieth century all led to substantial redefinitions of his mythic image.

Again, the point is not to deny the reality of the sixteenth century, but rather to note the historiographical distance that must be overcome to catch even a fleeting glimpse of the actual past. Given the weight of colonialism and its legacies on the construction of historical knowledge, it seems only prudent to urge caution and humility as we assess the past, from our various locations in the present.

Presents and Pasts

On October 26, 1990, the theater group "Juan Ruiz de Alarcon," directed by Mario Enríquez Torres, presented a dramatic rendition of the life of Don Vasco de Quiroga.[32] The performance was part of the ceremonial surrounding the transfer of his remains to their new and current location in the basilica of Pátzcuaro. It was staged at the Teatro Emperador Caltzontzín, which, as Manuel Toussaint remarked, incorporated elements of an ancient Augustinian monastery and received its "absurd name" when it was built in 1930.[33] The images presented appeared to conform to a classic morality play. Vasco de Quiroga humbly voiced reluctance to accept his nomination as bishop, because of the position's importance and status. However, after being requested to serve, he quickly challenged the tyranny of the cruel indigenous

32. Alejandro Aviles, "Presencia de Don Vasco en el Arte Teatral," *La voz de Michoacán,* October 26, 1990, 1B.

33. Toussaint, *Pátzcuaro,* 130.

elite, and directly interceded on behalf of the Indians to halt beatings administered by the brutal conquistador Nuño de Guzmán. Much to the delight of the audience—composed largely although not entirely of Purhépecha women and children—Nuño de Guzmán was finally led off in chains, and peace and harmony reigned. To the visitor's eye, one of the most notable features of the audience of Purhépecha women was their distinctive, predominantly blue shawls interlaced with lines of white, a much more beautiful pattern than the one permitted by Vasco de Quiroga's *Reglas*.[34]

Following the play, a different crowd, distinguished by pressed shirts, ties, and modest skirts, filed in to hear Silvio Zavala, the illustrious Mexican historian. Zavala, whose work on Vasco de Quiroga has been definitive for over half a century, delivered a lecture entitled "Vasco de Quiroga in Defense of Pátzcuaro." In it, he demonstrated how Vasco de Quiroga utilized legal means to defend Pátzcuaro from the unjust exactions of the colonial state, and suggested that he remains a relevant example for more contemporary struggles.[35] After Zavala's speech, most of the dignitaries left Pátzcuaro and returned to Morelia, Mexico City, and Seville. Those of more modest means began the long walk home, or to the bus station on the outskirts of this increasingly popular tourist destination.

On a billboard near the bus station, a graffiti artist had spray-painted "Welcome to Pátzcuaro, Enjoy the Repression."[36]

34. On the complexity of Purhépecha textiles, see Ruth Lechuga, *El traje indígena de México* (Mexico City, 1985), 192–94.

35. Additional sources discussing Zavala's lecture, besides the author's notes, are *La Voz de Michoacán* (Morelia, México), October 26, 1990, 9-B, and *La Jornada* (Mexico City), October 28, 1990, 14.

36. On political violence and human rights violations in Michoacán during this time, see John Gledhill, *Neoliberalism, Transnationalization and Rural Poverty* (Boulder, Colo., 1995), 1–23, 68–78, and Pascal Beltrán del Río, *Michoacán, ni un paso atrás* (Mexico City, 1993), 149–84.

Primary Sources

Acosta, P. Joseph de. *Historia natural y moral de las Indias.* Edited by Edmundo O'Gorman. Mexico City, 1960.

Acuña, René. *Vasco de Quiroga. De Debellendis Indis. Un tratado desconocido.* Mexico City, 1988.

Aguayo Spencer, Rafael, ed. *Don Vasco de Quiroga: Documentos.* Mexico City, 1940.

Basalenque, Diego de, O.S.A. *Los augustinos, aquellos misioneros hacendados.* Edited by Heriberto Moreno. Mexico City, 1985.

———. *Historia de la provincia de San Nicolás de Tolentino de Michoacán del orden de N.P.S. San Agustín.* Mexico City, 1673.

———. *Historia de la provincia de San Nicolás de Tolentino de Michoacán del orden de N.P.S. San Agustín.* 1673. Edited by Jose Bravo Ugarte. Mexico City, 1963.

Beaumont, Fray Pablo. *Crónica de Michoacán.* Ca. 1788. 3 vols. Mexico City, 1932.

The Chronicles of Michoacán. Translated and edited by Eugene R. Craine and Reginald C. Reindorp. Norman, Okla., 1970.

Cortés, Hernán. *Letters From Mexico.* Translated and edited by A. R. Pagden. New York, 1971.

Cuevas, P. Mariano, S.J. *Documentos inéditos del siglo XVI para la historia de México.* 1914. Mexico City, 1975.

Díaz del Castillo, Bernal. *The Conquest of New Spain.* Translated by J. M. Cohen. London, 1963.

———. *Historia verdadera de la conquista de la Nueva España.* 2 vols. 5th ed. Edited by Joaquin Ramírez Cabañas. Mexico City, 1960.

Escobar, Matías de. *Americana Thebiada, crónica de la provincia franciscana de los apostoles San Pedro y San Pablo de Michoacán.* 1729. Introduction by Nicolás de Navarrate. Morelia, Mexico, 1970.

Espinoza, Isidro Félix de. *Crónica de la provincia franciscana de los apostoles San Pedro y San Pablo de Michoacán.* Edited by Nicolás León and José Ignacio Dávila Garibi. Mexico City, 1945.

Fuentes, Patricia de, ed. and trans. *The Conquistadores: First-Person Accounts of the Conquest of Mexico.* New York, 1963.

Gilberti, Maturino. *Arte de la lengua de Michoacán.* 1558. Edited by J. Benedict Warren. Morelia, Mexico, 1987.

——. *Diccionario de la lengua tarasca.* 1559. Introduction by José Corona Núñez. Morelia, Mexico, 1983.

Gómara, López de. *Historia de la conquista de México.* 1552. Caracas, 1979.

Guzmán, Nuño de. *Memoria de los servicios que habia hecho Nuño de Guzmán, desde que fue nombrado gobernador de Panuco en 1525.* Edited and annotated by Manuel Carrera Stampa. Mexico City, 1955.

——. *Testamento de Nuño Beltrán de Guzmán.* Edited by Jorge Palomino y Cañedo. Mexico City, 1973.

"Juicio seguido por Hernán Cortés contra los Lics. Matienzo y Delgadillo año 1531." *Boletín del Archivo General de la Nación* 9, no. 3 (1938): 339–407.

Las Casas, Bartolomé de. *Brevísima relación de la destrucción de las Indias.* Edited by André Saint-Lu. Madrid, 1984.

León, Nicolás, comp. *Documentos ineditos referentes al ilustrísimo señor Don Vasco de Quiroga.* Mexico City, 1940.

Moreno, Juan José. *Fragmentos de la vida y virtudes de V.ILMO Y RMO. Sr. D. Vasco de Quiroga primer obispo de la santa catedral de Michoacán y fundador del real y primitivo colegio de S. Nicolas Obispo de Valladolid.* In Aguayo Spencer, *Don Vasco de Quiroga: Documentos.*

John Paul II. *Ecclesia en America.* http://www.vatican.va/holy_father/john_paul _ii/apost_exhortations/documents/hf_jp-ii_exh_22011999_ecclesia-in-america _en.html

Quiroga, Vasco de. "Carta al Consejo de Indias (14 de agosto de 1531)." In Aguayo Spencer, *Don Vasco de Quiroga: Taumaturgo de la organización social,* 77–83.

——. *Don Vasco de Quiroga y su Información en Derecho.* Edited by Paulino Casteñeda. Madrid, 1974.

——. *La Información en Derecho.* 1535. Edited by Carlos Herrejón. Mexico City, 1985.

——. *La Información en Derecho.* In *Colección de documentos inéditos relativos al descubrimiento, conquista y organización de las antiguas posesiones españoles en América y Oceania,* 10:333–525. Madrid, 1868.

——. *La Información en Derecho.* In Aguayo Spencer, *Don Vasco de Quiroga: Documentos,* 289–406.

——. *La Información en Derecho.* In Aguayo Spencer, *Don Vasco de Quiroga: Taumaturgo de la organización social,* 85–239.

——. *Reglas y ordenanzas para el gobierno de los hospitales de Santa Fe de México y de Michoacán.* In Aguayo Spencer, *Don Vasco de Quiroga: Taumaturgo de la organización social,* 242–69.

————. "Testamento de Don Vasco de Quiroga Primer Obispo de Michoacán, 24 de enero de 1565." In Miranda, *Don Vasco de Quiroga y su Colegio de San Nicolas,* 281–303.

————. *La utopía en América.* Edited by Paz Serrano Gassent. Madrid, 1992.

La Relación de Michoacán. Edited by Francisco Miranda. Morelia, Mexico, 1980.

Relación de Michoacán. Edited by José Tudela, preliminary study by José Corona Núñez. Morelia, Mexico, 1977.

Scholes, France V., and Eleanor B. Adams, eds. *Proceso contra Tzintzincha Tangaxoan el Caltzontzín, formado por Nuño de Guzmán, año de 1530.* Mexico City, 1952.

Tello, Fray Antonio. *Crónica miscelanea de la sancta provincia de Xalisco.* Guadalajara, Mexico, 1968.

Torquemada, Juan de. *Monarquía Indiana.* 7 vols. Edited by Miguel León Portilla. Mexico City, 1977.

Veracruz, Alonso de la. *The Writings of Alonso de La Veracruz.* 5 vols. Edited and translated by Ernest J. Burrus. Rome, 1968.

Secondary Sources

Adas, Michael, ed. *Islamic and European Expansion.* Philadelphia, 1993.

Adorno, Rolena. "Arms, Letters and the Native Historian in Early Colonial Mexico." In Jara and Spadaccini, *1492–1992,* 201–24.

————. "Discourses on Colonialism: Bernal Díaz, Las Casas, and the Twentieth-Century Reader." *MLN* 103, no. 2 (March 1988): 239–58.

————. "Introduction." In Leonard, *Books of the Brave,* ix–xl.

————. "Reconsidering Colonial Discourse for Sixteenth- and Seventeenth-Century Spanish America." *Latin American Research Review* 28, no. 3 (1993): 135–52.

Aguayo Spencer, Rafael. *Don Vasco de Quiroga: Taumaturgo de la organización social.* Mexico City, 1970.

Aguilar Camín, Héctor, and Lorenzo Meyer. *In the Shadow of the Mexican Revolution.* Translated by Luis Alberto Fierro. Austin, Tex., 1993.

Aguirre Beltrán, Gonzalo. *La población negra de México.* 1946. Mexico City, 1972.

Ahmad, Aijaz. *In Theory.* New York, 1992.

Ai Camp, Roderic. *Crossing Swords.* New York, 1997.

Aiton, Arthur Scott. *Antonio de Mendoza: First Viceroy of New Spain.* Durham, N.C., 1927.

Alberro, Solange. *Del gachupín al criollo.* Mexico City, 1992.

Alonso, Ana María. *Thread of Blood.* Tucson, Ariz., 1995.

Anderson, Benedict. *Imagined Communities.* London, 1983.

Andrews, George Reid. "Spanish American Independence: A Structural Analysis." *Latin American Perspectives* 44 (Winter 1985): 105–32.

Annis, Sheldon. *God and Production in a Guatemalan Town.* Austin, Tex., 1987.

Aristotle. *The Politics.* Edited by Stephan Everson. Cambridge, England, 1988.

Arrom, Sylvia Marina. *The Women of Mexico City, 1790–1857*. Stanford, Calif., 1985.
Attridge, Derek, Geoff Bennington, and Robert Young, eds. *Post-Structuralism and the Question of History*. Cambridge, England, 1987.
Aviles, Alejandro. "Presencia de Don Vasco en el arte teatral." *La Voz de Michoacán* (Morelia), October 26, 1990, 9-A, 1-B, 9-B.
Bancroft, Hubert Howe. *History of Mexico*, vol. 2, *1521–1600*. San Francisco, 1886.
Barabas, Alicia M. *Utopias indias*. Mexico City, 1987.
Barbosa Sánchez, Araceli. *Sexo y conquista*. Mexico City, 1994.
Barthes, Roland. "Historical Discourse." Translated by Peter Wexler. *Social Science Information* (International Social Science Council) 6, no. 4 (August 1967): 145–55.
———. "What Is Criticism?" In *Critical Essays*, trans. Richard Howard, 255–60. Evanston, Ill., 1972.
Barrett, Elinore M. *The Mexican Colonial Copper Industry*. Albuquerque, 1987.
Baruch, Elaine Hoffman. "Women in Men's Utopias." In Rohrlich and Baruch, *Women in Search of Utopia*, 209–19.
Bataillon, Marcel. "Don Vasco de Quiroga Utopien." *Moreana* 4, no. 15 (1967): 385–94.
———. *Erasmo y España*. 1937. Mexico City, 1950.
———. "Vasco de Quiroga et Bartolomé de Las Casas." *Revista de Historia de America* 33 (1952): 83–95.
Baudot, Georges. *History and Utopia in Mexico*. Translated by Bernard de Montellano and Thelma Ortiz de Montellano. 1980. Niwot, Colo., 1995.
Bauer, Arnold. "The Colonial Economy." In Hoberman and Socolow, *The Countryside in Colonial Latin America*, 19–48.
Bayle, Constantino, S.J. *El clero secular y la evangelización de America*. Madrid, 1950.
———. *El IV centenario de don Fray Juan de Zumárraga*. Madrid, 1953.
Beals, Ralph L. "The Tarascans." In *The Handbook of Middle American Indians*, vol. 8, no. 2, pp. 725–73. Austin, Tex., 1969.
———. *Cheran*. Washington, D.C., 1946.
Beals, Ralph L., Pedro Carrasco, and Thomas McCorkle. *Houses and House Use of the Sierra Tarascans*. Washington, D.C., 1944.
Becker, Marjorie. *Setting the Virgin on Fire*. Berkeley, Calif., 1995.
Beezley, William H., Cheryl English Martin, and William E. French, eds. *Rituals of Rule, Rituals of Resistance*. Wilmington, Del., 1994.
Beltrán, Ulises. "Estado y sociedad tarascos." In Carrasco et al., *La sociedad indígena*, 45–62.
———. "Tarascan State and Society in Prehispanic Times: An Ethnohistorical Inquiry." Ph.D. diss., University of Chicago, 1985.
Beltrán del Rio, Pascal. *Michoacán, ni un paso atrás*. Mexico City, 1993.
Benjamin, Walter. *Illuminations*. Edited by Hannah Arendt, translated by Harry Zohn. New York, 1968.
Bennett, Tony. "Texts in History." In Attridge, Bennington, and Young, *Post-Structuralism and the Question of History*, 63–81.

Bentley, Jerry H. *Old World Encounters*. New York, 1993.
Berryman, Philip. *Stubborn Hope*. New York, 1994.
Best, Steven, and Douglas Kellner. *Postmodern Theory*. New York, 1991.
Beverly, John, and José Oviedo, eds. "The Postmodernism Debate in Latin America." *boundary 2* 20, no. 3 (Special Issue 1993).
Bhabha, Homi K. *The Location of Culture*. London, 1994.
Biermann, Benno, O.P. "Don Vasco de Quiroga y su tratado *De Debellendis Indis (II)*." *Historia Mexicana* 18, no. 4 (April-June 1969).
Biersack, Aletta. "Local Knowledge, Local History: Geertz and Beyond." In Hunt, *The New Cultural History*, 72–96.
Bitterli, Urs. *Cultures in Conflict: Encounters Between European and Non-European Cultures, 1492–1800*. Translated by Ritchie Robertson. Cambridge, England, 1989.
Blackburn, Robin. *The Making of New World Slavery*. New York, 1997.
Borges, Pedro. *Métodos misionales en la cristianización de America*. Madrid, 1958.
———. "Vasco de Quiroga en el ambiente misionero de la Nueva España." *Missionalia Hispanica* 67 (1966): 297–340.
Bourdieu, Pierre. *The Logic of Practice*. Translated by Richard Nice. Stanford, Calif., 1990.
———. *Outline of a Theory of Practice*. Translated by Richard Nice. Cambridge, England, 1977.
Brading, David. *Church and State in Bourbon Mexico*. Cambridge, England, 1994.
———. *The First America*. Cambridge, England, 1991.
Brand, Donald D. "Ethnohistoric Synthesis of Western Mexico." In *The Handbook of Middle American Indians*, vol. 2, pp. 632–56. Austin, Tex., 1971.
———. *Quiroga: A Mexican Municipio*. Assisted by José Corona Nuñéz. Washington, D.C., 1951.
Bravo Ugarte, José. *Diocésis y obispos de la iglesia mexicana (1519–1965)*. Mexico City, 1941.
———. *Historia sucinta de Michoacán*. 3 vols. Mexico City, 1962.
Brown, Peter. *The Body and Society*. New York, 1988.
Burdick, John. *Looking for God in Brazil*. Berkeley, Calif., 1993.
Burke, Peter, ed. *New Perspectives on Historical Writing*. University Park, Pa., 1992.
Burkholder, Mark A., and Lyman L. Johnson. *Colonial Latin America*. Oxford, 1990.
Cabrera V., Ma. del Refugio, and Benjamín Pérez González. *El estado p'urhepecha y sus fronteras en el siglo XVI*. Morelia, Mexico, 1991.
Callens, Paul L., S.J. *Tata Vasco*. Mexico City, 1959.
Carr, Barry. *Marxism and Communism in Twentieth-Century Mexico*. Lincoln, Nebr., 1992.
Carrasco, Pedro. *El catolicismo popular de los tarascos*. Mexico City, 1976.
———. "Economia y política en el reino tarasco." In Carrasco et al., *La sociedad indígena*, 63–102.
———. "Parentesco y regulación del matrimonio entre los indios del antiguo Michoacán, México." *Revista Española de Antropología Americana* 4 (1969): 219–22.

————. *Tarascan Folk Religion*. New Orleans, 1952.

Carrasco, Pedro, et al. *La sociedad indígena en el centro y occidente de México.* Zamora, Mexico, 1986.

Caso, Alfonso. "Presencia de Don Vasco." *Cuadernos Americanos* 141, no. 4 (July-August 1965): 139–47.

Castro-Leal, Marcia, Clara L. Díaz, and Ma. Teresa García. "Los tarascos." In Florescano, *Historia General de Michoacán*, 1:191–304.

Certeau, Michel de. *Heterologies.* Translated by Brian Massumi. Minneapolis, 1986.

————. *The Practice of Everyday Life.* Translated by Steven F. Rendell. Berkeley, Calif., 1984.

————. *The Writing of History.* 1975. Translated by Tom Conley. New York, 1988.

Cervantes, Fernando. *The Devil in the New World.* New Haven, Conn., 1994.

Cevallos-Candau, Francisco Javier, et al. *Coded Encounters.* Amherst, Mass., 1994.

Chang-Rodríguez, Raquel. "Cultural Resistance in the Andes and Its Depiction in *Atau Wallpaj P'uchukakuyninpa Wankan* or *Tragedy of Atahualpa's Death.*" In Cevallos-Candau et al., *Coded Encounters*, 115–34.

Chartier, Roger. "Intellectual History or Sociocultural History? The French Trajectories." In LaCapra and Kaplan, *Modern European Intellectual History*, 13–46.

————. "Texts, Printings, Readings." In Hunt, *The New Cultural History*, 154–75.

Chiapelli, Fredi, ed. *First Images of America: The Impact of the New World on the Old.* Berkeley, Calif., 1976.

Chipman, Donald E. *Nuño de Guzmán and the Province of Panuco in New Spain.* Glendale, Calif., 1967.

Christian, William. *Local Religion in Sixteenth-Century Spain.* Princeton, 1981.

The Church in Latin America, 1492–1992. Maryknoll, N.Y., 1992.

Cleary, Edward L. "The Journey to Santo Domingo." In Hennelly, *Santo Domingo and Beyond*, 3–23.

Clendinnen, Inga. *Ambivalent Conquests: Maya and Spaniard in Yucatán, 1517–1570.* Cambridge, England, 1987.

————. *The Aztecs.* Cambridge, England, 1991.

————. "The Cost of Courage in Aztec Society." *Past and Present* 107 (May 1985): 44–89.

————. "Disciplining the Indians: Franciscan Ideology and Missionary Violence in Sixteenth-Century Yucatán." *Past and Present* 94 (February 1982): 27–48.

————. "Fierce and Unnatural Cruelty": Cortés and the Conquest of Mexico. *Representations* 33 (Winter 1991): 65–100.

Clifford, James. *The Predicament of Culture.* Cambridge, Mass., 1988.

Clifford, James, and George E. Marcus. *Writing Culture.* Berkeley, Calif., 1986.

Collier, George A., Renato I. Rosaldo, and John D. Wirth, eds. *The Inca and Aztec States, 1400–1800.* New York, 1982.

Comaroff, John, and Jean Comaroff. *Ethnography and the Historical Imagination.* Boulder, Colo., 1992.

Coronil, Fernando. "Listening to the Subaltern: The Poetics of Neocolonial States." *Poetics Today* 15, no. 4 (Winter 1994): 643–58.

Cooper, Frederick. "Conflict and Contention: Rethinking Colonial African History." *American Historical Review* 99, no. 5 (December 1994): 1516–45.

Cooper, Frederick, et al. *Confronting Historical Paradigms.* Madison, Wis., 1993.

Cope, R. Douglas. *The Limits of Racial Domination.* Madison, Wis., 1994.

Crosby, Alfred W. *The Columbian Exchange.* Westport, Conn., 1972.

———. "The Columbian Voyages and Their Historians." In Adas, *Islamic and European Expansion,* 141–64.

———. *Ecological Imperialism.* Cambridge, England, 1986.

Cuevas, P. Mariano, S.J. *Historia de la Iglesia en México.* 2 vols. Mexico City, 1921.

Davis, Natalie Zemon. "Poor Relief, Humanism and Heresy." In *Society and Culture in Early Modern France.* Stanford, Calif., 1975.

Dealy, Ross. *The Politics of an Erasmian Lawyer, Vasco de Quiroga.* Malibu, Calif., 1976.

Dillon, Sam. "A Rebel Creed, Stifled by the Pope, Flickers Still." *New York Times,* January 21, 1999, A4.

Don Vasco de Quiroga y Arzobispado de Morelia. Mexico City, 1965.

Dussel, Enrique. *The Invention of the Americas.* Translated by Michael D. Barber. New York, 1995.

Eagleton, Terry, Fredric Jameson, and Edward W. Said. *Nationalism, Colonialism and Literature.* Minneapolis, 1990.

Eagleton, Terry. *Literary Theory.* Minneapolis, 1983.

Edwards, Emily, and Manuel Álvarez Bravo. *Painted Walls of Mexico.* Austin, Tex., 1966.

Estrada, Genaro. "Introducción a la 'Utopia' de Tomas Moro en la Nueva España (1937)." In Zavala, *Recuerdo de Vasco de Quiroga,* 160–65.

Farriss, Nancy. *Maya Society Under Colonial Rule.* Princeton, 1984.

Fernandez, Justino, and Edmundo O'Gorman. *Santo Tomas Moro y "La utopia de Tomas Moro en la Nueva España."* Mexico City, 1937.

Florescano, Enrique. *Memory, Myth and Time in Mexico.* Translated by Albert G. Bork with the assistance of Kathryn R. Bork. Austin, Tex., 1994.

———, ed. *Historia general de Michoacán.* 4 vols. Morelia, Mexico, 1989.

Foster, George M. *Tzintzuntzan.* Boston, 1967.

Foster, George M., assisted by Gabriel Ospina. *Empire's Children.* Washington, D.C., 1948.

Foucault, Michel. *Discipline and Punish.* Translated by Alan Sheridan. New York, 1979.

———. *The History of Sexuality.* Translated by Robert Hurley. New York, 1978.

———. "Nietzsche, Genealogy, History." In *The Foucault Reader,* ed. Paul Rabinow, 76–100. New York, 1984.

———. *The Order of Things.* 1966. New York, 1970.

Franco, Jean. *Plotting Women: Gender and Representation in Mexico.* New York, 1989.

———. "Remapping Culture." In Stepan, *Americas,* 172–88.

French, Howard W. "Dissent Shadows Pope on His Visit." *New York Times,* October 14, 1992, A15.

Friede, Juan. "Las Casas and Indigenism in the Sixteenth Century." In Friede and Keen, *Bartolomé Las Casas in History*, 127–234.

Friede, Juan, and Benjamin Keen, eds. *Bartolomé Las Casas in History*. Dekalb, Ill., 1971.

Friedrich, Paul. *The Princes of Naranja*. Austin, Tex., 1986.

Fuentes, Carlos. *Valiente mundo nuevo*. Madrid, 1990.

Galeano, Eduardo. *Memory of Fire*. 3 vols. Translated by Cedric Belfrage. New York, 1985–88.

Gallegos Rocafull, José M. *El pensamiento mexicano en los siglos XVI-XVII*. Mexico City, 1951.

Gampel, Benjamin R. *The Last Jews on Iberian Soil*. Berkeley, Calif., 1989.

García Canclini, Nestor. *Las culturas populares en el capitalismo*. Havana, 1982.

———. *Hybrid Cultures*. Translated by Christopher L. Chiappari and Silvia L. López. Minneapolis, 1995.

Gardiner, C. Harvey. *Martín López*. Lexington, Ky., 1958.

Geertz, Clifford. *Works and Lives*. Stanford, Calif., 1988.

Geoghegan, Vincent. *Utopianism and Marxism*. London, 1987.

Gerhard, Peter. *A Guide to the Historical Geography of New Spain*. Norman, Okla., 1993.

Gibson, Charles. *The Aztecs Under Spanish Rule*. Stanford, Calif., 1964.

———. *Spain in America*. New York, 1966.

Ginzberg, Carlo. *The Cheese and the Worms*. Translated by John Tedeschi and Anne Tedeschi. Baltimore, 1980.

———. *Clues, Myths, and the Historical Method*. Translated by John Tedeschi and Anne Tedeschi. Baltimore, 1989.

Gledhill, John. *Neoliberalism, Transnationalization and Rural Poverty*. Boulder, Colo., 1995.

Goldberg, Jonathan. *Sodometries*. Stanford, Calif., 1992.

———. "Sodomy in the New World: Anthropologies Old and New." *Social Text* 29 (1991): 46–56.

Gomes Moreira, José Aparecido. *Conquista y conciencia cristiana*. Quito, 1990.

Góngora, Mario. *El estado en el derecho indiano*. Santiago, Chilé, 1951.

González Echevarría, Roberto. *Myth and Archive*. Cambridge, England, 1990.

González, Luis. *San José de Gracia*. Austin, Tex., 1972.

———. "Viaje a las crónicas monásticas de Michoacán en busca de los purépecha." In Miranda, *La cultura Purhé*, 50–70.

———. *La vuelta a Michoacán en* 500 libros. Zamora, Mexico, 1994.

Gorenstein, Shirley, and Helen Perlstein Pollard. *The Tarascan Civilization*. Nashville, Tenn., 1983.

Gramsci, Antonio. *Selections from the Prison Notebooks*. Edited and translated by Quintin Hoare and Geoffrey Nowell Smith. New York, 1971.

Grayson, George W. *The Church in Contemporary Mexico*. Washington, D.C., 1992.

Greenblatt, Stephan, ed. "The New World: Essays in Memory of Michel de Certeau." *Representations* 33 (Special Issue, Winter 1991).

Gruzinski, Serge. *The Conquest of Mexico.* 1988. Translated by Eileen Corrigan. Cambridge, England, 1993.

———. *Man-Gods in the Mexican Highlands.* Translated by Eileen Corrigan. Stanford, Calif., 1989.

Gutiérrez, Gustavo. *Las Casas.* Translated by Michael D. Barber. New York, 1995.

Gutiérrez, Ramón. "Honor Ideology, Marriage Negotiation, and Class-Gender Domination in New Mexico, 1690–1846." *Latin American Perspectives* 44 (Winter 1985): 81–104.

———. *When Jesus Came, the Corn Mothers Went Away.* Stanford, Calif., 1991.

Hamilton, Nora. *The Limits of State Autonomy.* Princeton, 1982.

Hanke, Lewis. *Aristotle and the American Indians.* Chicago, 1959.

———. "A Modest Proposal for a Moratorium on Grand Generalizations: Some Thoughts on the Black Legend." *Hispanic American Historical Review* 51, no. 1 (1971): 112–27.

———. *The Spanish Struggle for Justice in the Conquest of America.* Philadelphia, 1949.

Haring, C. H. *The Spanish Empire in America.* Oxford, 1947.

Harris, Max. "Disguised Reconciliations: Indigenous Voices in Early Franciscan Missionary Drama in Mexico." *Radical History Review* 53 (1992): 13–25.

Harvey, David. *The Condition of Postmodernity.* Oxford, 1989.

Hassig, Ross. *Mexico and the Spanish Conquest.* London, 1994.

Hebblethwaite, Peter. "Bid to Beatify Isabella Will Ignite Furor." *National Catholic Reporter,* January 18, 1991, 10.

Hemming, John. *The Conquest of the Incas.* London, 1970.

Hennelly, Alfred T., S.J. "A Report from the Conference." In Hennelly, *Santo Domingo and Beyond,* 24–36.

———, ed. *Santo Domingo and Beyond.* Maryknoll, N.Y., 1993.

Henning, E. M. "Archaeology, Deconstruction, and Intellectual History." In LaCapra and Kaplan, *Modern European Intellectual History,* 153–96.

Herrejón, Carlos. "Dos obras señaladas de Don Vasco de Quiroga." In *Don Vasco de Quiroga y Arzobispado de Morelia,* 63–106.

———. "*La Información en Derecho* de Vasco de Quiroga como fuente para el estudio de los indios." In Carrasco et al., *La sociedad indígena,* 129–39.

———, ed. *Humanismo y ciencia en la formación de México.* Zamora, Mexico, 1984.

Hill, Elizabeth Boone, and Walter D. Mignolo, eds. *Writing Without Words.* Durham, N.C., 1994.

Himmerich, Robert Theron. "The Encomenderos of New Spain, 1521–1555." Ph.D. diss., University of California, Los Angeles, 1984.

Hispanic American Historical Review 79, no. 2 (May 1999). *Special Issue: Mexico's New Cultural History: ¿Una Lucha Libre?*

Hoberman, Louisa Schell, and Susan Midgen Socolow, eds. *The Countryside in Colonial Latin America.* Albuquerque, 1996.

Hu-Dehart, Evelyn. *Missionaries, Miners and Indians.* Tucson, Ariz., 1981.

Hulme, Peter. *Colonial Encounters.* London, 1986.

Hunt, Lynn. "Introduction." In Hunt, *The New Cultural History*, 1–24.
———, ed. *The New Cultural History*. Berkeley, Calif., 1989.
Hutcheon, Linda. *The Politics of Postmodernism*. London, 1989.
Israel, J. I. *Race, Class, and Politics in Colonial Mexico, 1610–1670*. Bath, 1975.
Jacoby, Russell. "A New Intellectual History?" *American Historical Review* 97, no. 2 (April 1992): 405–24.
Jara, René, and Nicholas Spadaccini, eds. *1492–1992: Re/Discovering Colonial Writing*. Minneapolis, 1989.
Jarnes, Benjamin. *Don Vasco de Quiroga, obispo de utopia*. Mexico City, 1942.
Kadir, Djelal. *Columbus and the Ends of the Earth*. Berkeley, Calif., 1992.
Kaplan, E. Ann, ed. *Postmodernism and Its Discontents*. London, 1988.
Kaplan, Steven, ed. *Indigenous Responses to Western Christianity*. New York, 1995.
Katz, Friedrich, ed. *Riot, Rebellion and Revolution*. Princeton, 1984.
Keen, Benjamin. "The Black Legend Revisited: Assumptions and Realities." *Hispanic American Historical Review* 49, no. 2 (February 1969): 703–19.
———. *A History of Latin America*. 5th ed. Boston, 1996.
Kellog, Susan. "Hegemony out of Conquest: The First Two Centuries of Spanish Rule in Central Mexico." *Radical History Review* 53 (1992): 27–46.
Kemper, Robert V. "Urbanización y desarrollo en la región tarasca a partir de 1940." In De la Peña, *Antropología social de la región purépecha*.
Kenyon, Timothy. *Utopian Communism and Political Thought in Early Modern England*. London, 1988.
Klor de Alva, Jorge. "The Postcolonization of the (Latin American) Experience: A Reconsideration of 'Colonialism'." In Prakash, *After Colonialism*, 241–75.
———. "Spiritual Conflict and Accommodation in New Spain: Toward a Typology of Aztec Responses to Christianity." In Collier, Rosaldo and Wirth, *The Inca and Aztec States*, 345–66.
———. "Spiritual Warfare in Mexico: Christianity and the Aztecs." Ph.D. diss., University of California, Santa Cruz, 1980.
Kobayashi, José María. *La educación como conquista (empresa franciscana en México)*. Mexico City, 1974.
Kohut, Karl, ed. *De conquistadores y conquistados*. Frankfurt am Main, 1992.
Kramer, Lloyd S. "Literature, Criticism, and Historical Imagination: The Literary Challenge of Hayden White and Dominick LaCapra." In Hunt, *The New Cultural History*, 97–128.
Krippner-Martínez, James. "Invoking Tata Vasco: Vasco de Quiroga, 18th–20th Centuries." *The Americas* 56, no. 3 (January 2000): 1–28.
———. "The Politics of Conquest: An Interpretation of the *Relación de Michoacán*." *The Americas* 47, no. 2 (October 1990): 177–98.
———. "The Vision of the Victors: Power and Colonial Justice." *Colonial Latin American Review* 4, no. 1 (1995): 3–28.
Kselman, Thomas A. "Ambivalence and Assumption in the Concept of Popular Religion." In Levine, *Religion and Political Conflict in Latin America*, 24–41.
Kumar, Krishan. *Utopia and Anti-Utopia in Modern Times*. Oxford, 1987.

LaCapra, Dominick, and Steven L. Kaplan, eds. *Modern European Intellectual History.* Ithaca, N.Y., 1982.

LaCapra, Dominick. "Intellectual History and Its Ways." *American Historical Review* 97, no. 2 (April 1992): 425–39.

———. "Rethinking European History and Reading Texts." In LaCapra and Kaplan, *Modern European Intellectual History,* 47–85

Lacas, M. M. "A Social Welfare Organizer in Sixteenth-Century New Spain: Don Vasco de Quiroga, First Bishop of Michoacán." *The Americas* 14 (1957–58): 57–86.

Laclau, Ernesto, and Chantal Mouffe. *Hegemony and Socialist Strategy.* London, 1985.

Lancaster, Roger N. *Life Is Hard.* Berkeley, Calif., 1992.

Landa, Ruben. *Don Vasco de Quiroga.* Mexico City, 1965.

Langer, Erick, and Robert H. Jackson, eds. *The New Latin American Mission History.* Lincoln, Nebr., 1995.

Langguth, A. J. *Hidden Terrors.* New York, 1978.

Larson, Brooke. *Colonialism and Agrarian Transformation in Bolivia.* Princeton, 1988.

Lavrin, Asunción, ed. *Sexuality and Marriage in Colonial Latin America.* Lincoln, Nebr., 1989.

Lechuga, Ruth. *El traje indígena de México.* Mexico City, 1985.

Leitz, Paul S. "Don Vasco de Quiroga and the Second Audiencia of New Spain." Ph.D. diss., Loyola University, 1940.

Lejarza, Fidel de, O.F.M. "Don Vasco de Quiroga en las crónicas franciscanas." *Missionalia Hispanica* 23, no. 68 (1966): 129–256.

León, Nicolás. *El ylmo. señor Don Vasco de Quiroga primer obispo de Michoacán. Grandeza de su persona y su obra; estudio biográfico y crítico premiado en los Juegos Florales del estado de Michoacán el año de 1903.* Morelia, Mexico, 1903.

Leonard, Irving. *Baroque Times in Old Mexico.* Ann Arbor, Mich., 1959.

———. *Books of the Brave.* 1949. Berkeley, Calif., 1992.

Leonardo, Micaela di, ed. *Gender at the Crossroads of Knowledge.* Berkeley, Calif., 1991.

———. "Gender, Culture and Political Economy: Feminist Anthropology in Historical Perspective." In *Gender at the Crossroads of Knowledge,* 1–47.

Lerner, Gerda. *The Creation of Patriarchy.* Oxford, 1986.

Levi, Giovanni. "On Microhistory." In Burke, *New Perspectives,* 93–113.

Levine, Daniel H. "Conflict and Renewal." In *Religion and Political Conflict in Latin America,* 236–56.

———, ed. *Religion and Political Conflict in Latin America.* Chapel Hill, N.C., 1981.

Limerick, Patricia. *The Legacy of Conquest.* New York, 1987.

Liss, Peggy K. *Mexico Under Spain, 1521–1566.* Chicago, 1975.

Lockhart, James. *The Nahuas After the Conquest.* Stanford, Calif., 1992.

———. *Nahuas and Spaniards.* Stanford, Calif., 1991.

———. "Sightings: Initial Nahua Reactions to Spanish Culture." In Schwartz, *Implicit Understanding,* 218, 248.

Lombardo Toledano, Vicente. "Don Vasco de Quiroga fundador de la escuela de la acción." *Excelsior,* September 7, 1929, 5, 9.

———. *El problema de la educación en México.* Mexico City, 1924.

———. *El problema del indio.* Mexico City, 1973.

López Austin, Alfredo. *The Human Body and Ideology.* 2 vols. Translated by Thelma Ortiz de Montellano and Bernard Ortiz de Montellano. Salt Lake City, Utah, 1988.

———. *The Rabbit on the Face of the Moon.* Translated by Bernard R. Ortiz de Montellano and Thelma Ortiz de Montellano. Salt Lake City, Utah, 1996.

———. *Tarascos y Mexicas.* Mexico City, 1981.

López Lara, P. Ramón. "Los Hospitales de la Concepción." In Miranda and Briseño, *Vasco de Quiroga,* 112–28.

———. "El Oidor." In *Don Vasco de Quiroga y Arzobispado de Morelia,* 27–43.

López-Portillo y Weber, José. *La conquista de la Nueva Galicia.* Mexico City, 1935.

López Sarrelangue, Delfina Esmeralda. *La nobleza indígena de Pátzcuaro en la época virreinal.* Mexico City, 1965.

Lynch, John. *The Spanish American Revolutions, 1808–1826.* 1973. New York, 1986.

Lumholtz, Carl. *Unknown Mexico.* 2 vols. New York, 1902.

Luna Arroyo, Antonio. *Juan O'Gorman.* Mexico City, 1973.

MacCormack, Sabine. "The Heart Has Its Reasons: Predicaments of Missionary Christianity in Early Colonial Peru." *Hispanic American Historical Review* 67 (1985): 443–66.

———. "Pachacuti: Miracles, Punishments, and Last Judgments: Visionary Past and Prophetic Future in Early Colonial Peru." *American Historical Review* 93, no. 4 (October 1988): 960–1006.

———. *Religion in the Andes.* Princeton, 1991.

Mackenthun, Gesa. *Metaphors of Dispossession.* Norman, Okla., 1997.

MacLachlan, Colin M. *Spain's Empire in the New World.* Berkeley, Calif., 1988.

Magner, James A. *Men of Mexico.* 1942. Freeport, N.Y., 1968.

Mallon, Florencia. *Peasant and Nation.* Berkeley, Calif., 1995.

———. "The Promise and Dilemma of Subaltern Studies: Perspectives from Latin American History." *American Historical Review* 99, no. 5 (December 1994): 1491–1515.

Maravall, José Antonio. *Culture of the Baroque.* Translated by Terry Cochran. Minneapolis, 1986.

Marcus, George E., and Dick Cushman. "Ethnographies As Texts." *American Review of Anthropology* 11 (1982): 25–69.

Martín Hernández, Francisco. *Don Vasco de Quiroga (Protector de los indios).* Salamanca, 1993.

Martínez, Herminio. *Diario maldito de Nuño de Guzmán.* Mexico City, 1990.

Martínez, Rodrigo. "Los inicios de la colonización." In Florescano, *Historia General de Michoacán,* 2:39–73.

Mazín, Oscar. *Entre dos Majestades.* Zamora, Mexico, 1987.

McNeill, William H. *Plagues and Peoples.* New York, 1976.

Mendieta y Nuñéz, Lucio, ed. *Los tarascos*. Mexico City, 1940.

Mendoza Briones, Marian Ofelia, and Marta Terán. "Repercusiones de la política borbonica." In Florescano, *Historia General de Michoacán*, 2:218–33.

Merino, Manual, O.S.A. "Don Vasco de Quiroga en los cronistas agustinianos." *Missionalia Hispanica* 23, no. 67 (1966): 89–127.

Meyer, Jean. *La cristiada*. 3 vols. Mexico City, 1973.

Meyer, Michael, and William Sherman. *The Course of Mexican History*. Oxford, 1991.

Mignolo, Walter D. "Afterword: Writing and Recorded Knowledge in Colonial and Postcolonial Situations." In Hill and Mignolo, *Writing Without Words*, 293–313.

———. "Colonial and Postcolonial Discourse: Cultural Critique or Academic Colonialism?" *Latin American Research Review* 28, no. 3 (1993): 120–34.

———. *The Darker Side of the Renaissance*. Ann Arbor, Mich., 1995.

———. "Literacy and Colonization: The New World Experience." In Jara and Spadaccini, *1492–1992*.

———. "The Movable Center: Geographical Discourses and Territoriality During the Expansion of the Spanish Empire." In Cevallos-Candau et al., *Coded Encounters*, 15–45.

Miranda, Francisco. *Don Vasco de Quiroga y su Colegio de San Nicolas*. Morelia, Mexico, 1972.

———. "Vasco de Quiroga, artifice humanista de Michoacán." In Herrejón, *Humanismo y ciencia*, 131–49.

———, comp. *La cultura Purhé: II coloquio de antropología e historia regionales*. Zamora, Mexico, 1980.

Miranda, Francisco, and Gabriela Briseño, comp. *Vasco de Quiroga: Educador de adultos*. Pátzcuaro, Mexico, 1984.

Miranda, José. "La fraternidad cristiana y labor social de la primitiva iglesia mexicana." *Cuadernos Americanos* 141, no. 4 (July-August 1965): 148–58.

———. *El tributo indigena en la Nueva España durante el siglo XVI*. Mexico City, 1952.

Moheno, César. *Las historias y los hombres de San Juan*. Zamora, Mexico, 1985.

Montrose, Louis. "Professing the Renaissance: The Poetics and Politics of Culture." In Veeser, *The New Historicism*, 15–36.

———. "The Work of Gender in the Discourse of Discovery." *Representations* 33 (Winter 1991): 1–41.

Moran Alvarez, Julio Cesar. *El pensamiento de Vasco de Quiroga*. Morelia, Mexico, 1990.

Moraña, Mabel, ed. *Relecturas del barroco del Indias*. Hanover, N.H., 1994.

Morin, Claude. *Michoacán en la Nueva España del siglo XVIII*. Mexico City, 1979.

More, St. Thomas. *Utopia*. Edited by Edward Surtz, S.J. New Haven, Conn., 1964.

Morse, Richard. "The Heritage of Latin America." In *The Founding of New Societies*, ed. Louis Hartz et al., 123–77. New York, 1964.

———. "Towards a Theory of Spanish American Government." *Journal of the History of Ideas* 15, no. 1 (January 1954): 71–93.

Muriel, Josefina. *Hospitales de la Nueva España*. 2 vols. Mexico City, 1956.

Nelson, Cary, and Lawrence Grossberg, eds. *Marxism and the Interpretation of Culture*. Urbana, Ill., 1988.

Novick, Peter. *That Noble Dream*. Cambridge, England, 1988.

O'Brien, David J., and Thomas A. Shannon. *Renewing the Earth*. New York, 1977.

O'Brien, Patricia. "Michel Foucault's History of Culture." In Hunt, *The New Cultural History*, 25–46.

O'Gorman, Edmundo. *La idea del descubrimiento de America*. Mexico City, 1952.

———. *The Invention of America*. Bloomington, Ind., 1961.

———. "Lewis Hanke on the Spanish Struggle for Justice in the Conquest of America." *Hispanic American Historical Review* 29 (1949): 563–71.

O'Malley, Ilene V. *The Myth of the Revolution*. Westport, Conn., 1986.

Ortner, Sherry B. "Resistance and the Problem of Ethnographic Refusal." *Comparative Studies in Society and History* 37, no. 1 (January 1995): 173–91.

Pagden, Anthony. *European Encounters with the New World*. New Haven, Conn., 1993.

———. *The Fall of Natural Man*. Cambridge, England, 1982.

———. "Rethinking the Linguistic Turn: Current Anxieties in Intellectual History," *Journal of the History of Ideas* 49 (1988): 519–29.

———. *Spanish Imperialism and the Political Imagination*. New Haven, Conn., 1990.

———. *The Uncertainties of Empire*. Aldershot, England, and Brookfield, Vt., 1994.

Pagden, Anthony, and Nicolas Canny. *Colonial Identity in the Atlantic World*. Princeton, 1987.

Pagels, Elaine. *Adam, Eve and the Serpent*. New York, 1988.

Palmer, Colin. *Slaves of the White God: Blacks in Mexico, 1570–1650*. Cambridge, Mass., 1976.

Paredes M., Carlos S. "El tributo indígena en la region del lago de Pátzcuaro." In Paredes Martínez et al., *Michoacán en el siglo XVI*, 23–104.

Paredes Martínez, Carlos S., Marcela Irais Piñon Flores, Armando M. Escobar Olmedo, and María Trinidad Pulido Solis. *Michoacán en el siglo XVI*. Morelia, Mexico, 1984.

Parry, J. H. *The Audiencia of New Galicia in the Sixteenth Century*. 1940. Cambridge, England, 1968.

Pastor, Beatriz. "Silence and Writing: The History of the Conquest." In Jara and Spadaccini, *1492–1992*, 121–63.

Pastor, Rodolfo, and María de los Angeles Frizzi. "Expansión económica e integración cultural." In Florescano, *Historia General de Michoacán*, 2:163–91.

———. "El crecimiento del siglo XVIII." In Florescano, *Historia General de Michoacán*, 2:195–211.

Peña, Guillermo de la, comp. *Antropología social de la región purépecha*. Zamora, Mexico, 1987.

Pérez de Mendiola, Marina. "The Universal Exposition Seville 1992: Presence and Absence, Remembrance and Forgetting." In *Bridging the Atlantic*, 187–204.

———, ed. *Bridging the Atlantic*. Albany, N.Y., 1996.

Perry, Mary Elizabeth. *Gender and Disorder in Early Modern Seville*. Princeton, 1990.

Phelan, John Leddy. *The Millennial Kingdom of the Franciscans in the New World*. Berkeley, Calif., 1956.

Pollard, Helen Perlstein. "Ecological Variation and Economic Exchange in the Tarascan State." *American Ethnologist* 9, no. 2 (May 1982): 250–68.

———. "Prehispanic Urbanism at Tzintzuntzan, Michoacán." Ph.D. diss., Columbia University, 1972.

———. *Taríacuri's Legacy*. Norman, Okla., 1993.

Poole, Stafford. "The Declining Image of the Indian Among Churchmen in Sixteenth-Century New Spain." In Ramírez, *Indian-Religious Relations in Colonial Spanish America*, 11–19.

———. *Our Lady of Guadalupe*. Tucson, Ariz., 1995.

Poovey, Mary. *Uneven Developments*. Chicago, 1988.

Powell, James M, ed. *Muslims under Latin Rule 1100–1300*. Princeton, 1990.

Powell, Philip Wayne. *Soldiers, Indians and Silver*. Berkeley, Calif., 1952.

Prakash, Gyan. "Introduction: After Colonialism." In Prakash, *After Colonialism*, 3–17.

———, ed. *After Colonialism*. Princeton, 1994.

Prescott, William H. *History of the Conquest of Mexico*. Philadelphia, 1860.

Pupo-Walker, Enrique. *La vocación literaria del pensamiento histórico en América*. Madrid, 1982.

Purnell, Jennie. *Popular Movements and State Formation in Revolutionary Mexico*. Durham, N.C., 1999.

Rabasa, José María. "Dialogue as Conquest: Mapping Spaces for Counter-Discourse." *Cultural Critique* 6 (1987): 131–59.

———. "Fantasy, Errancy and Symbolism in New World Motifs: An Essay on Sixteenth Century Spanish Historiography." Ph.D. diss., University of California, Santa Cruz, 1985.

———. *Inventing America*. Norman, Okla., 1993.

———. "Writing and Evangelization in Sixteenth-Century Mexico." In Williams and Lewis, *Early Images of the Americas*, 65–92.

Rafael, Vicente. *Contracting Colonialism*. Ithaca, N.Y., 1988.

Ramírez, Susan E, ed. *Indian-Religious Relations in Colonial Spanish America*. Syracuse, N.Y., 1989.

Ramírez Montes, Mina. *La catedral de Vasco de Quiroga*. Zamora, Mexico, 1986.

Ranke-Heinemann, Ute. *Eunuchs for the Kingdom of Heaven*. Translated by Peter Heinegg. New York, 1990.

Refugio, Ma. del, and Benjamín Pérez González. *El estado p'urhepecha y sus fronteras en el siglo XVI*. Morelia, Mexico, 1991.

Reich, Peter Lester. *Mexico's Hidden Revolution*. South Bend, Ind., 1995.

Ribadeneira, Diego, and Richard Chacón, "Throngs Welcome Pope to Mexico City: In Nation Where Church is Losing Ground, Pontiff Speaks of Rebirth." *Boston Globe* January 23, 1999, A1.

Ricard, Robert. *Conquête Spirituelle du Mexique*. Paris, 1933.

————. *The Spiritual Conquest of Mexico.* Translated by Lesley Byrd Simpson. Berkeley, Calif., 1966.

Ricouer, Paul. *Time and Narrative.* Vol. 3. 1985. Translated by Kathleen Blarney and David Pellauer. Chicago, 1988.

Riding, Alan. "Carlos Fuentes Trades His Pen for Television." *New York Times,* December 31, 1990, 11 and 14.

Rivas Palacio, Vicente. *México a través de los siglos.* Vol. 2. Barcelona, 1888–89.

Rivera, Luis. *A Violent Evangelism.* Louisville, Ky., 1992.

Rodríguez O., Jaime E. *The Revolutionary Process in Mexico.* Los Angeles, 1990.

Rodríguez Prampolini, Ida. *Juan O'Gorman arquitecto y pintor.* Mexico City, 1982.

Rohrlich, Ruby, and Elaine Hoffman Baruch, eds. *Women in Search of Utopia.* New York, 1984.

Rojas Gonzales, Francisco. "Los tarascos en la época colonial." In Mendieta y Nuñéz et al., *Los tarascos,* 53–102.

Rosa, Martín de la, and Charles A. Reilly, eds. *Religión y política en México.* Mexico City, 1985.

Rowe, William, and Vivian Schelling. *Memory and Modernity.* London, 1991.

Ruggiero, Guido. *The Boundaries of Eros.* Oxford, 1985.

Ryan, Michael T. "Assimilating New Worlds in the Sixteenth and Seventeenth Centuries." *Comparative Studies in Society and History* 23, no. 4 (October 1981), 519–38.

Said, Edward. *Culture and Imperialism.* New York, 1993.

————. *Orientalism.* New York, 1978.

————. *The World, The Text, and the Critic.* Cambridge, Mass., 1983.

————. "Yeats and Decolonization." In Eagleton, Jameson, and Said, *Nationalism, Colonialism and Literature,* 1990.

"Sainthood Bid for Queen Isabella Stirs Debate." *New York Times,* December 28, 1990, A5.

Sánchez López, Ma. del Socorro, et al. *Ixiti juchiti irieta: Asi es mi pueblo.* Morelia, Mexico, 1987.

Schacht, Richard. *Hegel and After.* Pittsburgh, 1975.

Schondube, Otto B. "Las exploraciones arqueológicas en el área tarasca." In Miranda, *La cultura Purhé,* 16–30.

Schwaller, John Frederick. *The Church and Clergy in Sixteenth-Century Mexico.* Albuquerque, 1987.

Schwartz, Stuart B., ed. *Implicit Understanding.* New York, 1994.

Scott, James C. *Domination and the Arts of Resistance.* New Haven, Conn., 1990.

Scott, Joan Wallach. "Experience." In *Feminists Theorize the Political,* ed. Judith Butler and Joan Wallach Scott, 22–39. London, 1992.

————. *Gender and the Politics of History.* New York, 1988.

————. "Women's History." In Burke, *New Perspectives,* 42–66.

Seed, Patricia. *Ceremonies of Possession in Europe's Conquest of the New World.* Cambridge, England, 1995.

————. "Colonial and Postcolonial Discourse." *Latin American Research Review* 26, no. 3 (1991): 181–200.

————. "More Colonial and Post-Colonial Discourses." *Latin American Research Review* 28, no. 3 (1993): 146–52.

————. "Taking Possession and Reading Texts: Establishing the Power of Overseas Empires." In Williams and Lewis, *Early Images of the Americas,* 111–47.

————. *To Love, Honor and Obey in Colonial Mexico.* Stanford, Calif., 1988.

Semo, Enrique. *Historia del capitalismo en México.* Mexico City, 1973.

Sepúlveda y H., María Teresa. *Los cargos políticos y religiosos en la región del lago de Pátzcuaro.* Mexico City, 1974.

Sheridan, Susan, ed. *Grafts.* London, 1988.

Sider, Gerald. "When Parrots Learn to Talk and Why They Can't: Domination, Deception and Self-Deception in Indian-White Relations." *Comparative Studies in Society and History* 29 (1987): 3–23.

Siller, Clodomiro. "La Iglesia en el medio indígena." In Rosa and Reilly, *Religión y política en México,* 213–39.

Silverblatt, Irene. "Interpreting Women in States: New Feminist Ethnohistory." In Leonardo, *Gender at the Crossroads of Knowledge,* 140–71.

————. *Moon, Sun, and Witches.* Princeton, 1990.

Simpson, Leslie Byrd. *The Encomienda in New Spain.* Berkeley, Calif., 1950.

————. *Many Mexicos.* 1941. Berkeley, Calif., 1960.

Skursi, Julie. "The Ambiguities of Authenticity in Latin America: Doña Barbara and the Construction of National Identity." *Poetics Today* 15, no. 4 (Winter 1994), 605–42.

Sobrino, Jon. "The Winds in Santo Domingo and the Evangelization of Culture." In Hennelly, *Santo Domingo and Beyond,* 165–235.

Spalding, Karen. *Huarochirí.* Stanford, Calif., 1984.

Spence, Jonathan D. *The Memory Palace of Matteo Ricci.* New York, 1983.

Spivak, Gayatri Chakravorty. "Can the Subaltern Speak?" In Nelson and Grossberg, *Marxism and the Interpretation of Culture.*

————. *In Other Worlds.* New York, 1987.

————. *The Post-Colonial Critic.* New York, 1990.

————. "The Rani of Sirmur: An Essay on Reading the Archives." *History and Theory* 24, no. 3 (1985): 247–72.

————. "Subaltern Studies: Deconstructing Historiography." In *Selected Subaltern Studies,* ed. Ranajit Guha and Gayatri Chakravorty Spivak. Oxford, 1988.

Steck, Francis Borgia, O.F.M. *Motolinia's History of the Indians of New Spain.* Washington, D.C., 1951.

Stepan, Alfred, ed. *Americas.* Oxford, 1992.

Stepan, Nancy Leys. *The Hour of Eugenics.* Ithaca, N.Y., 1991.

Stern, Steve J. "Africa, Latin America, and the Splintering of Historical Knowledge: From Fragmentation to Reverberation." In Cooper et al., *Confronting Historical Paradigms,* 3–20.

————. "Feudalism, Capitalism, and the World-System in the Perspective of Latin America and the Caribbean." *American Historical Review* 93, no. 4 (October 1988): 829–97.

————. "Paradigms of Conquest: History, Historiography, and Politics." *Journal of Latin American Studies* 24 (1992): 1–34.

————. *Peru's Indian Peoples and the Challenge of Spanish Conquest: Huamanga to 1640*. Madison, Wis., 1982.

————. *The Secret History of Gender*. Chapel Hill, N.C., 1995.

————, ed. *Resistance, Rebellion and Consciousness in the Andean Peasant World, 18th–20th Centuries*. Madison, Wis., 1987.

Stevenson, Robert. *Music in Mexico*. New York, 1952.

Stoler, Ann Laura. "Rethinking Colonial Categories: European Communities and the Boundaries of Rule." In *Colonialism and Culture*, ed. Nicholas B. Dirks, 319–52. Ann Arbor, Mich., 1992.

Stoll, David. *Is Latin America Turning Protestant?* Berkeley, Calif., 1990.

Stone, Cynthia Leigh. "A Fragile Coalition: The 'Relación de Michoacán' and the Compiling of Indigenous Traditions in Sixteenth-Century Mexico." Ph.D. diss., University of Michigan, 1992.

————. "Rewriting Indigenous Traditions: The Burial Ceremony of the *Cazonci*." *Colonial Latin American Review* 3, no. 1–2 (1994): 87–107.

Stone, Lawrence. "The Revival of Narrative: Reflections on a New Old History." *Past and Present* 85 (November 1979): 3–24.

Sweet, David. "The Ibero-American Frontier Mission in Native American History." In Langer and Jackson, *The New Latin American Mission History*, 1–48.

Szeminski, Jan. "Why Kill the Spaniard?" In Stern, *Resistance, Rebellion and Consciousness*, 166–92.

Tangeman, Michael. *Mexico at the Crossroads*. Maryknoll, N.Y., 1995.

Tapia Santamaría, Jesus. *Campo religioso y evolución política en el bajío zamorano*. Zamora, Mexico, 1986.

Taylor, William B. "Banditry and Insurrection: Rural Unrest in Central Jalisco." In Katz, *Riot, Rebellion and Revolution*, 205–48.

————. "Between Global Process and Local Knowledge: An Inquiry Into Early Latin American Social History, 1500–1900. In Zunz, *Reliving the Past*, 115–90.

————. *Drinking, Homicide and Rebellion in Colonial Mexican Villages*. Stanford, Calif., 1979.

————. *Landlord and Peasant in Colonial Oaxaca*. Stanford, Calif., 1972.

————. "Santiago's Horse: Christianity and Colonial Indian Resistance in the Heartland of New Spain." In Taylor and Pease, *Violence, Resistance and Survival in the Americas*, 153–89.

————. "The Virgin of Guadalupe in New Spain: An Inquiry into the Social History of Marian Devotion." *American Ethnologist* 14 (1987): 9–33.

Taylor, William, and Franklin Pease G.Y. *Violence, Resistance and Survival in the Americas*. Washington, D.C., 1994.

Tena Ramírez, Felipe. *Vasco de Quiroga y sus pueblos de Santa Fe en los siglos XVIII–XIX*. Mexico City, 1977.

Tenenbaum, Barbara A. "Streetwise History: The Paseo de la Reforma and the Porfirian State, 1876–1910." In Beezley, Martin, and French, *Rituals of Rule, Rituals of Resistance*, 127–50.

Thomas, Hugh. *Conquest.* New York, 1993.

Todorov, Tzvetan. *The Conquest of America.* 1982. Translated by Richard Howard. New York, 1984.

Toussaint, Manuel. *Pátzcuaro.* Mexico City, 1942.

Trexler, Richard C. *Sex and Conquest.* Ithaca, N.Y., 1995.

Trouillot, Michel-Rolph. *Silencing the Past.* Boston, 1995.

Tudela De La Orden, José. "La pena de adulterio en los pueblos precortesianos." *Revista de Indias* 31, no. 123–24 (January-July 1971): 377–88.

Tuñon Pablos, Julia. *Mujeres en México.* Mexico City, 1987.

Valdés, Mario J., and Linda Hutcheon. *Rethinking Literary History—Comparatively.* American Council of Learned Societies (ACLS) Occasional Paper No. 27. New York, 1994.

Vanderwood, Paul J. "Explaining the Mexican Revolution." In Rodríguez O., *The Revolutionary Process in Mexico,* 97–114.

Van Young, Eric. "Conclusion: The State as Vampire—Hegemonic Projects, Public Ritual, and Popular Culture in Mexico, 1600–1990." In Beezley, Martin, and French, *Rituals of Rule, Rituals of Resistance,* 343–74.

———. "Conclusions." In Ramírez, *Indian-Religious Relations in Colonial Spanish America,* 87–97.

———. "The Cuautla Lazarus: Double Subjectives in Reading Texts on Popular Collective Action." *Colonial Latin American Review* 2, no. 1–2 (1993): 3–26.

———. *Hacienda and Market in Eighteenth-Century Mexico.* Berkeley, Calif., 1981.

———. "Material Life." In Hoberman and Socolow, *The Countryside in Colonial Latin America,* 49–74.

Van Zantwijk, R.A.M. *Servants of the Saints.* Assen, Netherlands, 1967.

Vasco de Quiroga y Obispado de Michoacán. Morelia, Mexico, 1986.

Veeser, H. Aram, ed. *The New Historicism.* London, 1989.

Verastíque, Bernardino. *Michoacán and Eden.* Austin, Tex., 2000.

Versényi, Adam. *Theatre in Latin America.* Cambridge, England, 1993.

Vidal, Hernán. "The Concept of Colonial and Postcolonial Discourse: A Perspective From Literary Criticism." *Latin American Research Review* 28, no. 3 (1993): 113–19.

Villanueva, Margaret A. "From Calpixqui to Corregidor: Appropriation of Women's Cotton Textile Production in Early Colonial Mexico." *Latin American Perspectives* 44 (Winter 1985): 17–40.

Wachtel, Nathan. *Gods and Vampires.* Translated by Carol Volk. Chicago, 1994.

Warren, J. Benedict. *La administración de los negocios de un encomendero en Michoacán.* Mexico City, 1984.

———. *The Conquest of Michoacán.* Norman, Okla., 1985.

———. *La conquista de Michoacán.* Translated into Spanish by Agustín García Alcaraz. Morelia, Mexico, 1977.

———. "Los estudios linguisticos en Michoacán en el siglo XVI: Una expresion del humanismo cristiano." In Herrejón, *Humanismo y ciencia,* 113–24.

———. "Fray Jerónimo de Alcalá: Author of the *Relación de Michoacán?*" *The Americas* 27, no. 3 (January 1971): 307–26.

———— (Fintan B.). *Vasco de Quiroga and His Pueblo-Hospitals of Santa Fe.* Washington, D.C., 1963.

————. "Writing the Language of Michoacán: Sixteenth Century Franciscan Linguistics." In *Franciscan Presence in the Americas,* ed. Francisco Morales, O.F.M., 308–44. Potomac, Md., 1983.

Weeks, Jeffrey. *Sexuality and Its Discontents.* London, 1985.

West, Robert C. *Cultural Geography of the Modern Tarascan Area.* Washington, D.C., 1948.

White, Hayden. *The Content of the Form.* Baltimore, 1987.

————. "The Historical Text as Literary Artifact." In *The Writing of History,* ed. Robert H. Canary and Henry Kozicki, 41–62. Madison, Wis., 1978.

————. *Metahistory.* Baltimore, 1973.

————. "The Noble Savage Theme as Fetish." In Chiapelli, *First Images of America,* 121–35.

————. *Tropics of Discourse.* Baltimore, 1978.

Williams, Jerry M., and Robert E. Lewis, eds. *Early Images of the Americas.* Tucson, Ariz., 1993.

Williams, Raymond. *Towards 2000.* London, 1983.

Winn, Peter. *The Americas.* Berkeley, Calif., 1992.

Winter, Sylvia. "1492: A New World View." In *Race, Discourse, and the Origin of the Americas,* ed. Vera Lawrence Hyatt and Rex Nettleford, 5–57. Washington, D.C., 1995.

Wolf, Eric. *Sons of the Shaking Earth.* Chicago, 1959.

Zavala, Silvio. "En busca del tratado *"De Debellendis Indis* de Vasco de Quiroga." *Historia Mexicana* 18, no. 4 (April-June 1968).

————. "En torno del tratado *"De Debellendis Indis* de Vasco de Quiroga." *Historia Mexicana* 17, no. 4 (April-June 1969): 623–26.

————. *Los esclavos indios en Nueva España.* Mexico City, 1967.

————. *Recuerdo de Vasco de Quiroga.* Mexico City, 1965.

————. "La utopia de America en el siglo XVI." *Cuadernos Americanos* 141, no. 4 (July-August 1965): 130–38.

————. "Vasco de Quiroga ante las comunidades de indios." In Herrejón, *Humanismo y ciencia,* 27–35.

Zavala Paz, José. "Vasco de Quiroga, padre de los indios." In *Don Vasco de Quiroga y Arzobispado de Morelia,* 45–61.

————. *D. Vasco de Quiroga.* Morelia, Mexico, 1964.

Zunz, Olivier, ed. *Reliving the Past.* Chapel Hill, N.C., 1985.

continued from front flap

the *Relación de Michoacán*; and assesses the writings of Michoacán's first bishop, the legendary Vasco de Quiroga, and their complex interplay of authoritarian paternalism and reformist hope. Part II, "Reflections," looks at how the memory of these historical figures is represented in later eras. A key text for this discussion is the *Crónica de Michoacán*, written in the late eighteenth century by the Franciscan intellectual Pablo de Beaumont.

Krippner-Martínez concludes with a critique of the debate that framed his investigation—the controversy between Latin Americans and Europeans over the colonialist legacy, beginning with the Latin American Bishops Conference in 1992.

JAMES KRIPPNER-MARTÍNEZ is Associate Professor of History at Haverford College.